LAND, SEA OR AIR?

Land, Sea or Air?

Military Priorities: Historical Choices?

Michael D. Hobkirk

St. Martin's Press   New York

© Royal United Services Institute 1992

All rights reserved. For information, write:
Scholarly and Reference Division,
St. Martin's Press, Inc., 175 Fifth Avenue,
New York, N.Y. 10010

First published in the United States of America in 1992

Printed in Hong Kong

ISBN 0-312-07493-X

Library of Congress Cataloging-in-Publication Data
Hobkirk, Michael D.
Land, sea or air? : military priorities, historical choices? /
Michael D. Hobkirk.
p. cm.
Includes bibliographical references and index.
ISBN 0-312-07493-X
1. Armed Forces—History. 2. Military policy—History. 3. Sea
–power—History. 4. Strategy—History. I. Title.
UA14.H6 1992
355'.009—dc20 91-32013
CIP

For my father, who would have liked to see this

Contents

List of Maps		viii
Acknowledgements		ix
Foreword by Field Marshal Sir Nigel Bagnall, GCB, CVO, MC		x
1	Strategic Choices	1
2	The Ancient World	9
3	The Ottoman Assault on the West	32
4	The Rise and Decline of the Dutch Republic	52
5	Britain and France: The Whale and the Elephant	86
6	Before the First World War	122
7	Planning for the Second World War	142
8	The Cold War – and After?	186
Bibliography		198
Index		202

List of Maps

1. Greece and Sicily during the Persian and Peloponnesian Wars   10
2. The Western Mediterranean during the Punic Wars   22
3. The Ottoman Assault on the West   33
4. Spain, England and the Dutch Republic   53
5. The Netherlands during the Wars of Independence   57
6. The Pacific Theatre 1941–45   167

Acknowledgements

A number of friends and colleagues have been good enough to read and comment on parts of this book. They have helped me greatly and saved me from some bad mistakes, but I am reluctant to name those who have seen only part of this study in case they are unfairly blamed for the whole. Anthony Bennell, however, has read the whole book in draft and given me much wise advice. I owe him a special debt of gratitude but must stress that the remaining errors are my own.

Finally I must record my admiration and gratitude to the students and staff of the former National Defence College at Latimer in Buckinghamshire and of the National Defense University, Washington, DC. I served on the staff of the former and was a Research Fellow at the latter. These two institutions first introduced me to that wide and wild country known as defence studies. However I must absolve them from any responsibility for the results of my studies there.

April 1990   MICHAEL D. HOBKIRK

Foreword

As Michael Hobkirk clearly portrays, over the centuries identifying a nation's future strategic priorities has proved to be a very imprecise art, and as a result peacetime force structures have seldom proved relevant when put to the test of war. As two examples show, both politicians and military commanders have tried their hand without either of them displaying any marked superiority for objective thinking.

Before Rome precipitated the First Punic War with Carthage by seizing Messina in 264 BC, hereditary factional party interests, represented by three influential family clans, had divided the Senate's strategic thinking and prevented any changes to the country's force structure. Rome had then remained a land power without a navy, which, following her opportunistic act of expansion across the straits of Messina, had provoked a war with a great maritime nation. The responsibility for Rome's lopsided force structure clearly lay with the Senate, and Rome was fortunate that Carthage possessed equally unbalanced forces: a powerful navy in being but a mercenary army which required considerable expansion before it was ready to take the field in a major war.

Some 2000 years later Michael Hobkirk provides an example of muddled strategic thinking by German military commanders when, at the beginning of the twentieth century, the Reichstag acquiesced to the construction of a great navy without having identified any clear strategic priorities. The forceful Admiral Tirpitz was able to convince both the Kaiser and the Reichstag that a powerful navy was essential if Germany were to play a major role in world affairs. As a result manpower and money were syphoned off for the construction of a surface fleet which played no significant part in the First World War, while arguably depriving the army of the resources which would have achieved victory by ensuring the success of the Schlieffen plan.

Throughout history only a continental land power – such as Mongolia when Ghenghis Khan swept over most of China, into the Middle East, Russia and Eastern Europe – can ignore the need for a navy. For the rest of us it is a matter of getting the balance right. Whether this was achieved

Foreword

during the Cold War is a matter yet to be researched and then judged with hindsight, but certainly it looks as though the Soviets made the same mistake as the Germans in constructing a large surface fleet which has had difficulty in fitting into a land-dominated strategy. Climatic conditions and problems of access to the high seas forced the Soviets to maintain and operate three essentially self-contained fleets. Moreover, the need to achieve strategic surprise before unleashing a land campaign would have prevented the navy from being deployed to the Atlantic before a war started.

Today, with a less clearly identifiable threat and the imposition of an arbitrary financial ceiling on defence expenditure, the problem of getting future force structures right presents a major challenge, and one which is further complicated by alliances of uncertain durability and rapid technological developments. For those trying to determine their country's military priorities in the coming decades, Michael Hobkirk's thoughtful book provides an historical perspective which makes it essential reading.

FIELD MARSHAL SIR NIGEL BAGNALL, GCB, CVO, MC

1 Strategic Choices

> War is too serious a business to be left to soldiers.
> *Georges Clemenceau*

Clemenceau's dictum has been used so often and been subject to so many different interpretations that the edge of its paradox has been lost. Yet there is one truth in his remark which is almost self evident, widely applicable, but rarely studied. For many nations war cannot be left to soldiers because these nations must fight on sea as well as on land and latterly in the air as well. It would be very unwise to leave defence budgeting entirely to soldiers. Politicians, very often Heads of States themselves, must undertake the thankless task of dividing available resources between their generals, admirals, and latterly air commanders as well. It is not very likely that Clemenceau had this point in mind when he made the remark, although the strategic choice between land and naval forces did matter to France during the long struggle with Britain in the eighteenth century, and after his death, with the coming of nuclear weapons, her politicians would have to decide how to allocate resources between nuclear and conventional forces. Perhaps this book should have been called 'Left to Politicians'.

Not all great powers of the past needed to make a serious choice between their land and sea forces in pursuit of security or conquest. Continental powers such as China for most of her history, nineteenth-century Russia and the Austrian Empire, depended for power and protection on their armies and could afford to neglect their navies. However, France, another continental power, built up her navy to secure colonies and trade in the seventeenth and eighteenth centuries. Even Russia on one occasion built up a modern navy during the nineteenth century, but her experience was disastrous; the fleet which she assembled in European waters and sent east to counter the Japanese attack on her Far Eastern possessions was utterly defeated at Tsu Shima in 1905. The Mediterranean provides an interesting special study of the use of naval power. Before the expansion of Europe overseas in the fifteenth and sixteenth centuries and thereafter, the focus of the great powers of Europe and part of the Near East tended to be this inland sea. Many of them, though predominantly land powers like Persia under Darius and Xerxes, Sparta, Rome and the Ottoman Empire, had to take to the sea to defeat or try to defeat their enemies. This was at least partly because communications round the periphery of the Mediterranean were so poor on account of the terrain, that before the coming of railways and modern roads nations were often compelled to build navies and take to the sea in order to reach the enemy homeland.

These and others examples of strategic choice between land, sea and air will be discussed in this study, which cannot claim to be comprehensive; and one of the most puzzling has been omitted. Chinese emperors had built up a powerful navy for use on rivers and in the China Sea as early as the twelfth century, but it was not until the fifteenth century that the ruling Ming dynasty began to extend Chinese naval power further. Between 1405 and 1433 the famous admiral Cheng-ho led powerful fleets into the Indian Ocean and with tribute and trade exchanges asserted Chinese suzerainty from Borneo and Malaysia to Ceylon and then to the shores of the Red Sea and the eastern coast of Africa. No naval opponent stood in the admiral's way and his ships were apparently four times as large and powerful as the Portuguese ships which would make similar voyages in the Indian Ocean shortly after. Yet no new voyages to this area were made after 1433 and in 1436 a decree was issued forbidding the construction of new seagoing ships. The reason for this withdrawal from the chance for increased trade and wealth is not easy to divine. China did, it is true, face serious threats from invaders on land, but it is also likely that innate Chinese suspicion of the disturbing influences of foreigners engaged in trade also played a part. Whatever the reasons, China has never again tried to expand as a sea power and provides a unique instance of a great power withdrawing from mastery of the seas around her without pressure from a maritime rival.

Nations which have depended on maritime power have usually been those which needed to protect either seaborne trade or the raw materials from colonies on which their wealth depended; occasionally these maritime empires, such as Athens and Great Britain, needed to import food as well as raw materials for manufacture and re-export. Those which opposed them in war were either other maritime nations like themselves competing in the scramble for colonies and trade, or continental land-based powers intent on destroying a rival which happened to depend on sea power for wealth and security. Whatever the form of rivalry, it was rare for these wars to be fought wholly at sea, the Anglo-Dutch wars of the late seventeenth century being a notable exception. As the following chapters will show, on most

Strategic Choices 3

occasions nations had a hard choice to make in allocating their resources between their armies and navies; in addition, air power would have to be considered in the twentieth century. The maritime power might have important allies on land which had to be supported and armies would also be needed to attack the enemy's colonies overseas or to defend its own. In those instances when the continental power had no overseas possessions, a maritime opponent would often seek allies on land to exhaust the continental power, which in its turn might seek to extend its influence on land in order to deny a maritime enemy access to harbours or sources of naval stores. As one looks back over Europe's turbulent history since the late fifteenth and early sixteenth century, it is surprising how few major wars were fought only at sea or indeed only on land. On most occasions the great powers had to make choices between land and sea (and later air) when deploying resources for war.

Of course, the very idea of defence resources which could be switched between land, sea and later air forces, is a relatively new one which has achieved acceptance as the costs of war increased dramatically and the concepts of economics (including that of opportunity cost) became more widely known. For much of history, even European history, the war resources of a nation were not liquid assets, but men, perhaps bound to give some limited military service under a feudal system or its equivalent, indigenous resources such as horses and minerals to make metal weapons, with a very limited supply of currency to support what forces could be raised. Increasing wealth from trade in the fifteenth century enabled cities in Italy to hire mercenary soldiers to fight for them; these had the great advantage of disposability, they could be discharged when the war was over, a great saving in cost. When the Dutch were fighting for their independence they developed the mercenary system to create the first modern standing army of paid professionals trained in the latest weapons (which were now firearms) and ready for duty at all times. At about the same time, cannon were developed to fire accurate broadsides from ocean-going warships built specially for this purpose. These needed at least some trained crews, and professional navies on a reasonably permanent basis also came into existence. These changes are discussed in more detail in Chapter 4, but for the present it is enough to note that both these new professional forces required money to sustain them; neither a feudal system of military duty in exchange for land, nor an abundance of natural resources were enough. In consequence taxes in cash had to be raised (and a permanent civil service recruited to collect and administer them). When collected, this cash could be spent on either an army or a navy. Those nations with access to the sea had a genuine strategic choice, often for the first time. This Age of the Professionals, lasting say from the middle of the sixteenth to the middle of the nineteenth century, marks a new era in strategic planning.

The next change which extended strategic choice between land and sea came with the development of railways. This changed the face of war by enabling the great powers of Europe to mobilise and deploy their forces at the start of a war in a fraction of the time it had previously taken. The staff officers and the complex military bureaucracy created to plan this had also to function in peacetime. Their plans and agreements or disagreements with their opposite numbers in the sister service imperceptibly but inevitably fixed the allocation of defence resources and hence their country's strategy for the coming war. This is discussed in Chapter 6; for the moment the Age of the Staff Officer can be noted as the next stage in the development of strategic planning.

By 1945 the advent of nuclear weapons, the growth in the cost of all weapons and the limited budgets available to pay for them in peacetime, forced both the Superpowers and the medium-sized powers to regard resources available for national security, not as the sum of separate shares for the army, navy and air force, but as defence resources to be shared amongst the three services in accordance with a coherent defence policy, with the implication that if the policy changed, then the share allocated to each service might change. Moreover, as President Truman perceptively remarked, 'Strategy, programmes and budget are all aspects of the same basic decisions.' Nations had to decide their strategies and order weapons system with a long-term strategy in mind, and if funds ran short they might have to change their strategy. It is clear that nations have not always followed this advice since the Second World War; nevertheless to recognise the change which came over strategy with the arrival of nuclear weapons and the other factors just mentioned, the period since 1945 can be known as the Age of the Defence Staff Officer. This interplay of land, sea and air strategy can then be recognised as a separate field of strategy subordinate to Grand Strategy, which comprehends all the resources of the nation; its alliances and political objectives. Since 1945, defence strategy, in which civilians, both politicians and the subordinate and possibly permanent civil servants, play their part with service staff officers, covers resource allocation decisions taken on an inter-service basis, but it could and in this author's opinion should, be extended to cover all the choices between land, sea and air strategies which are the subject of this book, although the term 'defence' was not normally applied to war strategy before the start of the twentieth century. The term 'military strategy' has been and is sometimes still used to include maritime and air strategy; this use would clearly be misleading in this study and therefore 'military strategy' will be used here only in connection with military operations on land.

As this is a study of the alternative uses of the resources available for war it must sometimes pose and try to answer a series of hypothetical questions, such as: if country X had strengthened its fleet at the expense of its army, would it have won the war? This is a hazardous practice, frowned on by historians but if this study is to be of any value it must sometimes seek out alternatives and try to deduce their likely consequences. It must also from time to time pose strategic options, without necessarily accepting the political objections to them which were, and perhaps still are, seen as overriding. Again this could be criticised. Strategists are often taken to task for ignoring political factors (and this book will on occasion do so) but if political factors are used at the outset as a reason for circumscribing strategic choices, then the strategies proposed may well be less effective. It is surely the job of the defence planners in all ages to propose the best options within the resources available and leave it to their political masters to reject those which entail political risks which are too great.

Whatever the composition of the teams within the defence bureaucracies which plan future strategy, the doubt must still remain whether the study of past strategic decisions will help them to do better in the future. Presumably few would claim in 1989 that members of the intelligence community or those who study and teach history, politics, or international relations can be relied on as prophets with power to see the future. If history were studied only for its power of prediction then its stock would now be very low. No intelligence organisation or academic institution known to the author has publicly and authoritatively forecast the particular combination of social and economic factors which have created the recent fundamental changes in the Soviet Union. The extent to which the subsequent changes in Eastern Europe were foreseen by George Kennan when he expounded the policy of Containment will be mentioned in Chapter 8, but even he did not predict the manner in which Communism would collapse within the Soviet Union. The strategist who studies history cannot expect to learn about the next change either to society or to the art of war.

In his address 'The Use and Abuse of Military History' Michael Howard advises the service officer approaching the subject to study in width, in depth and in context. Study in width will show, for instance, how warfare has developed over a long period and this, as Professor Howard points out, shows what does and what does not change in the evolution of war. Study in depth will require the student to take a single campaign and study it thoroughly, not only from official and academic histories, but also from memoires, letters, diaries and the like, which catch some of the confusion and horror of a campaign which has been drily analysed by the historian. Finally, study in context shows that wars are not conducted in total detachment from the rest of the activities of mankind. Rather they are conflicts between societies, and the ultimate cause of victory or defeat may be political, social or economic. Professor Howard cites the collapse of Prussia in 1806 and France in 1870 as occasions when political and social factors were im-portant elements in the ultimate military defeat.

This wise advice should surely be followed as far as possible by those who try to write about history and strategy. This study is not, as any historian will soon discover, a work of historical research, but an attempt to put into a broad historical context some important strategic decisions which have been taken in the past. It is therefore necessary to look both wide, in Michael Howard's phrase, and in context. Whenever it is relevant the technological development of warfare will be traced and, equally important, the political, economic or social context will be sketched in, if this will help to explain the reasons why certain strategic decisions were taken. One cannot follow Professor Howard's advice as far as depth is concerned. The wars discussed are so numerous and often so long that only a bare outline of the important campaigns can be given. If the history of a war is likely to be unfamiliar to the general reader, then it will be described in more detail but never to the extent that individual battles are described, unless the technology or tactics used had a marked effect on subsequent strategic decisions. This omission has one unfortunate result; much of the horror and confusion of war is lost. It follows also, that in a review of strategy there is little or no place for a record of either the gallantry or the suffering of both combatants or non-combatants. They must be virtually ignored. It may seem harsh to omit any mention of, for instance, the suffering of the Dutch population at the hands of the Duke of Alva's troops at the start of the Dutch revolt, or the bravery of RAF Bomber Command aircrew in the 1942 to 1945 bombing offensive against Germany, but if one is to try to determine the merits of strategic decisions, neither bravery nor suffering are relevant. If admiration or sympathy takes the place of judgement, the conclusion is likely to be flawed.

Any judgement on past strategic decisions is bound to involve hindsight. This affords knowledge of the actual, as opposed to the anticipated, consequences of the strategy in question and, as important, awareness of what was happening 'on the other side of the hill'; that is, in the enemy camp, when the strategy was being planned. On this basis a strategy can be judged as successful or unsuccessful, but those who planned it cannot be criticised if their plans are disrupted by wholly unforeseen, and unforeseeable events. There are from time to time great discontinuities in the history

Strategic Choices

of war when the nature of warfare seems to change abruptly, rendering past methods and weapons obsolete. If the military (and other) staffs planning strategy in all combatant countries fail to forecast the change, it is perhaps unfair to blame those who planned the strategy beforehand. An example is the type of warfare which developed on the Western Front between 1914 and 1918, taking all those in charge of military operations in 1914 by surprise. It therefore seems right to judge the pre-war plans of 1914 without reference to the stalemate which was in force by the end of that year. On other occasions the discontinuity results because one side develops a battle-winning weapon or technique and the other fails not only to make the same discovery, but also to find out what the enemy is developing and planning. This double failure is almost certain to merit criticism. Chapter 7 discusses several examples of such failures during the Second World War. Some of these can be attributed to faulty intelligence, however it is astonishing how often the failure lay not in the intelligence reports, but in those who ignored them, or read them with blinkers on. One argument for a study of past strategic decisions is that it may induce an attitude which is sceptical of current strategic dogma and also a burning desire to find out more about what is happening 'on the other side of the hill'.

Another reason for studying the strategy in the past is best explained by analogy. In his 1985 Reith Lectures, David Henderson memorably described a phenomenon which he termed 'Do-It-Yourself Economics'. By this he meant ideas about economic issues, events and relationships which, though broadly held and influential, are largely intuitive and unconnected with the professional economist's way of thinking. Is there not also a form of Do-It-Yourself History which has in the past influenced those concerned with national security and no doubt still does today? A possible British example is that view of strategy, widely held before the coming of aircraft, which maintained that all Britain needed was a strong navy with which to protect herself from attack and to safeguard her trade and Empire, and that whatever happened in Europe was of no concern to Britain. Chapters 4–7 will try to show that this is a seriously distorted view of Britain's strategic aims from Elizabeth I to the present century, but echoes of this DIY view could still be found in print, even after the last war. The lesson for students of strategy is surely that if they wish to use history in order to profit from experience, they must take good care to get their history right.

There is one argument which supports analysis of the past which is special to studies like this. It would stress the need to realise that defence strategy as defined here, and the need for many nations to share available resources between two or more armed services, has been part of European history since the invention of the trireme. The debate about this aspect of strategy has involved not only those who expected to direct the battles to come, but also the civilian side of government which would have to ensure that resources were found to sustain the armies and fleets required. The Defence Ministers in governments today face decisions about the allocation of resources which are similar to those faced by Neville Chamberlain's government in the 1930s and by others in former times stretching back to the citizens of the Athenian Assembly in the fifth century BC. Those who face this task in the future could perhaps spare some time to consider how their predecessors tackled the problem. They are bound to make mistakes, but these could be lessened if they acknowledge what has happened before.

2 The Ancient World

Athens may not have been the first power to gain wealth and dominion from overseas trade, but she was probably one of the first to found both on the ability to wage war at sea. There are examples in earlier history of nations such as the Minoan empire in Crete, growing rich by trade, but Athens is surely the first for which we have unequivocal evidence of a nation whose very existence, towards the end of her supremacy, depended on the power of her navy.

THE PERSIAN INVASION

Surprisingly enough the birth of Athenian naval power was abrupt and in many ways unexpected. The first Persian invasion of Greece in 490 BC was defeated by the Athenian army at Marathon without any naval encounter at all. After this success the Greeks realised that an empire as proud and as powerful as Persia was certain to repeat the attempt to subdue and punish those Greek cities which had encouraged their fellow Greeks in Asia Minor to revolt against Persian rule. Themistocles, the Athenian politician who played a leading part in resistance to the second Persian attack, persuaded his fellow countrymen to use the new-found wealth from a recently discovered seam of silver in the state mines at Laurium to build a war fleet of triremes instead of, as previously, diverting the wealth to their own pockets. No doubt many of those who supported Themistocles remembered the forced march in heavy armour back to Athens after the victory at Marathon to confront the Persian fleet on the shore of Phaleron Bay. After their defeat the Persians had sailed their fleet round Cape Sunium hoping to capture Athens while her only army was away at Marathon. The forced march was as important for the future as the battle and it clearly demonstrated to quick-witted Athenians the need for a war fleet. The superiority of the Greek heavily armed hoplite infantry, as shown at Marathon, was not enough in the face of vastly superior numbers of the Persian army, if they could mask the Greek forces with part of it and land the remainder behind the 'front

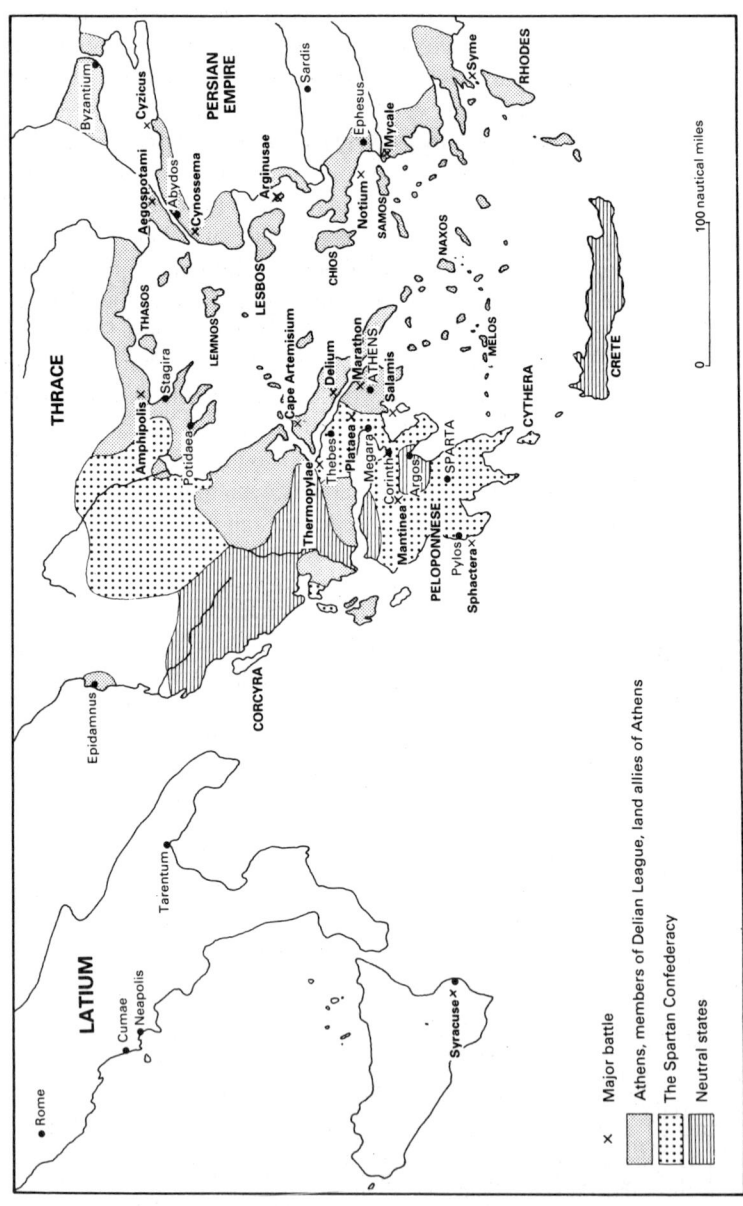

1. Greece and Sicily during the Persian and Peloponnesian Wars

line' to attack Greek cities and their inevitably limited areas suitable for food production. The Athenians decided to build a large fleet of triremes. When Darius's successor Xerxes marched his army of more than 200 000 men into northern Greece in 480 BC, a fleet of perhaps over 500 warships accompanied the army round the coast of Thrace and Macedonia. When the Persians destroyed the legendary defence of the Spartans at Thermopylae, they met a Greek fleet off Artemisium in an indecisive engagement after which the Persians suffered serious losses from storm and shipwreck. As a result, at the decisive naval battle of Salamis, the fleets were rather more evenly matched, with about 350 ships on the Persian and some 310 on the Greek side; but the Athenians evacuated to the island of Salamis for safety were not likely ever to forget that almost half of the Greek fleet, whose crucial victory they watched from the shore, was paid for and manned by Athenians. It is no wonder that from that day on for the rest of her pre-eminence Athens was wedded to the idea of seapower.

After this defeat Xerxes returned to Persia, leaving a smaller but good-quality army under his best general, Mardonius, who took up a position in Boeotia just north of Attica. Here he was defeated at Plateia in 479 BC by a combined Greek army under Pausanias, a Spartan. The Athenian contribution of hoplite infantry (8000) was second only to that of the Spartans (10 000). The Athenians could well feel proud of their part in finally disposing of this, the second and final attempt by Persia to conquer mainland Greece. On the same day as the battle of Plateia, a Greek expeditionary force defeated a Persian force at Mycale near Miletus in Asia Minor and destroyed almost the entire Persian fleet of 300 ships which were beached at the time; this is an early example of a naval victory on land which would be a feature of galley warfare in the Mediterranean. Mycale, rather than Plateia, opened the way for a Greek counter-attack on Persia. Before considering the strategic dilemma faced by Athens for the remainder of the fifth century there are a number of important points to note about Athenian strategy in the Persian Wars.

In the first place it is quite wrong to think of the Athenians as a nation with a long tradition of seafaring, turning to its ships when threatened by an invading army. The first Persian invasion came by sea, met no resistance, and was defeated on land. However, the victorious Athenian Army had to march back from Marathon as fast as it was able to defend Athens against a threatened attack by troops disembarked from the undefeated Persian fleet. The Athenian Army arrived just in time to protect the undefended city. By the time the Persians launched their second invasion ten years later, Athens, a sophisticated and wealthy state, had been able to acquire a powerful fleet based on the latest technology, the trireme, (the guided missile of its day), and learn how to use it effectively. The trireme was faster than its predecessors and with a skilled crew, including oarsmen, could ram and sink enemy ships without exposing itself to the risks of grappling and boarding its opponent. The victory at Salamis was won by the new fleet, acquired after widespread public debate in Athens. Of equal importance, however, was the subsequent decision by the Athenians, regarding the Persian Army in northern Greece. Sophisticated enough to agree to reduce their fleet by half and to send 8000 hoplites to fight at Plateia, they show how the democratic process in Athens could produce some very shrewd strategic decisions.

It was sometimes assumed that, as much of Athenian industry was run by slave labour, this was also used to propel her war fleet. It is clear that the motive power was provided, not by slaves or convicts, but by paid oarsmen drawn from the poorer class of free Athenian voters and that this form of paid and seasonal employment was increasingly popular with them. This block of voters could be said to have a vested interest in maritime strategy. Opposition to this preference for war by sea came from some of the wealthier middle classes and those with income from land or agriculture, who could afford to serve as hoplite heavy infantry for which the soldier had to provide armour and arms at his own expense (at a cost equivalent to that of a small car for a middle-class family in Britain in the 1930s). Consequently, this early example of inter-service rivalry could also be seen as an instance of social division and class rivalry within the Athenian state. However interpreted, this evidence surely shows that Athens had a choice of fighting on land or sea during the Persian war, and later, and that the choices selected by popular vote were as effective and as flexible as many similar decisions made since by emperors, kings, dictators and bureaucrats.

ATHENS AND SPARTA

This will be apparent from a study of Athenian strategy during her long war with Sparta and her allies which ended with the defeat of Athens in 404 BC.

The rivalry between the two city-states did not turn into open war until 431, but from the time that Athens built her fleet and became the foremost naval power in Greece she inevitably aroused the suspicion of Sparta and the implacable hostility of Corinth – after Athens the greatest commercial power on the mainland of Greece. This hostility became apparent when, after Plateia, Athens began to rebuild her city walls. Sparta suggested that it would be unwise for any city north of the isthmus of Corinth to re-fortify as this would provide shelter to the enemy if there were another Persian invasion. Under the urging of Themistocles, the Athenians temporised while using all able-bodied citizens to raise the walls to a defensible height. When this was done the Spartan proposal could be safely rejected. Before they began to rebuild, the Athenians had debated whether they should move the city to an adjacent island to avoid the danger of a land attack. This option was rejected, but the point was taken and, after the city walls were rebuilt, the famous Long Walls were constructed, linking Athens to her port and naval base at Piraeus. These were by far the most formidable military works in Greece at that time and were considered impregnable if adequately manned (though it has to be said that during this period the Greeks were not very skilled at siege warfare). The Walls were a novel, but expensive, solution to the perennial security problem of a mainland sea power.

While the Long Walls were being planned, the war against Persia was pursued, at first by a combined expedition under Spartan command, which sought to exploit the destruction of the Persian fleet at Mycale in 479. Although the general objective was to liberate those Greek cities in Asia Minor whose revolt had been one of the reasons for the Persian invasion, it is interesting to find that one of the first to be freed was the Greek colony at Byzantium on the Bosphorus. Its capture in 478 not only cut off the remaining Persian garrisons in Macedonia and Thrace from their bases, but also restored the route between Athens and the Black Sea coast around the Crimea, from which Athens imported significant supplies of corn. After this the Spartans lost interest in freeing the rest of Ionia from Persian rule, and leadership passed to Athens. The city formed the allies, coming mainly from the islands of the Aegean and the liberated coast of Asia Minor, into the Confederacy of Delos. All members contributed ships or money towards the fight to liberate Ionia from Persian rule. As time went on, however, and this objective was almost achieved, it became more usual for the contribution to be made in cash, which was kept by Athens until it was spent on ships which made war on Athens' behalf. When, in the second half of the century, those cities which wished to leave the Confederacy were restrained by force (which on occasion involved the destruction of the defecting city) it was plain that the Confederacy had become the Athenian Empire.

However, before it became wholly subservient to Athens, the Confederacy did undertake one daring and ambitious expedition. In 459 BC an allied fleet of some 200 ships was about to attack the Persians in Cyprus when it received an appeal from a rebel Libyan prince in Egypt to help him to free that country from Persian domination. The invitation was accepted, despite the risk of engagement with superior land forces, and the town, but not the citadel, of Memphis was captured by the Greeks. In the end, Persian preponderance on land proved decisive and the whole expedition was destroyed in 454 BC. One can only marvel at the energy and enterprise of the Athenians who could start such an enterprise when they were already engaged on five other war fronts. By 449 BC, Athens – already in conflict with Sparta or her allies from time to time – made peace with Persia. Although the details are not clear, it seems likely that the Ionian Greek cities on the coast of Asia Minor were relieved of direct Persian domination and perhaps also of paying tribute to Persia.

During this period war with Sparta had begun. On most occasions during the intermittent hostilities Sparta was drawn into war by appeals from cities more exposed to Athenian attack such as Megara, Corinth, and cities in Boeotia. Thus, following the battle of Oenophyta in 456 BC, Athens extended her sway over Boeotia, and Megara was also under her control. Both were lost in 447 BC. Other defections, actual or potential, alarmed the Athenians and in 445 BC, a year after the Spartan invasion of Attica, Athens concluded peace (optimistically called the Thirty Years' Peace) with Sparta and her allies. This brought an end to Athenian attempts to dominate her immediate neighbours on the mainland of Greece. In the future, her energies would be directed more towards the sea and memories of her defeats on land during this period must have influenced her strategy when the next war against Sparta and her allies began.

In 431 BC, Athens started the struggle with Sparta which lasted (with one short interruption) until Athens surrendered in 404 BC. Sparta was drawn somewhat reluctantly into a war between Athens and her bitter trade rival, Corinth, over the island of Corcyra (Corfu) and the city of Potidaea in Chalcidice, which were both being attacked by Athens, despite their links with Corinth. I will not attempt to summarise a war which lasted on and off for twenty-seven years and affected the whole Greek world from Asia Minor to Sicily, but the strategies of the two main antagonists are clear and the contrast between them shows clearly the dilemma of any state which aims for power at sea. The Peloponnesian League, led by Sparta, was strong on land and at first in no position to challenge the Athenian fleet. Almost from the start, Sparta and her allies invaded Attica and laid it waste. As a result Athens could get no produce from her own farms and had to import all the food needed by both the inhabitants of the city and the refugees from the countryside of Attica. On the other hand, the Athenians were safe behind their city walls which also covered their port, the Piraeus, and the road leading to it. They seemed invulnerable, provided that they could import enough food and raw materials to keep their economy going. Part of their advantage, it should be stressed, arose from the fact that Greek armies of this period were not proficient at storming fortified places, because they lacked many archers and peltasts. Pericles, the politician who led the Athenians during their years of greatness, persuaded the electorate to follow a maritime strategy deliberately, hard as it was for the Attic farmers to watch from the city walls as their crops were ravaged and their homes destroyed each year by the enemy. Athens retaliated by numerous seaborne attacks on enemy coasts and cities but the Messenian plain, the Spartan base and bread basket in the centre of the Peloponnese was out of reach of the Athenian fleet. One stroke of bad fortune during the first part of the war damaged Athens more than many of her defeats; plague came to the city, imported with wheat from Egypt, and a quarter of the population (including Pericles and many other prominent citizens) died between 430 and 427 BC. The erratic policy and wayward strategy adopted by Athens during the second part of the war may well have been due to the fact that the plague took so many of her brightest and best. Increasing war-weariness persuaded Athens to make peace with the Peloponnesian League in 421 BC.

During the Ten Years War (431–421 BC) the fortunes of both sides were mixed. The number and range of operations carried out may seem large, but it should be realised that many were equivalent to present-day amphibious operations at battalion or at most brigade level. Athens had some success in land operations on her borders, undertaken in defiance, as it were, of the maritime strategy advocated by Pericles; but an ally and neighbour, Plateia was lost to the enemy in 427, after a two-year siege and an invasion of Boeotia led to a severe defeat at Delium in 424 BC. Further afield, Athens sent a first expedition to Sicily from 427–424 with no decisive results.The Periclean strategy had more success in Greek waters; Athens seized the headland of Pylos in southern Peloponnese as a base for raiding and blockade, and in 425 BC a Spartan force sent to retake it was captured. The island of Cythera was also taken by Athens and used as a base for raids. On the debit side, the newly founded and important Athenian colony of Amphipolis in Thrace was captured in 424 BC by the Spartan general Brasidas. Two major attempts to recapture it were made in subsequent years; in the second in 422 BC, both Brasidas and his Athenian opponent Cleon, a pro-war politician, were killed. The Athenian rout at this battle impelled them to peace, while on the Spartan side the desire to regain the prisoners captured near Pylos had for sometime made them anxious for an end to the war. Peace between the main opponents was concluded in 421, but Sparta's allies continued the fight. As a result Athens did not regain Amphipolis as agreed, but instead retained both Pylos and Cythera, which were to have been relinquished. Athens also seems to have retained minor territorial gains at the expense of her bitter enemies and neighbours, Megara and Corinth. On the whole, the

Periclean strategy had been a success and harassing attacks had been successful without delivering any mortal wounds. On the other hand, Athens' attempts to dominate Boeotia and to hold Thrace had failed at great cost. During the early years of the peace the Athenians debated strategy, but now without the guidance of Pericles. There was a growing body of opinion which argued that Athens should break out of the straitjacket imposed on her by her neighbours and use her seapower to conquer Sicily, which had many very prosperous Greek and Hellenised Sicilian cities. Sicily, Egypt and South Russia were the main exporters of corn in the ancient world, but Sicily had strong ties with the cities of the Peloponnesian League and most of her grain exports went to the Peloponnese. A blow at Syracuse, the leading city of the island, would therefore both damage Sparta and secure wealth for Athens. After much heartsearching at the magnitude of the effort entailed and the risk of failure, Athenians were seduced by the vision of an 'El Dorado' in the west and conveniently forgot the unsatisfactory outcome of the small expedition which they had sent there in 427–424. The die was cast and the climax of the war had come. They sent an expedition of some 175 ships and 45 000 men in 415 BC. By 413 the whole expedition and a reinforcing fleet from Athens had been destroyed outside Syracuse. Athens never recovered psychologically or materially from this disaster, which could be compared to what Britain would have faced if all Allied Forces had been destroyed in Normandy in 1944

The resilience of the Athenian people was amazing and makes one realise what power could have been invested in her maritime strategy if the Syracusan expedition had succeeded or never taken place. Despite being threatened by a permanent Spartan base at Decelia, (14 miles from Athens) established in 413 and maintained to the end of the war, Athens raised another fleet at great financial sacrifice and sent it to the approaches to the Dardanelles. There it had to contend with an enemy fleet led by the Spartans but paid for increasingly by the Persians, who aimed in this way to recover the Ionian coastal cities from Athens. What was mainly at stake for Athens at this stage was the corn supply route from the Black Sea, on which she largely depended for grain.

To add to her troubles, democracy in Athens gave way in 411 to an oligarchy which was lukewarm about the war against Sparta. The fleet based on Samos was firmly pro-war and after two years democracy was restored in Athens, but the bitterness between the rich peace party and the poor war party remained. Despite these handicaps, Athens managed to retain a precarious hold on the eastern Aegean between 411 and 405. At Cynossema in 411 her fleet gained a narrow victory over the fleet led by Sparta and subsidised by Persia and in the next year the Athenians gained a convincing victory at Cyzicus. In 407, however, the Athenian fleet was defeated at Notium (off Samos) and suffered a further reverse at Mitylene in the following year. As a result, the Athenians had nothing left to oppose the now greatly strengthened enemy fleet. The Athenians were shaken by these reverses and made a final supreme effort. Gold offerings in the temples were melted down, freedom was promised to slaves, and citizenship to foreigners who would fight. As a result, a new fleet was ready in a month and it defeated the Spartan-led fleet at the Arginusae Isles (off Lesbos). One is tempted to believe that if her fleet had remained in being, Athens might have forced a stalemate on Sparta and her allies, despite her loss of confidence, for although the Peloponnesian League continued to be funded by Persia, it was, running short of the men and materials needed for a war at sea. The end came, however, in 405 BC when the Athenian fleet was destroyed near the Dardanelles on the beaches of Aegospotami in a surprise attack by a Spartan army. Athens was besieged and surrendered in the following year: a sea power had been defeated by a land power supported by a navy paid for by a foreign power.

The question will always be asked 'Could Athens have won if she had waged a different kind of war, or had she no alternative?' Many have seen the fall of Athens as yet one more example of a state which became too powerful for her neighbours meeting defeat only when all combined against her. Others point to the deep and bitter social and class divisions in all Greek city states – there was a fifth column of oligarchs in Athens for most of the war – and most of Sparta's allies had democratic factions, more or less ready to cooperate with Athens. This, it is argued, made a long conflict inevitable and gave victory to the side which was prepared to put the class struggle above Greek patriotism (insofar as either term can be applied to fifth-century Greece) and take financial help from Persia, the strongest adjacent power. Helpful as these quasi-sociological insights may be, they seem less convincing when compared to an explanation based on economic facts.

Greece is a very beautiful, but relatively barren country and even before the fifth century could not feed a growing population. A partial response to this was the export of citizens to form colonies elsewhere. Those states, which controlled a fertile plain safe from enemy incursion, as Sparta did in the central Peloponnese, enjoyed considerable advantages, even so the Peloponnesian League needed to import grain during the war with Athens. Those who see the wars in fifth-century Greece as a kind of deadly musical chairs in which too many city-states fought for too few food producing areas, provide an invaluable starting point for examining Athenian strategy in the Peloponnesian War. As early as the sixth-century BC Athens was faced with the need to feed a growing population and it was probably well before the Persian Wars that she gave up growing wheat in Attica and instead turned to producing wine, olive oil and honey (the only sugar of the age) to trade for imported wheat. By the middle of the fifth century, with upwards of 350 000 mouths to feed, Athens was wholly dependent on foreign trade for survival. She not only needed wheat from overseas, but also timber for ships and metal for tools and weapons; her peacetime survival as well as her ability to wage war had come from overseas trade. In exchange for her imports she had two raw materials to trade – fine clay to make excellent pottery, but, above all, silver from the mines at Cape Laurium near Cape Sunium. Without the silver, she could not have built the fleet which made victory at Salamis possible, nor could she have subsequently continued to challenge Sparta and her allies for the hegemony of Greece. In the light of this dilemma, the argument that Athens should have adopted a land strategy and used her border forts like Decelia (subsequently used by the Spartans as a permanent base to raid Attica) on her frontiers to hold the Attic Plain against attack, does not convince. Even it were held against Sparta, it could never have made more than a marginal addition to Athenian food supplies: Athens had to survive by her fleet or not at all. Perhaps it was for this reason that those who started as pro-army became more and more for peace with Sparta. It is evident that the pro-navy party clearly saw the need to control a defensible food-producing area, as an examination of Athenian strategy in the wars of the fifth century will show.

It will be remembered that one of the first moves by the combined fleet after the victory at Mycale in 479 was to the Dardanelles, so that the route to the Black Sea and the plentiful grain supplies of the Crimea could be freed from Persian control. This was achieved, but no one, Greek or Persian, could control those turbulent Scythian princes who ruled the Crimea. Despite her best diplomatic efforts, Athens never gained influence or control over the Crimea. She had to trade, and could only do so if the Scythians wished. Unfortunately, the Scythians preferred to be paid in gold, a commodity which the Athenians lacked in the fifth century, but which the Persians could obtain in reasonable quantities. Hence the need for Athens to look elsewhere for safe and reliable supplies of wheat. It seems certain, if the archaeological evidence of coin and pottery finds is to be trusted, that Athenian trade with the Crimea did not reach its full extent until the fourth century, when Persian gold was available to that city, but not to Sparta.

It is not surprising, therefore, that Athens and the Delian Confederacy should seize the chance to intervene in Egypt in 459–454 BC. The control of the granary of the ancient world was a prize worth the risk of confronting the Persian Army on land not just in single campaigns, but year after year.

Indeed the effort – in terms of the forces involved and their distance from base – would not be equalled until the Sicilian expedition of 415. At this distance hindsight seems to make the Athenian defeat inevitable, but it is worth noting that it took four years and was brought about by a combination of an exceptionally active and effective Persian general and the very lukewarm support for Athens from the Egyptians. Even then the Greek forces could only be destroyed on the island to which they had retreated by the damming and diversion of the river channel protecting them.

With South Russia and Egypt beyond their grasp, the Athenians inevitably looked west to South Italy and Sicily, the remaining corn lands known to them. They may perhaps have had an exaggerated idea of the wealth there (as sixteenth and seventeenth century Europeans did of America) but from what they knew it was plain that the wheat in Sicily and South Italy was enough to supply all Athens' needs. Much of the Athenian war effort in the numerous wars and campaigns which preceded the final Peloponnesian War in 416, was directed towards controlling the route to Sicily. The constant war on Megara is explained by the need to find a way to the Gulf of Corinth (and thence westwards) avoiding using a route at the mercy of her arch-rival, Corinth. Much diplomatic and then military effort was also expended on Acharnania in north-west Greece in order to control the next stage of the voyage to the west. Finally Corcyra (Corfu), with its safe harbours, rocky coast and small but efficient navy, became the cause of the outbreak of the war. Neither Athens nor Corinth could afford to let the other control Corcyra and the crossing of the Adriatic to Italy.

It is sometimes supposed that the first Athenian expedition to Sicily was a sideshow outside the main strategy of the war. However, it is more likely that it was, on the contrary, a key part of Athenian strategy to secure Sicilian wheat for herself and deny it to the Peloponnese. Some forty ships were sent initially and reinforcements followed. Athens and her Sicilian allies gained control of both sides of the Straits of Messina, but there was no decisive battle with Syracuse, the most powerful city and main enemy there. In 424 the Athenians returned home after three years' fighting when the Sicilian city-states decided that Sicilian interests were not served by continuing the war. Athens learned from that expedition, and a later diplomatic mission, that to control Sicily she would have to conquer Syracuse and as she could not expect significant help from other Sicilians, she would have to do it alone.

The Sicilian Expedition which left the Piraeus in 415, the largest which Athens ever mounted, was no *folie de grandeur*; it was the last attempt by a great city to break from the straitjacket imposed on it by geography and economic circumstances. Athens had no practicable alternative strategy for the war with Sparta. She had to use her sea power to control the source of food and raw materials on which the life of her city depended. As usual we must let an anonymous Athenian have the last word, for they debated strategy as well as poetry, philosophy, science and every other subject under the sun. Harking back to the time after the Persian wars, when Athenians seriously considered refounding their city on Salamis, or some other nearby island, an Athenian is supposed to have said, 'If we were islanders, we could defy the world.'

ROME AND CARTHAGE

For the next 140 years, one state after another dominated Greece and the eastern Mediterranean. Sparta gave way to Thebes and Thebes to Macedonia, which under Alexander the Great extended its sway as far as India, but seapower was never an important, or even decisive element in the fight for domination. Alexander gained power at sea by capturing the naval forces of all enemies – actual or potential – from land. The only other notable power at sea besides the Phoenicians, was Rhodes, which was able to maintain a measure of independence when Alexander's empire was divided among his warring successors. This was mainly due to the rocky coastline of the island on which her cities were built and which also provided a few excellent harbours for her war and trading fleets.

By 264, however, the struggle shifted to the central Mediterranean, where Rome controlled all the Italian mainland up to the Appenines. By a skilful mixture of coercion and persuasion she had incorporated all the inhabitants into her military system, making alliances and extending the privilege of citizenship wherever it seemed advantageous to do so. As a result, at the time of the Punic Wars she could raise about 500 000 troops from citizens and allies. Fertile and prosperous Sicily was an obvious prize for an expanding power. Greek city-states maintained a precarious existence in the eastern part of the island while the remainder was under the sway of Carthage, the state which was to pose the greatest threat to Rome until she was overwhelmed by Goths and Vandals in the fifth century AD. The Punic Wars with Carthage were to last 120 years and cost many Roman lives, ending with the complete destruction of Carthage. The history of these wars can be complex, but an understanding of the strategy employed is relatively straightforward. In order to win, Rome – a land power – had to gain command of the sea. The surprise is that Rome, hitherto an almost invincible power by land, gained command of the sea at virtually her first attempt and rarely, if ever, lost it. On the other hand, Carthage which had exercised maritime control of the central Mediterranean almost unchallenged since the decline of Athens lost control to the Romans in under ten years, but in two successive wars produced two generals of genius, Hamilcar Barca and Hannibal, who inflicted defeats on the Romans which were unprecedented and were not repeated for another 500 years. The Punic Wars were Rome's greatest trial. To win she had to transform herself from a regional to a world power and in doing so she initiated what was probably an inevitable and irreversible change from a tolerably democratic republic into a slave-run capitalist autocracy.

Carthage was founded near present-day Tunis in the eighth century BC by Phoenician colonists from Tyre in the Levant. In the next century she far outstripped her mother-city as a commercial and naval power. Relying on mercenaries to fight for her on land, Carthage was as formidable an enemy to the Greek cities of the west as Persia was to those on the Greek mainland and in the Aegean. In 480 BC she joined forces with Persia to execute a giant pincer movement on Greece and Greek Sicily together during the second Persian invasion. This failed at the Battle of Himera in the same year. Despite subsequent efforts, Carthage never really controlled the cities of eastern Sicily, but by 264 BC she regarded herself, with some justice, as having all Sicily within her sphere of influence. Any move by Rome into that island would therefore bring her into conflict with the richest state in the Mediterranean, which was also one of the most powerful. Her seafaring traders knew and exploited every corner of the Mediterranean and had sailed into the Atlantic as far as Britain in the north and equatorial Africa in the south. Carthaginian warships were mainly quinquiremes, much heavier and better armed than Athenian triremes with archers and slingers. Consequently naval warfare again became a matter of grapple and board rather than manoeuvre and ram.

Although she had no fleet, Rome sent an army across the straits to Sicily in 264 BC to support the people in revolt against a Carthaginian garrison. Inevitably, Carthage replied by sending an army and a fleet to Sicily. In the following year Rome sent a large army to conquer the whole island; Syracuse was captured and a year later Agrigentum fell to the Romans. The Carthaginian army was formidable, but their fleet was more dangerous, ravaging the coast of Italy as well as Sicily, where it regained some towns captured by the Romans. It became clear that if Rome were to win she would have to take to the sea, and the stage was set for one of the most dramatic strategic changes in history.

Rome's decision was implemented in 261 and 260 BC when she built 20 triremes, similar to the Athenian type and 100 quinquiremes, using the captured wreck of a Carthaginian vessel as a model. It seems likely that

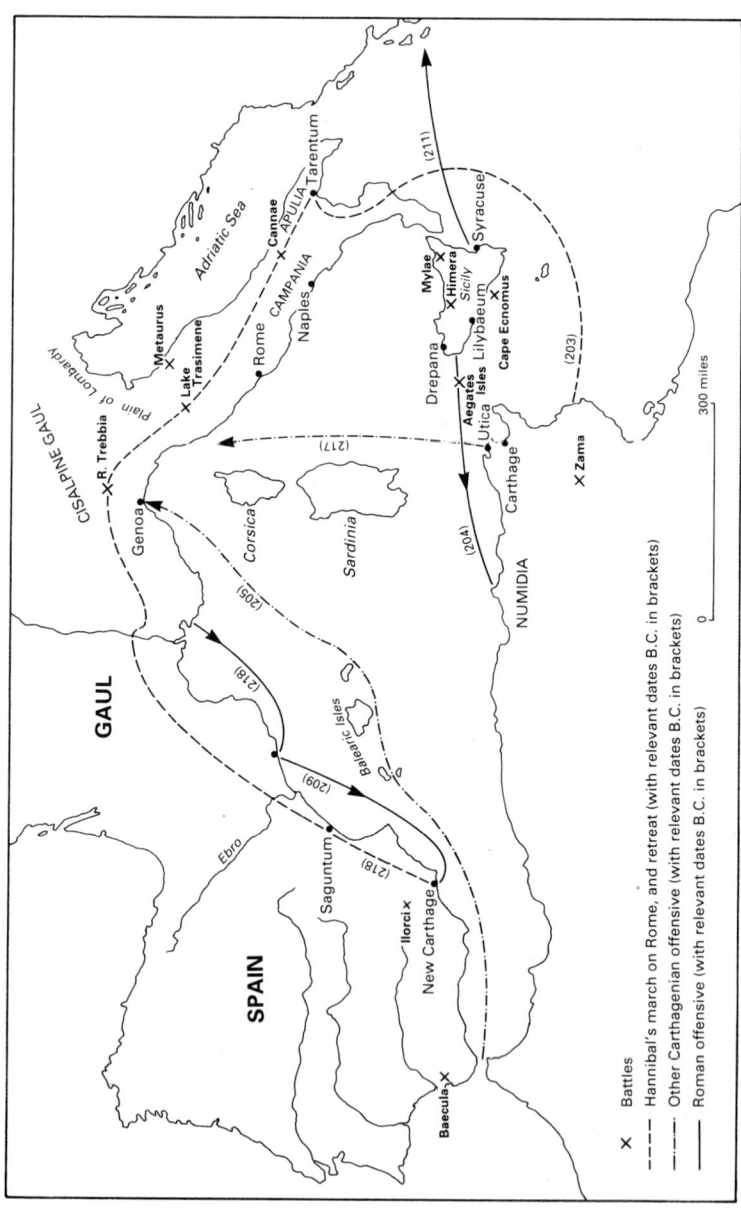

2. The Western Mediterranean during the Punic Wars

some form of prefabrication was used; certainly the fleet was finished very quickly, although there is doubt whether it was finished in a few months as was claimed later. The crews were trained to row on land while the ships were being built, but the most startling surprise for the Carthaginians was a new Roman invention. They devised a long gangplank slung from the mast with a large spike at the far end. At the critical moment when an enemy ship approached, the gangplank (called a *corvus* – a raven) was slammed down on the enemy deck where the spike fixed itself and the two ships were thus held together. As this happened the Roman marines stormed the enemy ship two abreast, with the sides of the *corvus* protecting them. After losing 17 ships on a detached mission the whole Roman fleet met the Carthaginian fleet off Mylae in north-east Sicily and defeated it. The Romans probably outnumbered their enemy by 140 to 130 ships and they destroyed 50 Carthaginian ships in gaining the victory. Another battle was won off Sardinia in 258, leading to the capture of Corsica. Then in 256 BC, the two fleets, each reinforced to about 300 ships, met off Cape Ecnomus in southern Sicily and the Carthaginians were decisively beaten. The way was now open for Rome's boldest move of the war. She sent two legions with her fleet to Africa to attack Carthage itself. The Carthaginian army sent against these legions was defeated and Regulus, the Roman general, overwintered his army in Africa. Making good use of this pause, the Carthaginians reinforced and retrained their troops under the guidance of a Spartan mercenary. As a result of this they destroyed the Roman army in 255 and captured Regulus. Rome's fortunes seemed to be fading. In that same year she lost over 200 ships in a storm when they were on their way to relieve Regulus and two years later another fleet was wrecked when returning from a raid on Africa. Clearly the Romans were not great seamen, whatever their ability as sea fighters. Rome was also facing difficulties in Sicily during this period. Although they had captured the great Carthaginian naval base and fortress at Panormus (Palermo) in 254, Roman forces could make no headway with their investment of Lilybaeum (Marsala) in 250 and in 249 the remains of their navy was destroyed by the Carthaginians in the adjacent harbour of Drepana. Rome was in a stalemate on land and, with a depleted treasury, had lost command of the sea, with seemingly little chance of regaining it.

If Carthage could have exploited the weakness of her opponent she could surely have won the war. The rich landowners who ruled her were, however, more concerned to extend their African dominions and hence their wealth, than to put money into fleets and armies for Sicily. The brilliant Carthaginian general Hamilcar Barca did what he could with the forces available. He held Lilybaeum against continued Roman assaults, supplying it by sea when necessary and harassing the Romans by both land and sea with great success. This was the limit of what he could do, lacking the strength to engage the Roman armies in a pitched battle. The Romans realised that to win they must regain command of the sea. At great financial sacrifice, in which all shared according to their means, another fleet was built and 200 ships put to sea. The Carthaginian fleet, however, had stayed idle and half-manned at Carthage since its last victory. When it finally appeared in 241 BC, undermanned and poorly trained, it was utterly defeated by the Romans near the Aegates Islands and the Carthaginians sued for peace. In 19 years the Romans had built and lost four fleets, but with the fifth they won the war. In future, the war strategies of both sides would be dictated by Rome's command of the sea.

Hamilcar Barca returned to Carthage from Sicily after peace had been agreed, but soon became disillusioned by the inertia and selfishness of those in power. He was therefore sent at his own request to Spain, which had been lost to Carthage at some stage between 264 and 237, in circumstances which are not now clear. It was vital for Carthage, relying as she did on mercenaries for her armies, to regain control of this source of plentiful and excellent recruits. Hamilcar largely succeeded in this in a series of campaigns between 237 and 229 when he died. His work was carried on by his son-in-law and then by his famous son Hannibal. All three had the same ambition – to renew the war with Rome and to win it. By 221, all Spain south of the Ebro was controlled by Hannibal and by 219 he was ready to renew the war with an army of African and Spanish mercenaries.

Having survived the war with Carthage, Rome had to fight another enemy, potentially as dangerous, this time from the north. Between 226 and 222 BC she had to face two major incursions by the Gauls. Both were repulsed at some cost, but they did not do serious harm south of the Appennines. Inevitably, Rome decided to push her frontier up to the Alps, which provided a far more defensible line than the Appennines. Roman colonies were also settled in the Lombardy plain, but the Gallic tribes living there would not be willing allies or subjects of Rome if one of Rome's enemies were to appear in their territory.

The Second Punic War really started in 219 BC, when Hannibal besieged and captured Saguntum (Murviedro) – the last possible Roman ally in Carthaginian Spain. His next move demonstrated for the first, but not the last, time in this war the great cost to Carthage of losing command of the sea, and not making serious and sustained efforts to regain it in the war which was just starting. In order to achieve his objective of invading Italy, Hannibal had to march his army from Spain and across southern France when a Roman army planned to intercept him, through the Alps, a formidable barrier in those days of primitive tracks, and then be ready to face a Roman army in the Lombardy plain. In the event the Alps themselves were not as serious a problem as the hostility of the tribes which lived there. They constantly attacked his rearguard and some historians estimate that he lost nearly half his army either by desertion or death before he reached the Lombardy plain. It is agreed that the Roman army which attempted unsuccessfully to intercept him in southern France did not cause the losses which the army suffered somewhere and somehow between Spain and Italy.

When Hannibal reached Lombardy in the autumn of 218, having left Spain in the spring, he was able to make good his losses by recruiting from the Lombardy Gauls who were already under arms resisting the establishment of further Roman colonies. By December he was ready to fight and at the Battle of the River Trebbia he defeated the first Roman army which he had met in open battle. Command of the sea passage between Spain and northern Italy would have enabled him to secure the same decisive result as the Trebbia on future occasions and would also have given him far greater strength for his subsequent operations in Italy. During his Italian campaign he followed an indirect strategy of seeking to detach Rome's allies from her instead of, as one might expect, assaulting Rome herself. This was surely at least in part due to the fact that he did not bring a siege train to Italy with him. It had to be left in Spain because there was no way of getting it across the Alps; the elephants were trouble enough on that journey and they had legs not wheels. Here again was a severe restriction imposed by the Carthaginians' loss of control of the sea. As we shall see, this handicap was to prove even more serious in the later stages of the war.

Since this is a study of the interaction of naval and military power there is no need to follow Hannibal's land campaign in detail, at any rate until the later stages, when the lack of a fleet became even more crippling. After the victory at the Trebbia in December 218 the Carthaginians overwintered north of the Appennines and recruited more Gauls to their army. In 217 Hannibal made his way south and in the hills south of Arezzo destroyed a second Roman army in the defiles by Lake Trasimene. Hannibal, in search of disaffected Roman allies and confederates, marched his army down the east side of Italy and wintered in Apulia where he was able to establish communication with Carthage, but this brought him neither reinforcements nor supplies. Here in 216 he won his greatest victory, at Cannae, which a later Roman historian described as Rome's greatest defeat until the Battle of Adrianople in AD 378. Roman losses have been estimated as low as 45 000 and as high as 75 000. On either estimate it seems that the legions broke and ran – a thing unheard of in Roman history till then – but nothing else would explain the casualties or the fact that the Roman Senate publicly disgraced and punished two legions. Now seemed the chance for Hannibal to march on Rome; his subordinates are said to have argued strongly for this but Hannibal refused. He was surely correct in this; without support from Carthage in the shape of reinforcements, supplies and above all a siege train, he could not hope to seize Rome with hostile armies at his back. Moreover, although Rome's defeat may reasonably be blamed on the tactical ineptness of her generals and the clumsiness of their manoeuvring on the field of battle, there was no doubt that the leaders of the Roman Senate had a very firm grasp of strategy and if Hannibal had chosen to invest Rome (he could not expect to take it at the first assault) the Romans could have used their superior numbers (it has been calculated that Rome could at this time draw on a manpower pool of some 500 000 citizens and allies in Italy) to trap Hannibal and crush him against the walls of Rome.

All this is conjecture; but what is not in doubt is the determination of the Roman people and their war-winning strategy, from which they would not be distracted. Their strategy was in effect threefold, or rather in three stages which sometimes overlapped, but were necessarily broadly sequential. Rome's first aim had to be to confine Hannibal to as small an area of Italy as possible given that the chance of a pitched battle in open ground had to be avoided until Hannibal was much weaker. The second aim was to deny Hannibal access to reinforcements from Spain, his main recruiting ground, and as soon as possible to take that country from the Carthaginians. The third aim was of course to take Carthage itself. At the heart of this strategy was command of the sea, and from now until the war's end it is unlikely that the strength of the Roman navy ever fell below 200 ships and 50 000 men. In addition Rome raised 25 legions, say 150 000 men, for many if not most of the remaining years of the war. By contrast Hannibal's army diminished in strength from Cannae onwards, since no major reinforcements ever reached it from either Spain or Africa.

The primary strategic task for Rome was that of containing Hannibal's army in as small an area of southern Italy as possible. Quintus Fabius persuaded the Romans to adopt the strategy of exhausting the enemy (the original Fabian tactics) without risking a pitched battle. It would impose a severe strain on Rome's resources, but it was surely the correct one in view of Carthaginian superiority in the open field. As H. H. Scullard writes, Rome had to 'conquer Hannibal as she had conquered Italy, by her roads and fortresses'. Much of southern Italy, including some of the Samnites, and most of Lucania, Apulia and Campania deserted to Hannibal. Most importantly, Capua, the chief city of Campania, and the second richest city in Italy, opened her gates to him and Hannibal made it his base. However, all the fortified Latin colonies, even in areas of disaffection remained loyal to Rome. Thanks to the excellent roads between them and Hannibal's lack of a siege train, they could normally resist attack long enough for a Roman army to arrive in time to threaten any Carthaginian force outside their walls. Moreover, much as he needed one, Hannibal was never able to capture a good harbour in southern Italy to receive supplies and reinforcements from Carthage. Rome was always able to use her fleet to reinforce any sea fortress which was threatened by Hannibal. Thus Naples resisted his attack in 212, and in 213, when he took the city of Tarentum, the citadel commanding the port, continued to hold out thereby denying him the use of it.

Any history of the Second Punic War is complex, both because of the various interlocking theatres of war and because the Romans had enough military power to carry out the first two stages of their threefold strategy, more or less simultaneously. Thus in 218, the year that Hannibal invaded Italy, two Roman legions landed in northern Spain and started the long process of wresting the whole peninsula from Carthaginian control. This would take many years, but at the start the Romans defeated an enemy fleet off the River Ebro. This was another key victory, for after a feeble demonstration off Italy in the same year, the Carthaginians abandoned any large-scale naval operations, leaving Hannibal isolated in Italy. A complicating factor for Rome was the enemy's counter-strategy: Hannibal's main aim after Cannae was to widen the war and Carthage tried to assist with a diversion. In 215 she prepared to help the Sardinians in revolt against Roman rule; but Rome forestalled her. Roman forces arrived and crushed the revolt before the Carthaginians arrived and when they did, vanquished them. Hannibal's own efforts were more successful, although in the event they did not provide him with much direct help in southern Italy. He concluded an alliance with Philip of Macedon in the year of Cannae, when Roman pressure in Spain was depriving him of any hope of reinforcements from there.

Philip's forces could well have tipped the balance in Italy, but they had to get there first, and the Roman fleet stood in the way. Elated by the alliance and induced to action by the victory at Cannae, Carthage prepared another fleet. However, instead of trying to take advantage of Macedonian aid she preferred to send fleets to Sardinia, with the aforementioned results, and to Sicily, where she had held sway in the past and might expect, if successful, to reap commercial benefits in the future. The war in Sicily lasted longer than her Sardinian venture and was more bitterly fought, but in the end was a failure for Carthage. Despite lack of Carthaginian help, Philip fought long enough to show what an asset he might have been if properly supported. Having made some inroads into Illyria, he was able by 214 to base a small fleet on the Adriatic. Rome responded quickly to this naval threat and Philip was defeated, forced to burn the rest of his fleet and retire to Macedonia. The Roman army followed and by diplomacy Rome combined Macedonia's many enemies in Greece against Philip. Nevertheless he fought four energetic campaigns against Rome and her Greek allies between 211 and 208, waiting in vain for help from Carthage. At length realising that Carthage was not interested in the alliance except for what she could get out of it in the short term, Philip concluded a separate peace with Rome in 205. Each nation kept the territories they held. Rome was obviously very glad to avoid war on this additional front by obtaining the neutrality of so formidable an enemy. Carthage lost in Philip of Macedon the only ally who might have altered the course of war.

The Sicilian campaign added to Rome's difficulties at a time when she was already heavily engaged in Italy, Spain and northern Greece. In 214, Hannibal was able to persuade the Syracusans to throw in their lot with Carthage, despite the longstanding hostility between the Greek cities of Sicily and the traditional overlord of western Sicily, Carthage. As soon as Syracusan intentions showed themselves Rome sent Marcus Claudius Marcellus (surely the best Roman general of the war, after Scipio Africanus) to intervene before there could be a general uprising in Sicily as a whole. Marcellus invested Syracuse in 213 after a Carthaginian army had managed to reach the city. Another army from Carthage operated in the rest of the island but her fleet failed after an abortive demonstration to relieve Syracuse. In 212 Marcellus captured a major part of the city, but the citadel commanding the harbour still held out. The Carthaginian fleet made another half-hearted attempt to relieve the city in 211 and then, in the aftermath of a plague which almost destroyed the Carthaginian army in the city, Syracuse fell to the Romans after a siege of two-and-a-half years. There was some small-scale fighting on the southern coast in 210, but at the end of it the whole island was under Roman control again. Once again the Carthaginian fleet had failed. The best bridge between Carthage and Hannibal in southern Italy was back in Roman hands.

In 212 after four years of Fabian tactics which had devasted that part of Italy on which the Carthaginian army but not the Romans relied for food, Rome felt strong enough to invest Capua, the largest city in Hannibal's possession. It fell in 211 after Hannibal had made desperate attempts to relieve it (he even made a feint at Rome). Thereafter the Carthaginian army was increasingly confined to south-east Italy and its strength began to diminish. Reinforcements were essential if he were to survive and these had to come from Spain, the only pool of manpower under Carthaginian control from which there was a land route to Italy. Spain was now the key theatre of the war and much depended on Hasdrubal (Hannibal's brother) who commanded the Carthaginian armies there. After the initial success of the Roman army in Spain in 218 the Romans seem to have been unable to make much headway against the Carthaginians. Part of this must be due to Hasdrubal, a skilful general and leader of troops, but he was absent from Spain for some years around 214 and the Romans did not make decisive progress in his absence. When he returned in 211 he inflicted two crushing defeats on the Romans at Ilorci and by the river Baetis and thereafter confined them to a small area in northern Spain. Rome, undeterred, then sent the man who was to be their best general of the war, to retrieve the situation. Publius Cornelius Scipio (later to be known as Scipio Africanus to commemorate his defeat of Hannibal) arrived in Spain in 210 and within a year had captured the main enemy base at New Carthage (Cartagena) by an operation using both fleet and army. This gave him access to plentiful supplies and control of the main silver mines in Spain, which was important because it deprived the Carthaginians of these resources which they could not replace without control of the sea. Scipio brought Hasdrubal to battle at Baecula in 208 and evidently had the better of the day, but Hasdrubal skilfully broke contact and started the long march to support his brother in Italy. This was Rome's worst crisis since Cannae.

Nonetheless, as before, Rome acted coolly and promptly to mend her fortunes. Scipio quite rightly stayed in Spain to complete its conquest (which he did by 206) and Rome deployed her two armies in Italy to contain Hannibal and defeat his brother. By good fortune the Roman generals intercepted letters between the two brothers and were therefore able to weaken the army facing Hannibal and reinforce that deployed to stop Hasdrubal. The ensuing battle in 207 on the banks of the River Metaurus in Umbria resulted in Hasdrubal's defeat and death. General Fuller ranks this battle along with Zama (Hannibal's final defeat in Africa) as among the decisive battles of the western world, ensuring Rome's dominance until the fourth century AD.

Hannibal's position was now serious. Carthage made two attempts during this period to assist him but both failed. In 205 reinforcements had been driven by a storm to Sardinia, and captured there. In the same year Mago, another effective Carthaginian general, sailed from the Balearics and landed an army on the shores of the Gulf of Genoa. He received reinforcements direct from Carthage but the Gallic tribes in the hinterland did not come to his support and he was defeated at a battle in the Po valley in 203 and withdrew to Africa.

The first two stages of Rome's strategy were now completed and she was ready for the third – the assault on Carthage itself. In 204 Scipio crossed from Sicily to Africa with about 25 000 men (he was denied a larger force because of jealousy in the Senate) and laid siege to Utica, a port some 15 miles west of Carthage. His sea passage from Sicily was unopposed, another failure by the Carthaginian navy. In 203, though forced to raised the siege of Utica, Scipio was able to defeat the Carthaginian and African armies sent against him in separate battles and to detach Numidia, a source of excellent cavalry, from the Carthaginian side. The end could not be delayed much further. In the same year Hannibal was ordered to withdraw from Italy and he was able to bring out between 15 000 and 20 000 men under a truce. The army available to him in Africa was much inferior to that facing him and the Roman general was their best. The final battle took place at Zama in 202 BC. The Carthaginian army under Hannibal was defeated. Peace terms were agreed which left the city of Carthage and her commerce intact but she was stripped of her power to make war; the fleet and dockyard were destroyed. After helping the city find the money to pay the large indemnity imposed, Hannibal went into exile and died without returning to his native city. The Third Punic War hardly deserves the name. It was started by Rome in 149 and ended with the complete destruction of Carthage in 146 BC. The war contributed nothing to Rome's security; it was an act of revenge on the city which had produced the general whom Rome most feared.

However ignoble Rome's final act of revenge against Carthage, few can fail to admire the wisdom and determination with which Rome selected her strategic goals and then pursued them despite setbacks which were often disastrous. In her first encounter with Carthage Rome soon realised that the key to victory lay in command of the Mediterranean. Despite negligible maritime experience she built a fleet and seized control of the central Mediterranean. Rome had to endure fearful losses by storm as much as by battle to maintain this control, but at crucial times she could dominate areas of importance, in both the First and Second Punic Wars. Without such mastery Rome could not have survived a hostile army in Italy for more than ten years. By contrast Carthage, despite the tactical brilliance of her generals and the excellence of her armies (always until Zama superior to their opponents in cavalry and in the ability to manoeuvre and their equal in infantry) never really exerted herself to contest for any long period Rome's power at sea. Fleets were raised, but they rarely fought to a finish or returned after a defeat to try for a victory to reverse a previous defeat. It was as if the Carthaginians could produce superb seamen but not sea fighters. The Second Punic War could well have been won by Carthage if she had had fleets prepared to fight at the right time and if beaten, to return to the fray again and again. The two expeditions sent to Italy in 205 (one of which was diverted to Sardinia by a storm and the other was sent to Mago in north Italy) show that aid to Hannibal could be sent by sea if temporary local control of the sea could be achieved. If this had been attempted earlier and a siege train and reinforcements could have reached him after Cannae, the course of the war might have been changed. Those who doubt whether intermittent mastery of the sea by a weaker fleet would have been practicable in those times are asked to suspend judgement until they have read the next chapter. It is possible that they are victims of what one writer, J. F. Guilmartin, has called the Mahanian fallacy, since they are applying the strategic principles and doctrine of Admiral Mahan to galley warfare in the Mediterranean, to which they are not wholly relevant.

3 The Ottoman Assault on the West

After the destruction of Carthage the Mediterranean reverted to its more normal role as a means of communication and trade between the countries surrounding it, particularly those on its northern shores. Fertile as many of these are, the land routes between them were so poor until the coming of railways and modern roads, that the best and often the only method of moving heavy goods and armies between them was by sea. Another factor increased the importance of the Mediterranean in the Middle Ages. During this period the all-important trade in spices from East Asia was for a number of reasons redirected to Syrian and Egyptian ports whence it was brought to Europe at great profit by the merchant fleets of the Italian city-states, of which Venice became the most powerful. The wealth which Venice gained through trade enabled her to become a naval power to be reckoned with when the Ottoman Turks began their assault on the West and sought supremacy in the Mediterranean.

After the division of the Roman Empire the Eastern, Byzantine half of its capital, Constantinople (founded in 330 AD), defended Europe from attack from the east and was also a key element in European trade with the East when that revived in the Middle Ages. Although the Byzantine emperors had never sought to restrict this trade and were even ready to give the Venetians valuable concessions, the Venetians wanted to have full control over this door to the spice trade and found the opportunity when the Fourth Crusade began to assemble in Italy in 1202. The crusade leaders agreed that in return for transport in Venetian ships to Syria, to go first to Constantinople and place a Venetian nominee on the Byzantine throne. In the event, Constantinople was sacked in 1204 and the crusading army never reached its true objectives in the Levant. A legitimate ruler was later restored to the Byzantine Empire, but it was so weakened by this attack from the west (not least because Venice seized from her a series of important bases in Greece and the Aegean) that her resistance to the attacks by the Seljuk Turks and other eastern powers gradually became less and less effective.

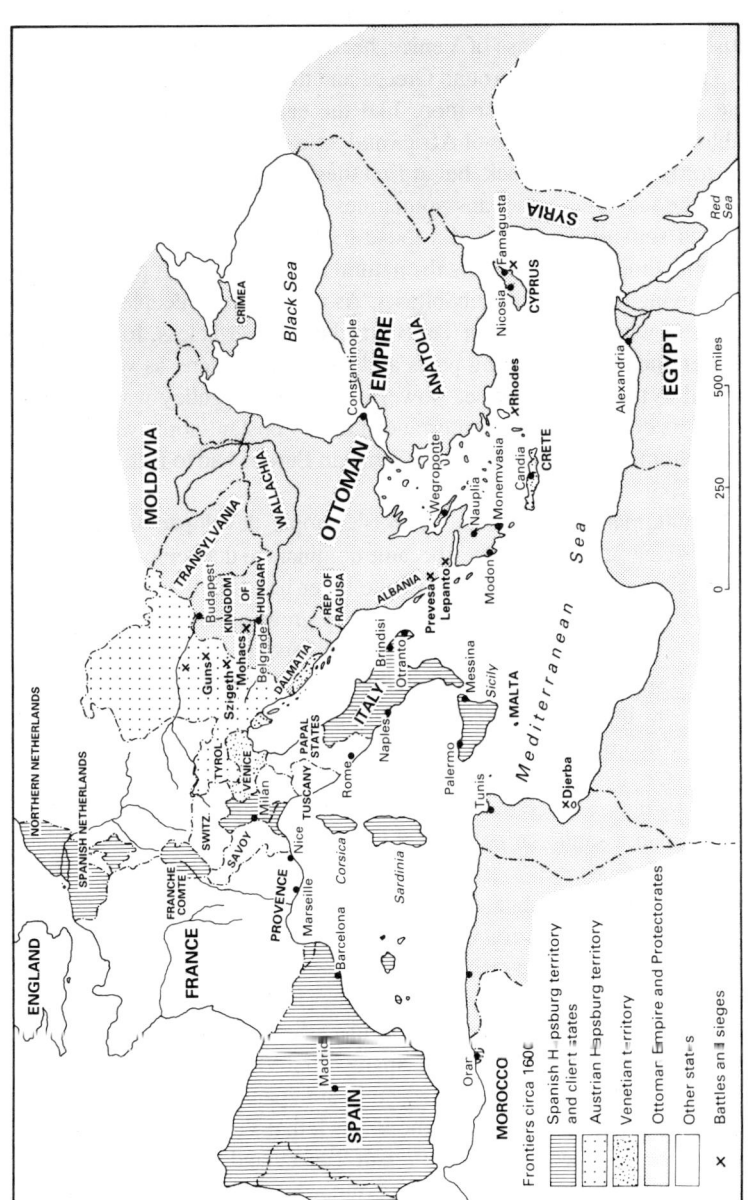

3. The Ottoman Assault on the West

The Venetian Empire is in some ways misnamed if the phrase is intended to convey the idea of a closely controlled dominion, like the rule of the British in India. In the case of Venice, her chain of fortified ports stretching down the Dalmatian coast round Greece and then into the Aegean and on to Crete and Cyprus, were far more like the early European trading posts established along the coasts of Africa and Asia which acted as entrepots and were fortified against attack, but at first they were incapable of dominating the hinterland. The Venetians sometimes established a feudal system of sorts and sometimes exercised a loose form of direct rule, but they gave little or no thought to exploiting the natural resources of their possessions or of improving the lot of the inhabitants. As a result they received little help from them when the Ottoman Turks attacked. Nevertheless, for as long as they were held, these staging posts and naval bases were, as we shall see, essential to the exercise of sea power in the type of galley warfare which reached its climax in the Mediterranean after Constantinople was captured by the Ottoman Turks in 1453, and Christian Europe had to face the Muslim assault from the East.

The Ottoman branch of the Turkish people developed from obscure origins in central Anatolia. They became dominant in that region by defeating their rivals, the Seljuk Turks, when the latter had finally expelled the last Crusaders from the mainland of Syria. They grew rapidly into a formidable military power with, it was generally acknowledged, the finest artillery in Europe. It was thanks to this weapon that Constantinople fell to their assault in 1453 and the way was open for an attack on the Balkans and central Europe, which they pursued for the next 150 years. This is a period of great strategic interest but also of great complexity, since the outcome was affected by unconnected events in countries as far apart as Persia and Peru. The Ottoman assault can be divided into three phases; 1) the land assault, 2) the maritime assault, 3) the stalemate. Neither side confined itself to one element in any of the phases, but the main emphasis on both sides was undoubtedly focused first on land and later on the sea. Three major questions confront those who try to make strategic sense of this period where so much remains unexplained. Firstly, why did the Turks turn from a land to a maritime strategy after their failure to take Vienna in 1529 and were they correct to do so? Secondly, was the Spanish and Venetian counter-offensive by sea correctly handled after their victory at Lepanto in 1571, and if so why was it not more decisive? Finally, how was it that Venice, a minor power in comparison with the warring empires of Turkey and the Hapsburgs, could play such a key role at various times and why were her interventions so infrequent? Answers to these questions will have to be found when the course of the war has been described, but first it is worthwhile to try to avoid some of the misconceptions which surround the phrase so commonly used to describe these wars, the Ottoman assault against Christendom. It is hardly fair to describe the Turkish offensives in this way when the second most powerful nation in the Christian world, the French, never fought against them. On the contrary, the main enemy of France was the Hapsburg Empire of Austria, Germany and Spain united under Charles V, and on his death, divided into the Spanish and Austro-German empires. These powers formed the main, indeed the only, effective bastion against the Ottoman assault, but in pursuit of its own national objectives, France was prepared to attack Hapsburg possessions in Germany or Italy when a Turkish assault was threatened. Moreover the Venetians, whose fleet could be a decisive factor in the Mediterranean, stood aside from the war against the Turks for long periods. The reasons for this were less discreditable than the cynical *Realpolitik* of the French, but the results of abstention by Venice were scarcely less damaging to those fighting against the Ottoman Turks. It is not correct, however, to see the Turkish assault as one uninterrupted attempt to expand westwards into Europe. During the period from the fall of Constantinople in 1453 until the peace treaty with the Hapsburg Emperor in 1606, the Ottoman Empire expanded south through Syria into Arabia and Egypt and west along the coast of North Africa as far as present-day Morocco. It also fought two major wars and several campaigns against the Savafid Empire of Persia and had to repel Portuguese incursions into the Red Sea. It was also necessary for it to quell revolts of restless subjects in Armenia and Anatolia from time to time. Since policy in the Ottoman Empire depended largely on the wishes of the ruling sultan there were also periods of peace when a pacific or indolent sultan ruled the Empire. It is not surprising therefore that the Ottoman threat of attack was sometimes lifted for considerable periods, much to the advantage of the Christian West.

THE ASSAULT BY LAND

After the capture of Constantinople (renamed Istanbul in the present century) by the Sultan Mahomet II, the Turks had a base from which they could attack the West by sea as well as by land. Not surprisingly they chose to continue to rely on their formidable army and in 1456 they opened an offensive in the Balkans where they had held territory before the capture of Constantinople. They attempted the capture of Belgrade, the main fortress guarding the southern approaches to Hungary, the border state protecting the Christian states in central Europe. When their attempt on Belgrade failed, the Turkish armies turned to the south, using their now numerous war galleys to transport siege materials and to raid enemy-held coasts. By 1470 when they captured Negroponte, the Venetian fortress on Euboea, they had already taken over most of the Greek mainland, and Albania had been under Turkish control since 1468. After 1470 the Turks extended their control up much of the Dalmatian coast of the Adriatic as far as Ragusa (Dubrovnik) which became a vassal state by 1479. In that year, facing the loss of her sea bases in the Adriatic, Venice was glad to make peace, despite the harsh terms. In the next year Mahomet sent his fleet to sack Otranto and let it be known that in 1481 he himself would sail to invade Italy. All Europe from Rome to Vienna seemed to be threatened by the Turks and the Christian rulers were woefully unprepared for an invasion. Fortunately for Christendom Mahomet died in that year and was succeeded by his son Bajazet, the only pacific ruler in the long line of Ottoman sultans who directed the assault on the West. Europe was spared a major invasion until after his death in 1512. Venice was able during this pause to acquire Cyprus from the last of its Frankish rulers but lost to the Turks two major fortified ports in the Peloponnese, Coron and Modon.

In 1512 Bajazet's successor Selim I turned east to try to deal with the growing power of Persia under the Savafid dynasty. He defeated the Persians at Tchaldiran in 1514 and sacked their capital Tabriz. The Persians, however, were not completely beaten and indeed were never subdued by the Ottoman Turks and always threatened, either as an unacknowledged ally or as a cobelligerent of the West, to encroach on eastern Turkey whenever the Ottoman Turks turned west. Selim spent the remainder of his time in the East far more profitably. Armenia and Syria were annexed and with the capture of Egypt in 1517, the Ottoman Empire could claim to be the richest and most powerful Muslim state of its time.

When he succeeded his father in 1520, Suleiman the Magnificent used that power for a serious and relatively sustained attack on the West. In 1521 he captured Belgrade, the fortress guarding the southern approach to Hungary which had withstood an Ottoman assault 65 years before. In 1522 he took an army by sea to besiege Rhodes, which the Knights Hospitaliers of St John had made one of the strongest fortresses in Europe. A Venetian fleet stood by while this outpost of Christendom fell in 1523, without taking any action to help the besieged. In 1526 Suleiman again turned his attention to the mainland and in his second invasion of Hungary utterly defeated the defending forces at Mohacs. In effect Hungary was eliminated as a border state defending the West. Christian Europe now lay open to Ottoman attack. Suleiman did not, as expected, try to exploit his victory at once since revolts broke out in Cilicia in the following year; but he was probably also hoping that a planned French invasion of Italy would divert the forces of Charles V, the Hapsburg Emperor of Austria and Spain, who also had extensive possessions in Italy and the Netherlands. The Hapsburg bloc, whether united into one empire under Charles V or separated into two (Spain with the Netherlands and parts of Italy in one, and Austria and parts of Germany in the other), was to be the main and sometimes the only European adversary of the Ottoman Turks, but as has already been mentioned the Hapsburg rulers were regarded by the rest of Europe not solely as the defenders of the Christian world but also, and probably more importantly, as potential overlords of all Europe. This was the predominant fear of the recently unified French kingdom, but there was another reason for hostility to the Hapsburgs and that was the confessional divide caused by the rise of Protestantism. As a result the peoples of Holland and north Germany were constant enemies of the Hapsburgs, against whom both Austrian and Spanish Hapsburgs were prepared to wage war whenever there was a pause in the Ottoman assault from the East. The key part which the Protestant Dutch played in the decline of the Spanish Empire will be discussed in the next chapter, but for the present it is important to remember that during much of the sixteenth century the Hapsburg bloc had numerous European and transatlantic enterprises in play and did not, and probably could not, give all its attention to the threat from the East. Although the Turkish wars with their alternating emphasis on land and sea are of great interest for the current study, they were not the only wars in the sixteenth century which would affect not only the history of war, but also that of Europe. Some of this will become apparent in the next chapter; for the present it is important to stress that the disappearance of Hungary as an effective marcher state entailed the direct involvement of the Hapsburg bloc; the Ottoman assault begins to have a pan-European dimension.

By 1529 Suleiman was ready to start his most ambitious operation in Europe. He planned to march his army from Constantinople to Vienna, capture it, overwinter there and continue his assault on central Europe in 1530. However, his reliance on the French holding Charles V and his army in Italy was unwise. The French were unreliable allies and concluded a separate peace with Charles V (the Peace of Cambrai) and by July 1529 the Hapsburg armies could be redeployed against the Turks. It was not possible for more than a small force of crack Spanish infantry to reach the Archduke Ferdinand in Vienna before it was invested by the Turks. These troops played an important part in the defence but the Archduke had to rely mainly on the Austro-German part of the Hapsburg dominions for troops to defend the vulnerable medieval walls of Vienna against the dreaded Turkish siege cannon which had demolished the defences of Constantinople and many other forts and cities.

Suleiman gathered his forces at the Bosphorus in May 1529, the earliest date after the winter by which the Turkish cavalry levies, the main element in the Ottoman army, could arrive from their homes in eastern Turkey. Suleiman started his long march at once but found that the rough country and poor communications caused him serious delay, impeded as he was by the all-important siege train of artillery. He did not reach Vienna until September and though he at once started operations against the two most vulnerable parts of the defending walls, his efforts were hampered by the aggressive defence conducted by the excellent Spanish and German infantry in the garrison. The Ottoman attacks were vigorously pressed until October when the onset of winter forced Suleiman to order a retreat; even so he was too late. A country which his army had ravaged on the outward march inevitably denied it food on its return and early snow in the Danube valley destroyed much of the cavalry whose horses were not inured to such cold. The expedition was a disaster and Suleiman's first serious strategic reverse. In view of the short Turkish campaigning season and the long distance of key European cities from the Ottoman bases it would seem that central Europe was, if adequately defended, beyond the reach of the Ottoman armies. Moreover the infantry which they would meet there – Spanish tercios and German landsknechts – were, unlike the brave but undisciplined Hungarian cavalry routed at Mohacs, a fair match for the crack Janissary infantry of the Ottoman Sultans.

After a two-year pause, no doubt to rest his levies and recoup his finances Suleiman again marched his army into Europe in 1532 but turned aside from the normal route up the Danube valley to Vienna and penetrated into the mountains to the west of the Danube where he failed to take Guns, a fort some 250 miles west of Budapest. The campaign was not a success since the Ottoman army consisted mainly of cavalry which could not achieve decisive results in mountainous country. In the following year Suleiman made peace with his Austrian adversary and turned against Persia. Baghdad was captured but once again the Savafid Empire of Persia remained unsubdued. It was during this period that Suleiman decided to continue his offensive against the West by sea as well as by land. The Ottoman sultans has built shipyards and started to create a galley fleet soon after their capture of Constantinople. It had, however, been used hitherto to blockade ports and coastal fortresses and to assist in transporting and supporting armies operating in the Aegean and Levant, as at Negroponte and Rhodes. The isolated raid on Otranto in 1480 was exceptional, otherwise the fleet generally operated in support of the army. However, with the appointment of a corsair admiral from North Africa in 1534 there comes a notable change in Turkish maritime operations.

THE MARITIME ASSAULT

In the early part of the sixteenth century the Spanish part of the Hapsburg bloc had been slowly extending its sway along the coast of North Africa, reaching Oran by 1509. The independent Muslim corsair rulers of this coast naturally felt alarmed by this threat from Spain and, to secure protection, offered their allegiance to Suleiman in 1519. Suleiman accepted their homage and thus secured the services of one of them – Khaireddin – known to the West as Barbarossa, who in the years to come was the most feared Muslim naval commander in Turkish service. In 1529 Barbarossa and his brother recaptured the fortress defending Algiers from Spain, and five years later seized Tunis from Spain's Moorish vassal. It was clear that Spain had lost the chance, thrown up by the disunity of the corsair rulers, to get control of the coast of North Africa from Gibraltar to Tripoli; this could have been of immense advantage during the long naval war with the Turks which was to last from 1538 to 1572. Indeed without the corsair fleet, its commanders, and its North African bases, it is hard to see how an Ottoman fleet based on Constantinople could have lasted so long in the central Mediterranean, it is more likely that it would have been confined to the Aegean, as it was for the most part after Lepanto. Of course Charles, the Hapsburg ruler of dominions in Austria, Germany, Flanders, and France as well as in Spain had many other calls on his limited military resources and could not give his African campaigns high priority when his enemies there were weak. The criticism then is not that Spain did not try to subdue the North African corsairs, indeed she did try to do so in subsequent campaigns with varying success. However, it is clear with hindsight that the main effort from Spain came too late. It should have been made before the corsairs and the Turks combined their fleets under the corsair admiral Barbarossa in 1533 and Suleiman switched his attack on the West from the land to the sea. As it was, Charles V was able to recapture Tunis in 1535 and restore it to a Muslim vassal sultan (whose descendants held it against the Turks until 1568) but he was not able to proceed against Algiers immediately and the corsairs of North Africa were now too strong to be disposed of without a long and concerted land and sea campaign. To anticipate a little, Charles led one last major assault against Algiers in 1541, but owing both to storms and fierce resistance it ended in almost total disaster. Thereafter Charles was forced to confine his attention to European affairs and, save for one brief intervention by Don John of Austria after Lepanto, Spanish domination of the North African coast steadily declined.

We must return to 1538 to trace the course of Suleiman's maritime offensive. The newly enlarged Turkish fleets combined with the corsairs and under the command of Barbarossa, put to sea with the aim of capturing Corfu, the Venetian fortress off northern Greece. If this fell to the Turks the Venetian ships would be confined to the Adriatic, destroying her commercial wealth and naval power at one stroke. Corfu had been invested in 1537, but its modern defences had withstood the Ottoman assault and for that year the Turkish forces were rebuffed. When the attack was renewed in 1538 the Turkish and Christian fleets were evenly matched but when they met in September Barbarossa drew up his fleet under the guns of Prevesa, a fortified port in northern Greece. He thus secured the strategic advantage, as was shown when the Christian fleet attempted to blockade the Turks in the gulf of Prevesa – a manoeuvre for which galley fleets were not designed. When in due course the Christians were forced through lack of supplies to withdraw, they lost a number of ships to the pursuing Turks and narrowly escaped complete destruction. Barbarossa had won a strategic victory but Corfu was still in Venetian hands and the Turks lost many ships in a storm on the way back to Constantinople. Despite this setback the Ottoman Sultan could feel satisfied with the first major fleet encounter between the Turkish and corsair fleets and their main rivals, the navies of Venice and Spain. The former, disgusted by the poor performance of the commander of the Christian fleet, sought and obtained a separate peace with the Ottoman empire, with the result that the Venetian fleet, the second most powerful on the Christian side, was not used against the Turks in a major engagement until 1571. Under the terms of the peace treaty, Venice accepted the loss of her fortresses in southern Greece but retained Cyprus, Crete and of course Corfu and her other ports on the Dalmatian coast.

In retrospect 1538 can be seen as the *annus mirabilis* of the Ottoman Empire. Not only did it outface the Christian fleet at Prevesa but on land the Sultan conquered Moldavia and started a counter-attack against the Portuguese in the Red Sea, in an attempt to win access to trade in the Indian Ocean. By now this empire, with 12 million inhabitants, was the greatest Muslim power in the world and it is estimated that the wealth it received from its carefully controlled system of vassals and military fiefs was as considerable as that accrued by Spain from the silver mines of America. If 1538 showed Ottoman power at its height, then 1543 was the crucial year in the Ottoman assault on the Hapsburg empires. This was in part because it was one of the few occasions when the Franco-Turkish entente was really working. By sea the Turkish-corsair fleet mounted its most wide-ranging offensive, as Barbarossa, in open alliance with the French, moved his fleet to the western Mediterranean, sacked Nice and overwintered in Provence. At the same time Suleiman himself invaded the Balkans and turned his Hungarian vassal state into a Turkish province under permanent military occupation. The threat to Vienna and central Europe was serious, but the Hapsburgs were saved once more by the fickleness of the rulers of France, who in 1544 signed a peace treaty with their enemies leaving Barbarossa isolated in the western Mediterranean. He therefore sailed home to Turkey after devastating the west coast of Italy on the way, as if to underline the cost to the Christian cause of the loss in 1541 of the Hapsburg fleet off Algiers and the continued neutrality of the Venetian fleet. Barbarossa's death on his return must have been greeted with many grateful prayers of thanks in the West.

The understanding between France and Turkey, whether covert or public, must have been of considerable help to the latter and after the collapse of Suleiman's plans for a further invasion of central Europe, he signed an agreement with Charles V in 1547. Almost at once both parties turned to other wars; Charles fought against the Protestants in Germany and the Sultan Suleiman against Persia, where he was occupied without any lasting success until 1555. In the meanwhile despite the peace agreement, Muslim and French ships raided unchecked in the central Mediterranean. Two important changes took place before the Ottoman assault was renewed. In 1559 the Peace of Cateau Cambrésis ended the struggle between the French Valois kings and the Austro-Spanish Hapsburgs which had begun in 1494. This was important in enabling the Hapsburgs to concentrate their resources on other pressing problems. Four years before, Charles V, Emperor of the Holy Roman Empire and King of Spain, who had previously been charged with solving these problems had abdicated, exhausted and disillusioned. He was succeeded on the Spanish throne by Phillip II, who also ruled in Italy and the Netherlands. Ferdinand ruled in Austria and parts of Germany. Both Hapsburg empires were of course still targets for Ottoman attack and acted together against the Turks. Inevitably there was not a complete harmony of interest between such large political units and their cooperation was less than perfect.

Phillip of Spain was an unworthy successor to Charles, his father, both as a politician and as a strategist and anxious as he was to pursue the war against the Turks he had little or no success. His attack on Djerba in North Africa in 1560 was initially successful, but soon his fleet was surprised and destroyed by the Turkish and corsair fleet and the army ashore was then destroyed. A second fleet was launched but this was lost in a storm in 1562. The Ottoman fleet was therefore dominant in the central Mediterranean, but this could not be beyond doubt as long as the Knights of St John held the island of Malta. Its capture by the Turks would also enable them to prevent any future junction of the Venetian and Spanish fleets; the Turkish sultans could then deal with each separately. Malta was therefore an obvious target for the Turks and ever since their expulsion from Rhodes the Knights of St John had been fortifying their new base to the limit of their abilities and according to the most modern principles. It seemed very unlikely that the fortress controlling the main Maltese harbour would fall to the first attack and it is fair to assume that Spain planned her strategy accordingly.

The Turkish expeditionary force of 130 galleys, 50 transports and 30 000 men landed on the island of Malta at the end of May 1565. As with the siege of Vienna, timing was critical if the Turks were to achieve their objectives before winter storms arrived to endanger the operations of galley fleets in the Mediterranean. They landed unopposed at a distance from the main harbour and fortified town and set to work to reduce the outlying fort of St Elmo commanding the best anchorage for the besieging fleet. This small fort held out until the end of June and it was almost July before the investment of the main fortified town could begin. Increasingly fierce attacks were launched by the Turks in August and early September, but all were beaten back by the garrison, which numbered no more than 2500 fighting men and 30 cannon of various calibres with 20 more on St Elmo. Meanwhile a Spanish fleet under Don Garcia de Toledo was collecting at Messina to relieve Malta. After one attempt, which was dispersed by a storm, a small relieving force was landed in September on the far side of the island, well away from the Turkish encampment. The defenders, who had been appealing for help since June, accused the Spaniards of deliberately delaying relief until the Knights of St John, potential adversaries of Spain in the future, were so weakened that they would not pose any threat after the war was over. This accusation was unfair and misunderstood the real reason for Spain's delay which was based on a clear understanding of galley tactics in the sixteenth century. Galleys were amphibious weapons in at least two distinct senses. They were by far the most effective means of transporting siege cannon across the sea and landing them on a hostile coast. In addition the galley crews (mainly the rowers), played a vital part in any subsequent siege, acting as sappers, siege engineers and generally supporting the assault force. It followed that if a besieging commander exhausted his limited stock of galley oarsmen by using them as sappers, and so on during a siege his fleet would be deprived of its motive power and could easily be destroyed by a weaker force. Admiral Garcia de Toledo had to time his approach very carefully; if he came too late Malta would have fallen and the Turkish fleet could have defied him from beneath its walls, but if he arrived too soon, before Turkish galley crews had suffered heavy casualties in the land fighting, then they could have been recalled to the fleet, which with its superior numbers could well have beaten the Spanish fleet. As it was the

Spanish admiral's timing was correct. As soon as the Spanish troops had secured a significant foothold on the island the besiegers withdrew without a fight. Although they were not seriously attacked by the Spanish troops it is thought that only 6000 out of the 30 000 who sailed from Turkey returned there. The last Turkish attempt to control the central Mediterranean had failed and the final phase of the Ottoman maritime assault on the West, which lasted from 1566 to 1572, would now begin.

Suleiman opened this phase with an assault on Szigeth, a strong fortress in Hungary, but he died before its capture. He was succeeded by his son Selim, who was not as good a general but keen to continue the war nonetheless. His first objective was the Venetian colony of Cyprus. The Venetians had expected such a move for a long time and both the capital, Nicosia, and the port, Famagusta, had been well fortified according to the most modern designs with cannonproof bastions themselves mounting cannon. Selim probably counted on the Spanish forces being detained at home by the Morisco revolt but by 1570 when the Turkish expedition sailed for Cyprus the Morisco revolt was crushed and Spain was free to respond to Venetian entreaties for help in relieving Cyprus.

The Turkish force succeeded in overrunning most of Cyprus in 1570; Nicosia succumbed in weeks rather than months as had been hoped. However Famagusta, though invested in September of that year, held out throughout the winter giving Spain and Venice a further chance to mount a relief expedition. This, if properly timed, might like the relief of Malta, have inflicted serious defeat on the Turks. At last in the summer of 1571 a fleet had been collected at Messina, after much negotiation, by Venice, Spain and the Papal States. It met the Turkish fleet off Lepanto in Western Greece but before the fleets had met, Famagusta had fallen.

In a sense therefore the battle of Lepanto was fought too late. Nevertheless this, the last great naval battle between galley fleets and the largest naval battle since the Battle of Actium (in 31 AD not many miles away on the same coast), was one of the most decisive of all the battles fought during the 150-year Ottoman offensive against the West. The Turkish fleet numbered some 300 ships and was competently led although it had no commander to equal their former admiral Barbarossa. The Allies appointed Don John of Austria to command their fleet which was about the same size although the Turkish fleet probably contained a higher proportion of galleys and had more soldiers embarked. It is worth noting that Venice provided 114 war galleys and galleases and Spain 81, with 32 coming from other sources. The size of the Venetian contingent has to be set alongside the fact that there had been no contribution from Venice to any Christian fleet since the Battle of Prevesa in 1538. If Venice had re-entered the fray sooner the Ottoman assault might have been stopped further east. To return, however, to Lepanto, Don John, though young, was experienced in war but not in sea fighting. Nevertheless he acquitted himself well and the hard-fought battle went his way. Only 40 Turkish ships escaped destruction and over 200 Christian ships were available to exploit the victory. The loss of all Turkish bases in Cyprus and possibly in the Aegean must have seemed likely.

The fact that the Turks did not have to face these losses is partly due to the nature of galley warfare (which will be discussed later) but also to the immense energy with which they tried to replace the losses suffered at Lepanto. These efforts were not matched on the Christian side by a comparable determination to exploit their victory. During the winter of 1571–72 the Turkish shipyards launched 160 galleys, a remarkable effort (comparable to the achievement of the Athenians in 406 BC after the reverse at Mitylene). This replacement fleet reached Modon, the fortified port in the Peloponnese, and by exploiting the defensive strength of a galley fleet backed by land defences as at Prevesa, it was able to defy the allied fleet of 200 galleys when it at last appeared in September 1572. Dilatoriness on the part of Philip of Spain who admittedly had many problems in northern Europe, is surely the main reason why the victory at Lepanto was not properly exploited. There can be little doubt that if the allied fleet had been at sea early enough to meet the Turkish fleet before it reached a friendly fortified port, they would have won another victory like Lepanto. As it was, the Turks were able to retain control of the eastern Mediterranean, but such were their losses in skilled sea captains and crews at Lepanto that they never again challenged Spanish or Venetian galleys to a pitched battle in the open sea. At the same time the corsair rulers of the north coast of Africa gradually withdrew their active support from the Ottoman navy and reverted to semi-independence and piracy.

THE STALEMATE

After 1572 Venice, unwilling as always to face a long war with Turkey and the consequent loss of her trade, made peace. She accepted the loss of Cyprus but through bases on Crete retained a hold in the eastern Mediterranean for nearly a hundred years more. The Spanish fleet under Don John seized Tunis in 1573, but it was again lost to the Turks and corsairs a year later. Thereafter, although the Ottoman fleet did not venture far outside the eastern Mediterranean, the corsair rulers extended their grip on the north coast of Africa until they acquired much of the Mediterranean coast of present-day Morocco by defeating the Portuguese at Alcazar in 1578. They remained a menace to merchant shipping for many years but did not seriously contend for mastery of the Mediterranean with the English, Dutch and Spanish sailing ships with cannon broadsides which increasingly sailed into the Mediterranean as the seventeenth century progressed. After Lepanto Spain became steadily more involved in the affairs of northern Europe as her struggle with the French, Dutch and English absorbed so much of her resources. The fact that she could with impunity ignore the Ottoman threat by sea was due to the Christian victory at Lepanto. This was sealed by a truce between Spain and Turkey in 1580.

Although the naval war died down, there was continued fighting in the Balkans towards the end of the sixteenth century. In the last great battle of the war the Turks defeated an army of the Austrian Hapsburgs at Kerestes in 1596. By strenuous efforts the Austrians recovered from this defeat within two years. Thereafter the Turks were again distracted by revolts in Anatolia which were not put down until after 1598. As time went on the Ottoman sultans were more and more reluctant to pit their light cavalry, the main part of their army for over 100 years, against the largely professional infantry armies of the Hapsburg German empire. The balance of advantage in battle had by the end of the century swung back in favour of well-disciplined infantry, now having firearms as well as pikes. In addition, the new system of fortifications developed to such good effect in the Mediterranean, was imposing severe restraints on Turkish offensives in the Balkans. The Hapsburg emperors had fortified a number of small towns and strong points along their frontier with the Ottoman Turks and these were often able to hold out long enough under attack to thwart a Turkish offensive. On a number of occasions the Ottoman commanders found that after the frontier town or fortress had been taken they could not advance further without facing the danger of being caught by winter in the Balkan countryside. This, as they knew from the disastrous retreat from Vienna in 1529, was likely to lead to the loss of most of their light cavalry horses. By the end of the century the Muslim rulers in Constantinople were ready to abandon the idea of a holy war against Christendom and contemplate a lasting peace between great powers of equal status. The Peace of Silva Torok was signed in 1606 and with it the Ottoman assault on the West was ended. It is true that in 1683 a Turkish army would again reach Vienna, but by then all danger to Europe as a whole had passed; indeed a generation after the second assault on Vienna the Turks were driven back across the Danube and all Suleiman's conquests had been lost.

CONCLUSIONS

The outcome of the Ottoman assault on the West was often in doubt and events could well have turned out differently, particularly if France, the second most powerful state in the West after the Austro-Spanish Hapsburg empire of Charles V, had agreed to combine with their Hapsburg enemy against the Turks. If this had happened there is little doubt that the Ottoman Turks could have been repulsed much earlier and probably driven out of Hungary and present day Bulgaria very soon after Suleiman's death. The course of the war in the Mediterranean, if France had cooperated with Spain and Venice, is more difficult to decide. This will become clear as the reasons behind the Ottoman decision to pursue their offensive by sea are analysed.

The Turkish Army was clearly the basis of the power of the Ottoman sultans; but the way in which that power was used was very much a matter for each sultan personally and the succession of a pacific or an incompetent sultan saved the Hapsburgs from further disasters on more than one occasion. Apart from the Janissaries, a crack body of infantry raised by, and directly responsible to, the sultan of the day, the main strength of this army lay in the timariot cavalry, light horse which were virtually unbeatable by other cavalry after the Hungarian cavalry had been destroyed at Mohacs. It is convenient to call the timariot horse feudal since they rendered military service in exchange for rights over land, but the Ottoman system appears to have been far more efficient than that used by medieval kings in Europe to collect an army.

It has been estimated that in the time of Suleiman the Magnificent an Ottoman ruler could in any one year collect for the use of the state as many resources (men and material) as were raised by Spain with the proceeds of American silver. However, like any state system of the period which relied for military service on those who were sustained by the agricultural economy, the Ottoman Empire had two grave weaknesses. If the timariot cavalry were called out either too often or for too long in any year the national wealth of the state declined. In consequence the campaigning season was short (May to October at best) and it was rare for the sultans to mount two major campaigns in two consecutive years. Moreover the timariot levies could not withstand a Balkan winter in the open because of their horses nor could they, because of the Anatolian winter, leave their lands in time to be ready for a European campaign before May at the earliest. Suleiman's march to Vienna, the relatively brief and unsuccessful siege and the disastrous retreat, showed the results of these limitations. Unless Vienna could have been captured quickly and relatively intact for use as a base over the winter of 1529–30, it looked as though central Europe was beyond the reach of Ottoman assault. It is therefore understandable that after 1530 Suleiman should consider whether the sea would not provide the best means of projecting Ottoman power far into Europe. It was certainly then, the best means of moving the artillery needed to destroy and capture fortified cities and ports.

It is of course one thing to wish to initiate a maritime strategy, and quite another to have the ships and experienced crews to execute it. As far as Suleiman was concerned, his recently-acquired vassals, the North African corsairs, filled this gap in the Ottoman armoury perfectly. As seamen and fighters, the corsairs, based on Algiers, Tunis, Tripoli and elsewhere along the north African coast, were the equal of any in the Mediterranean at that time. Their first battle under Suleiman's banner at Prevesa showed that their Admiral, Barbarossa, was a match for any of his Venetian, Genoese or Spanish counterparts. If Suleiman was correct to choose a maritime strategy for his westward expansion after 1530 then it is at first sight difficult to explain why he was not more successful after Prevesa and conversely why Spain and Venice were unable to exploit their victory at Lepanto more effectively. In order to answer these questions it is necessary to understand the special nature of galley warfare and this entails discarding, as it were, the spectacles which Admiral Mahan has given us for the study of naval strategy. Writing about the way in which the British used their superiority at sea to defeat the French in the eighteenth and early nineteenth centuries, Mahan offered what might be called a set of universal axioms on seapower which went roughly as follows:

(i) national wealth depends on overseas trade;
(ii) navies exist to defend overseas trade in peace and war;
(iii) in war navies will seek a decisive engagement as soon as possible in order to defend their seagoing commerce and eliminate that of their opponents;
(iv) after the decisive battle the victor imposes a maritime blockade upon the beaten enemy until his economy collapses.

As J. F. Guilmartin points out, in the sixteenth century and – one could argue, before then – these 'axioms' do not apply. For a start only one of the combatants, Venice, depended on Mediteranean trade, but in this case the land routes and ports through which this trade reached the Mediterranean were under the control of her adversary, Turkey. Neither Turkey nor Spain drew any significant part of their wealth from trade in the Mediterranean. The main difference, however, between later conflicts at sea and those which have just been described, lay in the Mediterranean galley itself. This warship bore no resemblance to the ships of Trafalgar on which Mahan based his thesis, it would be easier to compare it to a rowing boat with a cannon at the bow. For so long as cannon were cast in bronze and were for that and other reasons expensive and scarce, the galley with bow-mounted cannon (so that recoil could be absorbed down the length of the boat) was an effective weapon of war. It was, when in action, independent of wind and weather and could be beached during storms and returned to its base during the rough winter season. It had the great tactical advantage of being able to be beached in the face of a superior force. With its guns pointing seawards it could form with other galleys a position almost impregnable to attack from the sea. It was undoubtedly an effective warship in the right environment. Perhaps the best proof of this is that until the advent of cheaper, and therefore more plentiful, cannon (made from cast iron) no nation which fought for supremacy in the Mediterranean but also had experience of ocean-going ships (one thinks particularly of Spain, but Venice also possessed experience of sailing outside the Mediterranean) ever seems to have attempted to overcome galleys with sailing ships. Moreover the actions by Portuguese ocean-going ships against Mameluke and Ottoman galleys in the Red Sea in the early sixteenth century showed that the galley could hold its own at that time against ships which had sailed round Africa. Galleys only disappeared from the Mediterranean when merchant ships from England and the Netherlands entered these waters with broadsides of cast-iron cannon.

The main limitations of the galley were its lack of seaworthiness in bad weather and its limited motive power – the muscles of its rowers. These needed constant supplies of food and water which entailed frequent visits to land to bake bread and to draw water. Galleys could not stay long at sea or sail far from the coast. A standing blockade of an enemy port without a base nearby was out of the question. The replenishment needs of galley crews also limited the size and range of galley fleets since there were only a very limited number of places around the Mediterranean which could provide drinking water speedily to a fleet of over 50 galleys. These were naturally well known and would be held by one or other naval power. The powerful galley fleet was therefore limited in its range of action beyond the furthest friendly base. The value of the string of bases held by Venice is obvious.

Naval war was therefore a matter of acquiring bases and of using them like stepping stones across a river to advance towards an objective. There could be no question after Lepanto of a victorious fleet sailing direct to Constantinople and dictating peace terms to the Sultan. Naval engagements took on the character of amphibious operations. They usually took place near the shore and probably within reach of a fortified port belonging to one side or the other. If the battle was won by the side without a base nearby then it was essential to capture one in the area if the victor's radius of action and the depth of his sea defence was to be extended. Venetian bases along the Dalmatian coast were essential, not only to get her fleet into the Mediterranean proper, but also to hold hostile fleets at arm's-length from her city and arsenal. It is no coincidence that the two main naval battles of the whole Turkish war were fought off the eastern shore of the Adriatic. It is plain therefore that Prevesa was not more decisive as a Turkish victory both because the Christian fleet remained in being and because the Venetian fortress of Corfu could not be used by the Turkish fleet to extend their radius of action up the Adriatic. In sum the Turkish attempt to bottle the Venetian fleet in the Adriatic failed on this occasion.

For similar reasons the Turkish failure to take Malta in 1565 precluded any attempt to control the central Mediterranean with a galley fleet. Despite the availability of subsidiary bases on the north African coast, Malta was at the limit of range for a fleet of galleys based in Turkey. Possession of Malta would have extended their range dramatically and the damage which this could have done to the Christian cause is shown by the exploits of Barbarossa and his fleet when it overwintered in Provence. As has already been mentioned, the siege of Malta illustrated other aspects of amphibious galley warfare. Galleys were the ideal and often the only method of moving siege artillery on to a hostile coast: all that was needed was a suitable beach. Then, once a sea fortress (for want of a better name) was invested, the seamen and rowers formed an invaluable pool of labour for siege operations. The relieving Spanish well understood the reverse side of this; if the siege went on long enough the motive power of the besiegers' fleet was likely to be killed or maimed on land in front of the besieged fortress. A repulse could then be turned into a naval disaster.

Finally a study of the special nature of galley warfare solves the puzzle of why Lepanto was not exploited. The reconstituted Turkish fleet which appeared at Modon the next year was sufficient to prevent the Allied fleet when at last it appeared, from acquiring that, or any other suitable base in the Peloponnese, from which it could pursue either any subsequent offensive into the Aegean or prevent a Turkish fleet from leaving that sea. The victors' failure to exploit their victory better was the result of Philip of Spain's habitual indecisiveness. The failure of the Turkish fleet to venture again beyond the eastern Mediterranean was due to two factors. The first and most obvious was the heavy loss of skilled sea captains and seamen at Lepanto. It would take years of training to replace them. It was one thing to defy Don John and his fleet from beneath the walls of Modon; it would have been quite another to pit such a fleet against trained Spanish and Venetian crews on the open sea. Even more damaging from the Ottoman point of view was the fact that after Lepanto the corsair beys of North Africa gradually distanced themselves from their Ottoman overlords and ceased to fight as part of the Turkish fleet. They continued to prey on Christian ships and coasts but never again joined in any strategic offensive against the West. The loss of corsair ships and skills seriously weakened the Ottoman fleet and thereafter it never ventured outside the eastern Mediterranean for any significant time. The entry of English and Dutch merchant ships and privateers armed with broadside cannon heralded the end of the galley in the Mediterranean; the North African corsairs adapted to this change, but despite having experienced at Lepanto the effect of Venetian galleases (a cross between a sailing ship and a galley, heavily armed with cannon which could fire broadside), the Ottomans never built a powerful fleet of ships for cannon.

The ambiguous attitude of Venice during much of the Ottoman assault has already been briefly discussed. Since she alone of the Mediterranean combatants depended on the Mediterranean for her wealth and naval power she could not afford long wars and the Turks were content to make a separate peace with the Venetians in order to secure the neutrality of the Venetian fleet. The re-opening of their ports to Venetian ships trading for spice was a small price to pay for the absence of Venetian galleys in the opposing battle fleet. Mahanian doctrines of sea power and trade do not apply when a land power controls the land routes to the ports which generate seaborne trade.

Another factor also contributed to the strategic significance of Venice, despite her size in comparison with the empires of Turkey and the Hapsburgs. As has already been shown, fortified sea ports were an essential part of galley warfare since the galley fleets' radius of action depended crucially on the availability of supplies of food and water. Venetian naval power and commercial strength depended on the chain of fortress ports stretching down the Dalmatian coast round Greece and then up into the Aegean or across the open sea to Crete or Cyprus. At the fall of Constantinople in 1453 the Turks had the best siege cannon in the West and could have taken with ease any fortress built at the time, as their capture of the Venetian base at Negroponte in Euboea in 1470 showed. Fortunately for Venice, there was a lull in the Turkish offensive at the end of the fourteenth and the start of the fifteenth centuries and at that time two new developments came to the assistance of the defence. First, cannon became sufficiently plentiful to be available for defending, as well as for attacking, fortress and city walls. At the same time engineers began to devise the famous *trace italienne* of (nearly) cannon-proof fortifications. The Venetians, spurred on by the loss of their forts in Euboea and in the Peloponnese, eagerly adopted the new but very expensive system of bastion redoubts, which cost money but saved on manpower for garrisons. By the time that the Turks resumed their assault in earnest, the strength of Rhodes (not, of course, Venetian but belonging to the Knights of St John) and Corfu proved the value of the new system of fortification. The precursors of Vauban and Coehorn produced magnificent fortresses for the Venetians (and the Knights of St John) at Nicosia, Famagusta, Malta as well as for the Hapsburg rulers in the Balkans at Candia (Heraclion). The abundant manpower of the Turkish armies was to a significant extent nullified by the power of artillery to defend walls which were now built to withstand artillery attack which had been an important feature in Turkish siege warfare. Without these changes in military technology, which combined so well with the need of a galley fleet for a chain of fortified coastal bases, it is hard to see how Venice and Spain could have resisted so successfully the westward expansion of the Ottoman Turks in the Mediterranean. For Venice these changes only postponed an inevitable decline as her trade in eastern spices was lost first to Spain and Portugal, whose seafarers had discovered ocean routes which bypassed the Mediterranean and then to the Dutch, whose merchants were by the start of the seventeenth century beginning to seize control of the spice trade and then to colonise the Spice Islands themselves. For these and other reasons the Mediterranean became a backwater for world trade and would remain so – at least until the opening of the Suez canal. Both trade and the consequent fight for maritime supremacy moved to the Atlantic Ocean and the seas bordering western Europe and it is to these areas that we must now turn.

4 The Rise and Decline of the Dutch Republic

The struggle for political and religious freedom by the people who would later be called Dutch and their subsequent decline to the status of second-class power occupied about 150 years. It was just one element in the expansion of modern Europe in the sixteenth and seventeenth centuries but it is of great interest to the student of war for several reasons. Firstly the 80-year conflict between the Dutch and their Spanish overlords was the first truly global war, with battles being fought from China in the east to Brazil and Chile in the west. In this context strategic decisions became more complex and on occasion more far-reaching. Even more important for strategy, however, was the advent of standing armies and navies. This became possible because the states of Europe had access (owing to the growth of both commerce and colonial exploitation) to large sources of liquid funds. Permanent forces, and as important, the depots and dockyards to supply them became essential as warships and military weapons became more complex. The conjunction of this advance of military and naval technology with the means to pay for it explain European predominance in world affairs for the next 400 years. It clearly widened the range of strategic choice. If both armies and navies have to be bought instead of being conscripted or raised by some variant of a feudal system, then ob viously the purchaser may, if his state has access to the sea, choose which to buy. The history of the Dutch Republic illustrates these points very well. With few, if any, indigenous resources, it was able resist Spain, the foremost military power of the time, with all the wealth of her American colonies to support her fleets and armies.

It was not, of course, simply a war between the Spanish and the Dutch. From shortly after 1572, when Dutch privateers seized the port of Brill until Spain agreed peace terms in 1648, the Dutch had important but intermittent allies in the Protestant North. England provided essential help on more than one occasion but to the Spanish the main enemy was France. The threat from her neighbour state, which would eventually succeed Spain as the

53

4. Spain, England and the Dutch Republic

dominant power in Europe, had been the main preoccupation of Spanish foreign policy ever since France tried to seize control of Italy in 1494. This can be seen as dynastic rivalry between Hapsburg and Valois, but when the Emperor Charles V divided his empire on his abdication, hostility between France and Spain continued. His son Philip received Spain, the Netherlands, Franche-Comté and Savoy, all adjacent to and threatening France. Not surprisingly the Hapsburg Kings of Spain, rather than their cousins on the throne of the Holy Roman Empire, became the main enemy of France. However, even if Spain identified France as the most important of her many adversaries, it does not follow that France did most to bring Spain down. The Spanish Empire succumbed, as Paul Kennedy has pointed out, to 'imperial overstretch'; that is to say, it had too many unavoidable commitments for the resources available, and many then, and now, would argue that the war against the Dutch was the most damaging. We must consider later whether Spain might have survived as a great power if she had shed some of her more costly commitments, but before doing so we must trace briefly the course of the Dutch Revolt and see what strategic advantages enabled a small nation on the mainland of Europe to resist the power which dominated much of the remainder of that continent.

The 80 years of the struggle between these two protagonists were dominated by what has come to be called the 'Military Revolution' which combined the transformation of warfare on land and sea by the use of firearms (whether hand-held or on gun-carriages) with the advent of both cannon-proof fortifications on land and ocean-going sailing ships with cannon broadsides at sea. All these changes aided the Dutch. Their country (unlike Belgium, the other half of the Spanish Netherlands) was intersected by rivers and dykes and covered with many towns large and small which could afford the new cannon-proof fortifications known as the *trace italienne*. A powerful and victorious army could conquer most of the rolling countryside of Belgium in a day or two (as happened in 1815 and 1944), but unless ice froze the rivers and dykes or the air was used to outflank them, Dutch defences could force an attacker into a prolonged seige. The second factor working in favour of the Dutch was their relative isolation (and subsequent insulation) from the centres of Spanish power. Spain did not acquire the Netherlands as part of a strategy of aggrandisement, but accidentally, when the hereditary ruler of the Netherlands, Charles of Burgundy, became first Holy Roman Emperor and then King of Spain. Even at the best of times the military supply route to the Army of Flanders was problematic for Spain. The natural route for the bullion and manpower needed by the army was by sea, but it was flanked by two of Spain's enemies, France and England, both of whom possessed admirable deep-water harbours for raiding fleets while

Spain had none between the Iberian peninsula and the Netherlands. The alternative was to go by land along the famous Spanish Road from Spanish Italy through Savoy, Franche-Comté and Lorraine. In 1601 a section of this was occupied by France, whose territory it skirted, and a new military route was devised through the Valtelline (or the Engadine) to the Tirol and thence through southern Germany to Alsace. Both routes were difficult and in places fit only for infantry or pack mules, but this was sufficient because arms and equipment could be procured in the north, so that only men and specie travelled its length. The real cost of keeping the roads open was the intense diplomatic and military efforts which Spain had to undertake to persuade the allied and neutral states, through whose territory the roads passed, that it was in their interest to allow Spanish troops to use them. One is reminded of British efforts to secure the sea route to India before 1945, but in that case the advantage was more obvious. The final factor working in favour of the Dutch was their wealth. This was derived partly from the trade gained from their control of the mouths of the Rhine and the Maas, but from the 1590s onwards they developed an enormous bulk trade by sea from the Baltic to the rest of Europe. Finally in the 1600s Dutch privateering traders broke the Spanish and Portuguese monopolies on trade with America and the East. This economic growth was sustained by a large shipbuilding industry with the result that the infant Dutch Republic was strong enough to be a power at sea from the first and rich enough to raise and maintain one of the first permanent armies in Europe. The lack of natural resources and the long and vulnerable lines of communication to sources of raw materials were weaknesses which would handicap the Dutch in their subsequent wars with England, but were not decisive disadvantages in the struggle with Spain.

THE DUTCH REVOLT

The first revolt of the Dutch people of the Netherlands in 1565 was crushed two years later with the arrival of 10 000 Spanish troops under the Duke of Alva, who thereafter kept order with great brutality. The presence of an army from Spain in Northern Europe was viewed with great alarm by the Protestant nations there and goes a long way to explaining the policy of France and England for the next 80 years. The second revolt in 1572 marks the start of the real war between Spain and the Dutch Republic, as from that year the Republic always maintained forces to resist Spanish attack. The seizure of the port of Brill by Dutch privateers, in that year was followed up by an army of Dutch exiles from Protestant Germany led by William of

Orange. This double attack secured for the rebels the easily defended coastal provinces of Holland and Zeeland. Thereafter the Dutch never lost control of this strategic base, most of which was covered by the three rivers of the Rhine Delta in the south, by the Zuider Zee on the east and on the north and west by the North Sea. There a fleet of shallow draught ships defended the Dutch from a coastal attack and prevented Spain from reinforcing her armies by ferrying troops from Spain. After two attempts in 1572 and 1574 Spain did not try to move troops to Flanders by sea until 1588 when the Armada sailed to join forces with the Army of Flanders. During the whole period from 1568 until the English left the war in 1604 only 10 000 Spanish troops went by sea to the Netherlands, while over 100 000 used the Spanish Road to reach the same destination.

Almost inevitably, the main Spanish attack came by land. The first attacks were launched in 1572 and 1573 by the Duke of Alva with a ferocity that made no distinction between combatants and non-combatants. In those years five major cities on the periphery of rebel territory were taken after long and fiercely fought sieges and most of their inhabitants were slaughtered. This example of Spanish 'frightfulness' served to intensify Dutch resistance. The end seemed only a matter of time although the ultimate defeat was clearly going to be a long and costly business if progress so far was to be any guide. However, the strain on Spanish resources of her many commitments around the world was already so great that in 1575 the Spanish state was to all intents and purposes bankrupt. The Army of Flanders was deprived of both pay and supplies and either mutinied or deserted. William of Orange, by now the supreme military commander, took advantage of this reprieve to invade the southern Netherlands (present-day Belgium) since it was at that stage the intention of the rebels to unite all the Netherlands in one state free from Spanish rule. By 1577 most of this territory was controlled by the rebels.

This could be called the high point of the Dutch revolt, but in the next year the tide turned with the arrival of a new commander for the Army of Flanders. This was the Duke of Parma, one of the foremost generals of the age, whose aim was to recreate and command the Army of Flanders. He made it what it was to remain until 1643 (for as long as it was paid): the most formidable fighting force in Europe. One rebel town after another was starved (or sometimes bribed) into submission and by 1581 he was ready to embark on the strategy which would in four years double the size of the Spanish Netherlands and bring the Dutch to despair. Parma concentrated on securing the Flemish coast and ports, throttling the trade of the major Flemish towns needing access to the sea. Parma's plan paid handsome dividends and French intervention in 1583 on the side of the Dutch failed to

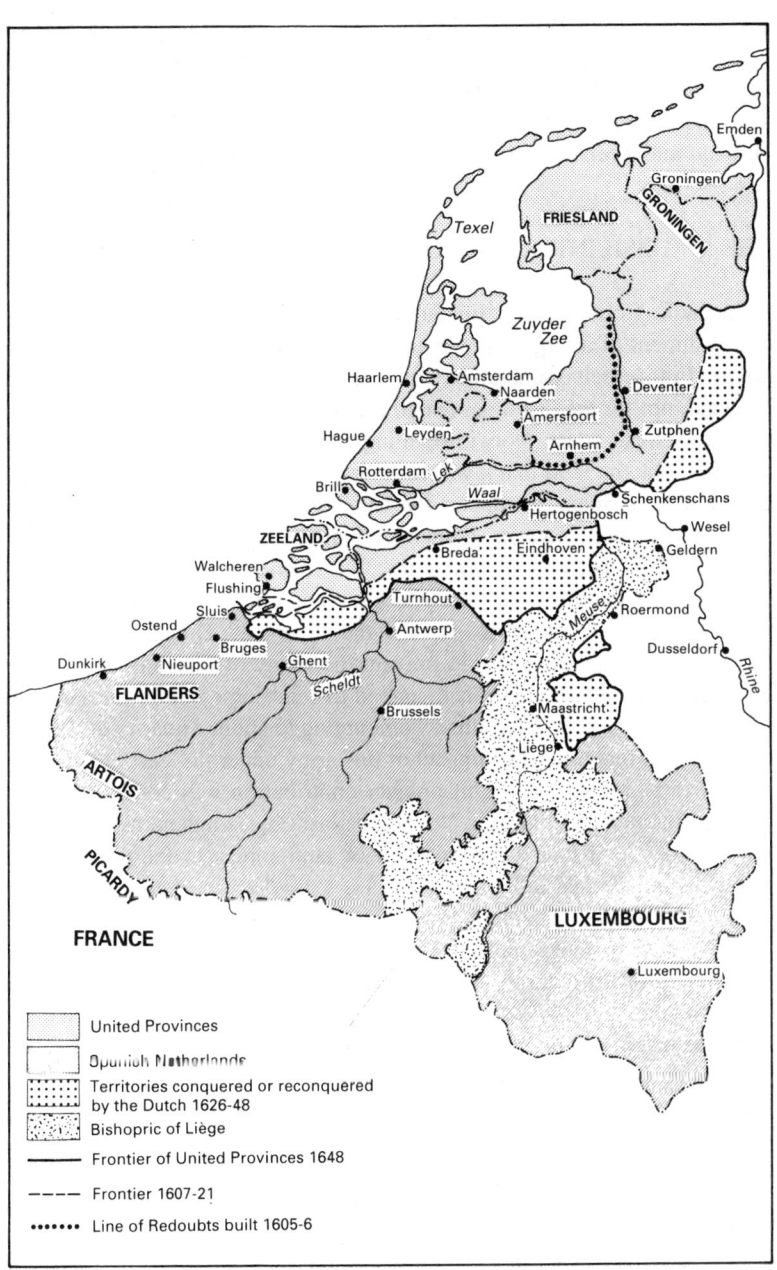

5. The Netherlands during the Wars of Independence

stop him. In 1585 Brussels and then Antwerp, the main trading port of Flanders, fell to Spain after a long siege. The Dutch, leaderless since the assassination of William of Orange the year before, were fast losing hope. They had been forced back to their fortified enclave in the provinces of Holland and Zeeland and were on the edge of bankruptcy.

THE ENGLISH INTERVENTION

Help came from outside. England as well as France had watched the establishment of a large army in the Spanish Netherlands with increasing alarm. France felt vulnerable with her main enemy on two sides and England, not for the last time, feared the presence of a hostile naval power on the Flemish coast. Notwithstanding this concern, Queen Elizabeth of England took the view that it was for France, the only land power in Europe comparable to Spain, to support the Dutch and curb Spanish expansion in northern Europe. However, France's collapse into civil and religious war in 1585 which became known as the War of the League, changed Elizabeth's mind. Spain seemed likely to intervene on the Catholic side and it was considered essential to support the Protestant Dutch, not only on grounds of religion, but also to prevent the Army of Flanders intervening in France. Accordingly Elizabeth agreed to send some 8000 troops to help the Dutch and to provide a subsidy amounting to about a quarter of the cost of the war at that time. The impact of this army under the Earl of Leicester proved to be small, but the manpower contribution was continued under other and better commanders. Not for the last time, England as a maritime power had found that a commitment of land forces to the continent of Europe was essential to her survival.

Philip of Spain responded promptly to this addition to his enemies. He decided that the way to defeat his Dutch subjects lay through England. If England could be neutralised and driven out of the war the defeat of the Dutch was certain. He therefore gave orders for the preparation of a large amphibious expedition against England. His recent accession to the throne of Portugal gave him control of the Portuguese fleet of ocean-going warships – one of the largest in the Atlantic – and therefore made his ambitious plans practicable. As a result the Armada (as it is known to the English) was the largest amphibious expedition which the world had ever seen, or would see again for several hundred years. A brilliant spoiling operation by Sir Francis Drake in 1587, when he burned shipping and stores at Cadiz, delayed the sailing of the Armada by one year but could not stop it. For that it would have been necessary to attack the main base at Lisbon which was too strong for Drake's forces. A similar spoiling attack was tried in 1588, but failed because of contrary winds, and the 130 ships of the Spanish Armada sailed for England in July of that year, with some 18 000 troops embarked.

The story of the Armada is well known, so well known in fact that the accretions to the Armada myth conceal rather than reveal both the difficulties and the achievements of the contestants. Above all, they do not explain why the war between Spain and England continued for another 16 years. The Spanish failure did not mark the end of her sea power, nor was that failure caused by cowardice or lack of seamanship. On the contrary, both sides displayed great bravery and skill. They were fairly evenly matched as regards the number of first-class warships (ships of the line or battleships to use later parlance) but the Spanish ships, especially some of the transports, were unable to sail close to the wind (which seriously restricted their power to manoeuvre) and for various reasons not all of which are clear today, the cannon fire from Spanish ships was remarkably ineffective except probably at close range. The plan laid down by Philip of Spain himself was for the Armada to sail from Spain direct up the English Channel, engaging the English fleet only if it tried to bar the way, to meet the Duke of Parma and his army embarked in flat-bottomed boats at Dunkirk and Nieuport and to escort them to the Kent coast near Margate. Once landed, this army of about 30 000 men (18 000 from the Army of Flanders and 10 000 from the Armada) all under Parma's command, was to march on London and compel Elizabeth to a separate peace under which she would stop helping the Dutch and allow freedom of worship to English Catholics. The plan was risky, given the lack of friendly harbours on the French coast, but was probably practicable if the naval opposition could be overcome or brushed aside.

The early engagements in the Channel gave both sides unpleasant surprises. The Spanish could find no way of closing with the English ships and boarding them and the English, although able to outmanoeuvre their opponents, could not damage them seriously with gunfire without coming within range of the heavier Spanish guns. In consequence the Armada proceeded up the Channel in unbroken formation but was unable (it is not clear whether this was by accident or English design) to find a safe anchorage off the English coast where it could wait until a rendezvous with Parma's forces had been arranged. When the Armada had anchored off Calais, an unsafe haven, without firm news of Parma's army, it was clear that Philip's strategic plan was in jeopardy. Nevertheless the fact remained that no Spanish ship had been sunk by gunfire and only three had been lost by accident. Then at Calais the fortunes of the Armada changed abruptly. It was dislodged from its anchorage by English fireships and fiercely attacked by the English ships which for the first time used their cannon to good effect. Complete disaster seemed inevitable since the wind was blowing the clumsy Spanish ships on to the dangerous shallows off the Flemish coast, known as the Banks of Flanders. A last minute change of wind saved the Armada from complete destruction off Gravelines but since the Spanish ships were unable to face the English ships or the contrary winds they could not return to Spain by the English Channel. Instead it was forced to make the dangerous voyage home round the north of Scotland through the fierce autumn storms of the north Atlantic. It was fortunate for the English that the action ended when it did, since their ships had used up all their powder and shot during the action off Gravelines. If the Armada had renewed the fight there would have been little or no opposition from the English fleet. As it was, the damage caused by English gunfire made the ships of the Armada even less capable of withstanding Atlantic storms, and of the 130 large ships which sailed, only 60 returned to friendly ports. Only 34 of these were major fighting ships and some of them were so damaged that they could never be used again.

The long-term effect on Europe of the destruction of the Armada will be discussed later but the reasons for its failure are worth looking at as they shed light on the next few years of maritime war between England and Spain. Philip of Spain made the correct strategic decision when he chose to try to neutralise England before launching a final assault on the well-defended Dutch 'redoubt' of Holland and Zeeland. However, his plan for achieving his objective was seriously flawed. The order to sail direct for the Flanders ports was questioned by some of his more experienced admirals who realised that their ships could well be lost in bad weather in restricted waters, particularly if they had been damaged in battle. They would have much preferred to seize a port like Falmouth, or an anchorage like the Solent, off the Isle of Wight, from which to operate in support of Parma's army but Philip forbade it. However, even if the Armada had reached the coast of Flanders in good order and in favourable weather, there was one obstacle which it had no means of overcoming. This was the Flemish Banks, a stretch of shallow and treacherous waters some 12 miles off the coast of Flanders. It was on these shoals that the Armada was nearly wrecked after the battle of Gravelines. The sea inside these sandbanks was patrolled by a squadron of Dutch shallow draught ships, which could certainly have summoned the remainder of the Dutch fleet at Flushing if any Spanish ships had entered these waters. It is hard to believe that Parma's fleet of barges (and the 18 000 men of the Army of Flanders) would have escaped destruction by the Dutch. The Dutch fleet would have made every effort to intercept Parma and his troops, for no other single action would have done more to guarantee the freedom of the Dutch Republic. As it was

The Rise and Decline of the Dutch Republic

the Army of Flanders lived to fight another day and the remains of Philip's great fleet limped home to Santander, San Sebastian, Corunna, and other ports of northern Spain. When at last the full extent of their victory became clear, the English were overjoyed and perhaps over confident. Certainly chances were missed and in consequence the war was prolonged. There was even talk of carrying the war to Spain in the autumn of 1588 when it was clear that the Armada was not hovering off Scotland, Ireland or France waiting to make another attempt on England, but the state of the English ships and crews and of the nation's finances precluded further action in that year. By 1589 the ships and crews were available but not the money to pay for them; the records show that Elizabeth's treasury was practically empty. As a result she had to resort – not for the first or last time – to the Tudor form of 'privatisation' and never can it have served her and England so ill. A sizeable fleet and landing force was prepared, with the state paying just over half and private enterprise the rest. The aim was first to destroy the remnant of the Armada in the Biscayan ports (which it had reached badly battered the previous year), then to capture Lisbon and destroy Spain's main naval base (and it was hoped start a revolt of the Portuguese against Spain). Finally the expedition was sail to the Azores and intercept the treasure fleet from America. The lure of gain was stronger than the needs of strategy; the first and most important task was barely attempted; the second attempted but not achieved; while the third and most profitable was attempted and botched, though some valuable cargo ships from the Hanseatic ports were unexpectedly collected as prizes.

After this missed opportunity Spain pressed on with the task of rebuilding her sea power. Progress was steady but ruinously expensive, especially since the maritime war with the English and increasingly the Dutch imposed another burden; the need to fortify the ports and coastal towns of the Spanish and Portuguese colonies in America and the East Indies and to base small fleets there to defend coastal trade and the *flota* (as the treasure fleet was more properly known) bringing valuable raw materials and goods to trade in Europe. From the early 1590s, most of the gold and silver bullion was carried back to Spain in specially built 30-gun frigates which could outsail more powerful ships and outgun ships which were faster than themselves. Moreover, after 1588 Spanish warship design tended to incorporate the best features of English ships, with the result that both sides were more evenly matched in subsequent fights. All these changes made England's maritime commitment more difficult and far less rewarding in terms of ships and cargoes captured. Nonetheless the strain on Spain was enormous; virtually all the materials needed to build ocean-going ships had to be imported to Spain, which was clearly costly and often difficult. Hanseatic and other north European traders and even some Dutch ships were willing to bring these materials to Spain, but to escape the English blockade in the Channel they had to sail round north Scotland and even then were often captured by English ships which were allowed by English decrees to regard anything destined for a Spanish warship as contrabrand. War at sea, then, was a great financial and logistic burden to both sides, but from the Protestant point of view the maritime struggle prevented Philip of Spain from concentrating enough resources to win outright victory in either France or the Netherlands. It will be convenient to follow the war at sea until England withdrew from the war in 1604 and then consider the land campaigns in France and the Netherlands.

In 1591 the annual *flota* from America was again the target of an unusually powerful English fleet, but it was too well defended by the revived Spanish fleet and in the fighting the *Revenge*, one the most powerful ships in the English fleet, was cut off and lost. In 1595 Drake and Hawkins attempted an attack on Panama and the Spanish Main in the old privateering style and were foiled not only by the advance warning which the Spanish had received, but also by the much improved Spanish defences. The year 1596 saw an amphibious attack on Cadiz which was highly successful in its own terms since the *flota* was burned in port to avoid capture and a large quantity of other shipping and stores was also destroyed. In the wider strategic view, however, the raid was really irrelevant; the Spanish war fleet was elsewhere, as were its main bases.

This was brought to the attention of the English when they learned later that year that Philip of Spain had sent an invasion fleet of 100 ships from Ferrol. This was destroyed by a storm with no intervention by English ships. In 1597 Philip prepared another invasion force known as the Third Armada, and an English force assembled to attack it in its base was frustrated because these forces had to be diverted to home defence by the threat of a raid by Spanish troops from Brittany. That raid did not materialise and the invasion force from Spain was again dispersed by storms. England had therefore on two occasions been very lucky with the weather. In 1599 Spain was able to assemble yet another invasion force but the warships had to be diverted to deal with a threat from the Dutch fleet against the *flota* and the Azores, an ominous warning for Spain that there were now two ocean-going war fleets to challenge her. Finally in 1601 Spain succeeded in landing an invasion force in the British Isles, at Kinsale in southern Ireland. Prompt action by considerable land and naval forces compelled them to surrender there before any serious Irish support for the invaders could materialise. The Kinsale campaign emphasised how serious a threat the earlier but abortive invasion attempts could have been. On those occasions far stronger forces had been employed and they were to have been directed at relatively undefended west coast ports such as Falmouth or perhaps Milford Haven. Judging by the large English forces employed to contain and destroy the Spanish at Kinsale, and the relative success enjoyed by a Spanish force raiding from Brittany, a sizeable Spanish force in say, Falmouth, might have been too strong for the English to expel. By 1603 England's ability to finance the war with Spain was stretched to the limit and after Elizabeth's death in that year there was little further action until the peace which her successor concluded with Spain in 1604.

One of the main reasons for England's weak response to both the threats and opportunities of the maritime war with Spain was the situation in France. Elizabeth regarded that nation, not unreasonably, as the main rival to Spain in Europe and therefore the nation which should and could do most to contain Spanish attempts to dominate northern Europe. It had been the virtual collapse of the French monarchy in 1585 which had persuaded Elizabeth to support the Dutch with troops and in 1589 things took a further turn for the worse. Henry III, the weak but legitimate king of the French, was assassinated and succeded by Henry, the Protestant king of Navarre. This was bitterly opposed by many of his Catholic subjects, who were eagerly supported by Philip of Spain. Elizabeth feared, quite rightly, that a Catholic victory aided by Spain would destroy any hope of having France as a countervailing power to Spain in Europe. Moreover, it could well lead to the appearance of Spanish garrisons in the ports of northern France, which would make it easy for Spain to launch a further amphibious attack on England with much greater chances of success.

In response to repeated requests from Henry IV, Elizabeth sent 3500 troops to Dieppe in 1590, from where they were able to prevent the Catholic forces from dominating the French side of the English Channel. The wider aim, of helping Henry and his forces to gain the upper hand in France as a whole, was never achieved, despite the fact that the English commitment to Protestant France was increased to the point where it exceeded, in terms of military strength, that which was provided for the Dutch. Henry's forces did not cooperate effectively with the English troops, as was plain when a desultory siege of Catholic-held Rouen in 1592–93 had to be abandoned as soon as Parma and the Army of Flanders marched to its relief. Even more disturbing from the English point of view was the landing of 3000 Spanish troops in southern Brittany in late 1590. These attempted in subsequent years to extend their control over the area and in particular to capture Brest, the finest port on the French side of the Channel. After two reverses had been suffered by the English forces in northern France Elizabeth sent a larger force of troops, many of whom had battle experience in the Netherlands. By late 1594 these troops had captured Fort Crozon, built by the Spanish to control access by sea to Brest. With this victory, the English contribution to the survival of France as a state independent of Spain was ended.

In fact by the time that the English left France in 1595 the objective which they had been sent to achieve had already been secured. This was mainly brought about by the agreement of Henry IV to accept the Catholic faith. By then the French people were thoroughly weary of war and even more of Spanish intervention in their affairs. An earlier conversion might not have persuaded French Catholics to accept him, but in 1593 the time was ripe. Henry was able to secure control of the whole of France and to expel the Spanish armies. In 1598 a peace treaty was signed between the French and Spanish Kings in which each undertook to respect the territorial integrity of the other. As a Protestant monarch, Elizabeth must have regretted the loss of a fellow monarch to the Catholic faith, but as a war leader she must have been quietly satisfied at the success of her strategy of preserving France as a counterpoise to Spain in Europe. Moreover, within a few years France would be at war with Spain and in the 1630s and 1640s it was France who played a decisive part in eliminating Spanish influence in northern Europe. Despite the cost to England, not only in men and money, but also in lost opportunities elsewhere, Elizabeth's strategy to keep Henry IV in power had been correct and, which is not always the same thing, it had succeeded.

THE DUTCH REPUBLIC SURVIVES

The defeat of the Armada was a turning point in the Dutch revolt. Dutch morale was improved, not only by the Protestant naval victory, but also by Parma's first reverse on land. In the autumn of 1588, when it became clear that there would be no invasion that year, he laid siege to Bergen-op-Zoom, (largely defended by English troops) but had to abandon it a month later. In the following year his attempt to breach the Dutch defences between the rivers Maas and Waal also failed when the unit leading the attack mutinied for lack of pay. It must have seemed to the Dutch that their survival was assured, they were able to believe that if they could survive they could win. However, the greatest change in the post-Armada years came on the economic front. During the 1590s trade blossomed in a most remarkable fashion. Part of this could be explained by the fact that Antwerp's trade was stifled by Dutch control of her outlet to the sea, and consequently Amsterdam and

The Rise and Decline of the Dutch Republic 65

other Dutch cities took over the entrepot trade and related financial business from her, but there was more to it than that. The Dutch were also able to take over from the cities of the Hanseatic League the trade from the Baltic in corn, naval stores (timber, pitch, etc.) and much else. Moreover, they carried these goods much further south than their predecessors; the Dutch traded with France, the Mediterranean countries and even with European colonies overseas. This intervention of the Dutch in the colonial trade of Spain had, as will be seen, major repercussions on the war between the two countries, but colonial trade was not at this stage anything like so important for the Dutch economy as the trade in the seas around Europe. The Dutch Republic had two essential advantages for a nation determined to expand its seaborne trade – it was a leading shipbuilder, and in due course it became the main financial centre and source of credit in Europe. Here then was the basis of the power of the Dutch to make war on land and sea, but they needed good generals and admirals to wield it. Fortunately a good general was at hand. Dutch morale was naturally very low after the death of the first William of Orange (known as William the Silent) and unfortunately neither of the two foreigners who came to lead them, the Earl of Leicester (sent by Queen Elizabeth) or the Duke of Anjou (who was invited to take the crown) were of any help at all, militarily or politically. It was a stroke of great good fortune that Prince Maurice of Nassau, the son of William of Orange, who succeeded his father as Captain General, proved to be one of the great generals of his time.

After his repulse in 1589 Parma was ordered to take the Army of Flanders south to France to restore the Catholic cause following defeats by Henry of Navarre in the battles of Arques and Ivry. This he was able to do in 1590 by saving Paris from capture by the Protestants but Maurice took advantage of the absence of the Army of Flanders to seize Breda by a surprise attack. The capture of this fortress gave an opening into the southern Netherlands should he need it. When Parma had to march south again in 1591 to save Rouen from capture by the English, Maurice did not try to advance into the southern Netherlands but instead concentrated in this, the first of several campaigns, on trying to clear the Spanish from the eastern flank of the Dutch river barriers (that is present-day north-east Holland), from which it would have been possible for them to turn the flank of the Dutch defences on the Rhine delta. In 1591 the Dutch captured Zutphen, Deventer and Nijmegen – useful steps towards this objective. In the following year Parma died and Philip lost his best general who had come closest of all to regaining the rebellious Netherlands for Spain. Until the arrival of Spinola in 1603 the Army of Flanders had no commander to compare with Maurice of Nassau. In the next four years Maurice steadily extended the Dutch grip on the north-east provinces, capturing Groningen, the most important fortified town there, in 1594. In 1597 Maurice surprised and defeated a Spanish force at Turnhout, his first notable success in open battle.

The peace treaty with France in 1598 allowed Spain once again to devote increased resources to the reconquest of the Netherlands and the first result was the recapture of the pivotal area around Cleves, from which either side could outflank the east/west defences built by both armies roughly along the present Dutch/Belgian border. Thereafter the Army of Flanders had to respond to a landing by the Dutch army on the coast of Flanders with the aim of capturing the privateer strongholds of Dunkirk and Nieuport which were becoming a serious menace to Dutch shipping. Both armies met on the beach at Nieuport in 1600 and although the Dutch could be said to have won, (their first victory against the formidable Spanish infantry in the open field when both sides were prepared for battle) Maurice rightly decided that the main objectives in the Flanders were beyond his reach and the Dutch withdrew behind their river barrier. Spain's resources were again reduced in 1600–1601 when the French invaded Savoy and thus cut the Spanish Road, the supply line from Italy.

However, the Spanish position in the Netherlands was unexpectedly revived in 1603 by the arrival of the Genoese banker Spinola, who was a superb organiser and became an excellent general. Ostend, which had been besieged by the Spanish with inadequate resources since 1601, was Spinola's first objective. He pressed the siege vigorously, refusing to be distracted when Maurice captured nearby Sluis in 1604, and finally in the same year Ostend fell to the Spanish. The withdrawal of the English from the war with Spain in 1604 allowed more resources to be allocated to Spinola and in 1605 he was appointed Commander-in-Chief of the Army of Flanders and superintendent of the treasury. In that year he took the offensive and captured three major fortresses on the eastern flank of the Dutch heartland and in the following year was given permission by Philip III, (who had succeeded his father on the Spanish throne in 1598) to open a decisive offensive against the Dutch heartland itself.

The Dutch for their part had been sufficiently alarmed by Spinola's success to build a chain of wooden fortresses connected by earth ramparts from the Zuider Zee along the river Ijssel to Arnheim and then west until the rivers of the Rhine delta were deep enough to be a sufficient defence. Spinola was able to force a passage of the Ijssel but made such slow progress that he had to abandon this offensive. He was, however, able to recapture two fortified towns in the east which had fallen to the Dutch during Maurice's earlier offensives. The real importance of the campaign was psychological. It shook the self-confidence of the Dutch, already bereft

The Rise and Decline of the Dutch Republic 67

of English support, and facing the prospect of Spanish warships in the Channel. They balked at the inevitable confrontation with Spain over their supposedly inviolable bases in the provinces of Holland and Friesland. For their part the Spanish were very disappointed by the failure of their offensive and again came up against serious mutinies, owing to the bankruptcy of the Spanish treasury formally declared in 1607. However, almost more worrying to Philip III and his advisers was a new threat – the Dutch incursions into Spanish and Portuguese colonies, and the accompanying naval threat from Dutch fleets.

THE TWELVE YEAR TRUCE

Expanding trade and commerce in the products of northern Europe had greatly strengthened the Dutch economy in the 1590s. Not surprisingly this success encouraged Dutch merchants to try to extend their trade to the East and West Indies and to South America which were, by papal decree, the monopoly of the Spanish and the Portuguese and the constant target of English and Dutch privateers. In 1602 the Dutch government, foreseeing that trade with these areas could not, owing to the high costs and risks involved, be left to free enterprise and cut-throat competition, sanctioned the creation of the East India Company and promised a measure of naval support. The aim was peaceful trade but it was accepted that defence of ships and trading posts against native rulers and European rivals would be necessary. This trade was far less valuable to the Dutch economy than the Baltic trade or the fishing industry; nevertheless it caught the imagination of the Dutch who pressed for the creation of a West India company with similar support from the Dutch navy. Of more importance, from the strategic and political point of view, this move into the East Indies (present-day Indonesia), the centre of the spice trade, was seen by the Spanish as the most serious threat that they had ever encountered to the colonial wealth on which their military power in Europe depended. Unlike the English with their policy of loot and burn, it was clear that the Dutch intended to stay in their overseas bases and wrest control of trade there from the Spanish and Portuguese. By 1606 the Dutch had secured virtual control over the trade of the Moluccas, the most valuable of the Spice Islands, and there was strong pressure in Spain for a peace treaty with the Dutch, on the condition that they evacuated the East Indies. This was rejected by the Dutch, who tried to exert further pressure by sending a fleet in 1607 to blockade Spain's Atlantic ports. The defeat of a Spanish fleet off Gibraltar did not hasten the peace process. Finally in 1609 a twelve-year truce was agreed as the differences over colonial trade and religious toleration were too great to be settled by a peace treaty. A standstill on Dutch expansion in the East Indies was broadly agreed (but never really implemented) and Spain recognised the independence of the northern Netherlands which were in future to be known as the United Provinces by friend and foe alike. (The Union of Utrecht in 1579 had united these Dutch provinces but neither Catholic allies of Spain, nor Spain herself could be said to recognise it until now).

Despite the terms of the truce, the Dutch and the Spanish continued to fight for the next few years in Africa, the East Indies and in South America; in most places where Spanish colonies and Dutch trading posts were contiguous. The most notable actions were a naval battle in the area of the Philippines, which the Dutch lost, and an extensive Dutch raid on Spanish colonies on the Pacific coast of South America, which was successful and in the longer run proved a profound and costly shock to the Spanish Empire in America. Although the Dutch made no lasting gains in the area, the Spanish were forced into the construction of extensive fortifications for their ports along that coast. Nearer home, both sides were more circumspect, although when a political crisis arose in the independent territories of Julich-Cleves in 1610, a key strategic area in the Rhineland, Spain put a garrison into Wesel, previously held by the Protestants, and the United Provinces occupied other towns in the area.

The main event affecting both Spain and the United Provinces was the outbreak of the Thirty Years War in Germany in 1618, between Catholics, led by the Hapsburg Emperor of Austria, and Protestants, first led by the Elector-Palatine, crowned King of Bohemia, then by Gustavus Adolfus of Sweden and finally by the Catholic kings of France. This war has been described as a civil war in Germany in which other countries got involved. The Dutch had promised help to the Elector-Palatine in his attempt to seize the throne of Bohemia, but were unable to fulfil this promise or to give much assistance later to the Protestant cause in Germany. The Spanish kings Philip III and his son Philip IV, however, gave considerable help to their Catholic cousins on the Hapsburg throne of Austria and in due course Germany became, as France had been before, the battleground on which France and Spain fought for the hegemony of Europe. The outcome of that fight was of course of crucial importance to the Dutch.

THE WAR RESUMED

The apparent eclipse of the Protestant cause in Germany by 1621 was one of the factors persuading the Dutch to renew the war, but certainly another powerful incentive to war was the prospect of immense wealth from trade and conquest in the East Indies and America. On the Spanish side there was a war and a peace party and much debate on the correct strategy to pursue if it came to war. The decision to build up the port of Dunkirk as a base for commerce and commerce raiders would cause many difficulties for the Dutch, but it was probably the activities of Spinola which caused most surprise at the start of the renewed hostilities. The Army of Flanders had been well prepared by Spinola during the truce and he was able to seize the initiative from Maurice of Nassau as soon as the truce ended in 1621. This second war with Spain was to last for another 27 years and would be fought on four fronts, of which the land front in Flanders was only sometimes the most active and important. By the time the final stage was reached it was economic strength and the outcome of the war between the Spanish and French – the closing stages of the Thirty Years War – which would decide the issue. This was not, it must be stressed, the return of the Dutch to Spanish rule, but rather their withdrawal from the Indies and America and their agreement not to support other Protestant or French causes in Europe. The war had four phases: 1621–25 – the Spanish offensive; 1626–33 – the Dutch counter-offensive; 1634–40 – stalemate; and 1641–48 – the final struggle; and it was fought in three main areas at the start and four at the finish. These were on land in the Low Countries, at sea off Europe, in the East Indies and lastly in America. It is simplest to consider each phase in each area in turn. Two other changes from the first (pre-truce) Spanish-Dutch war are worth noting for their effect on strategy. The neutrality of the English deprived the Dutch of an invaluable naval ally (even though neither side had fully appreciated the efforts of the other at sea in the past) and opened the English Channel to Spanish war fleets, thus providing Spain with another means of reinforcing the Netherlands. The second change was the growing unity and hence power of France; she was no longer an open battleground for Catholics and Protestants. The Spanish Road was no longer viable if France was hostile and a new route through the Valtelline to the east of Switzerland was therefore opened up and used extensively. However, even this was vulnerable when French power extended to Alsace in the 1630s, and was lost irretrievably in 1638 when Breisach was taken. As will be seen, these two factors would have a significant effect on this second Spanish-Dutch war.

One thing which had not changed when the war was renewed was the defensive complex of fortified towns, forts, earth ramparts and dykes which first the Dutch and then the Spanish had built along the boundary between the northern and the southern halves of the Netherlands. These greatly restricted the chances for large-scale manoeuvres by either army; in any case these fortifications needed some 30 000 men from each army, which was about half their available strength, to garrison them. Neither side had the strength to win the war on the land front in the Netherlands, but neither could afford to lose here either. The test for each was to allocate sufficient resources to avoid defeat and allocate enough either to the maritime war or to colonial campaigns to force the other to concede defeat.

THE SPANISH OFFENSIVE

Spinola's attempt to capture Bergen-op-Zoom in 1622 failed, with heavy losses, but in 1624 he laid siege to Breda, one of the best-defended towns in the Netherlands and took it after a nine-month siege. As Maurice of Nassau died during the siege, Spinola might have expected to be able to exploit the capture of one of the key cities in the Dutch defences, but Maurice's successor, his half-brother Frederick Henry, prevented any further Spanish advance and regained the initiative by skilful deployment along the eastern frontier. In any case the siege had exhausted Spanish resources, and in 1625 the Army of Flanders had to remain on the defensive.

At sea however Spanish expectations were higher. They hoped for great things from their Armada of Flanders, light draught commerce raiders based in Dunkirk and their main fleet based in southern Spain. These two fleets between them would, it was hoped, strangle Dutch trade with the Baltic and the Levant. The Dutch were thus faced with four conflicting tasks: to protect the Dutch merchant fleet at sea; to blockade Dunkirk; to intercept fleets of warships and troop transports sailing from Spain to Flanders; and finally to support Dutch efforts to establish trade and dominion in the Moluccas, China and South America. It was not surprising that quite frequently the Dutch could not afford to meet all these tasks. After an initial success in 1621 in attacking a Dutch convoy, the main Spanish fleet based on southern Spain failed against an escorted convoy of 80 ships returning from the Levant. Thereafter Spain concentrated her limited maritime resources on the Flanders coast, and the results were better from her point of view. The Dutch fleet blockaded Dunkirk as closely as it could but, despite this, Spanish ships ably assisted by privately financed privateers, did considerable damage to the Dutch merchant and fishing fleets. The strain of blockading the Flanders coast and of convoy protection was so great that the Dutch had to forgo the chance to attack Spain's Iberian bases such as Cadiz and Lisbon during the 1620s. In any case these ports had been so well fortified since the English raids in the 1580s and 1590s that a major expedition would have been needed to destroy them as bases.

The Rise and Decline of the Dutch Republic 71

The main Dutch offensive at sea was in the East Indies. By 1623 they had 90 ships and 20 major forts there. Spanish and Portuguese trade was frequently brought to a standstill and by 1623 the Dutch were ready to build on their success and expand their trading area. They attempted to seize control of the China Sea and thereby exclude Spain from the very lucrative silk trade. They failed to secure a port on the mainland but established a base at Taiwan in 1624 and developed a profitable trade with China from there. They did not oust Spain from the rest of Taiwan until 1642 but their success in the China trade was another severe blow to Spain's commercial wealth. In the West Indies the Dutch effort was on a smaller scale. In 1624 Dutch freebooters seized Bahia, capital of Brazil but, in an astonishingly swift reaction, the Spanish assembled a relief force for Brazil and recaptured it in the following year. Then the Dutch position in the west looked as unpromising as it was hopeful in the east.

THE DUTCH COUNTER OFFENSIVE

In the second phase of the war (1626–33) the Dutch army in the Netherlands outnumbered the Army of Flanders – a striking illustration of the extent to which Spanish resources were stretched. The Dutch made some useful gains on their eastern flank but their most ambitious project was an agreement with Denmark and England to raise a force to intervene in the Thirty Years War in Germany. By 1626 it looked as if the Catholic Hapsburg ruler of Austria, who was also Holy Roman Emperor, was going to dominate all Germany, leading to the complete eclipse of the Protestant princes of the Empire, who had in the past given much needed support to the Dutch. The plan was for the Danes to engage the army of the Catholic League under Tilly while two other Protestant armies were to evade the other Catholic army led by Wallenstein and march, one to liberate the Rhineland, and the other, Bohemia. If successful, this would have ended the Thirty Years War with a Protestant victory.

In the event the plan failed disastrously and the counter-strategy devised by Olivares, the Chief Minister of Philip IV of Spain, was potentially the most serious threat ever posed by Spain to the Dutch economy. The Danish attack in 1526 was easily beaten off and half their army destroyed at Lutter. The other two Protestant armies were largely ineffective so that by 1627 the two Catholic armies were ready to begin their offensive and put the strategy of Olivares into effect. The aim was to persuade the Hanseatic ports on the Baltic to deny entry to Dutch ships; in exchange for this, all Spain's trade from the Baltic would be carried in ships of the Hanseatic League. To reinforce this embargo Wallenstein's army was to deploy on the Baltic coast and a Spanish fleet was to assemble in the English Channel and then sail to the Baltic to support Wallenstein. The naval part of this strategy did not materialise, but on land everything went as planned; by 1628 Wallenstein had overrun Denmark and his army was besieging Stralsund – the only Hanseatic port on the Baltic not under his control. It looked as if the lifeline of the Dutch economy, the trade between Danzig and Amsterdam, would shortly be cut, but the tide of Catholic expansion had reached its limit. Danish and Swedish ships kept Stralsund supplied and in a few weeks Wallenstein abandoned the siege. Swedish intervention, however indirect, had halted the drive to the north and in 1630 there would be far more dramatic changes when Swedish troops under Gustavus Adolfus landed nearby at Peenemunde.

The avowed aim of Gustavus Adolphus, Sweden's king, and the brilliant general of her armies, was to defend the Protestant cause, but it was as important for Sweden to keep the Baltic free from Hapsburg domination. To that extent their aims coincided with those of the Dutch, but in any case the Swedish success in Germany did a great deal to relieve pressure on the Dutch. Within 18 months Gustavus Adolphus had defeated the Catholic army under Tilly at Breitenfeld and occupied the Rhineland thereby (at least temporarily) cutting the Spanish Road to Flanders. Although Gustavus himself was killed at Lutzen in 1632 when defeating the second Catholic army under Wallenstein the Swedish army remained a dominant force in Germany until 1634 when its fate was again linked to that of the Dutch.

With the failure of their ambitious plans for 1626 the Dutch were again forced to look to their own defences. By 1628 a Catholic army under Tilly had invaded East Friesland and threatened Emden which had a Dutch garrison. The danger of a close blockade of Dutch ports by Spanish ships based on East Friesland harbours caused real concern in the United Provinces. However, events elsewhere, notably the financial crisis in Spain caused by the loss of her silver fleet, and the threatened intervention by France against Spanish interests in Italy (which threatened the Spanish Road again), relieved pressure on the United Provinces. By 1629 the Army of Flanders was so short of funds that it was confined to the defensive and faced with a Dutch army almost half as large again. The Dutch used their advantage to lay siege to s'Hertogenbosch and were still strong enough to beat off a strong raid by Catholic League forces which seized and temporarily held Amersfoort near Utrecht in the centre of the Dutch heartland. Frederick Henry was not distracted from the siege, and s'Hertogenbosch fell a few months later. Wesel fell in the same year and the Dutch army advanced far enough down the Rhine in 1630 to threaten Dusseldorf, the main Spanish base remaining in the area. The Dutch offensive failed, however, and Frederick Henry spent the rest of 1630 consolidating, while abortive truce talks persuaded the Dutch to stay on the defensive. By 1631 Spain had ended her war in Italy to secure the Spanish Road and signed a peace treaty with the French; she was therefore ready to resume the offensive in Flanders. Her attempt to establish a blockading base on the Scheldt estuary was, however, thwarted and in the following year, 1632, the Army of Flanders was again weakened by the need to send troops to Germany to halt the advance of the Swedish Army. The Dutch profited by this to capture Venlo and Roermond on the eastern flank of both the Dutch and Spanish lines of defence and then laid siege to the great fortress city of Maastricht, the loss of which would isolate the remaining Spanish garrisons in this area, already almost totally cut off from the main bases in in the southern Netherlands. The now familiar double siege lines were built, one to keep the besieged in and the other to repel relieving forces. No less than three attempts at relief were thwarted and the city fell to the Dutch in August 1632 after less than three months of siege. Both sides were quiescent in 1633; the Dutch were recovering from the heavy financial burden of their successful offensive and the Spanish, who had brilliantly limited the local damage caused by their defeat at Maastricht, were collecting forces for a counter-offensive, to offset one of the most damaging defeats that they ever suffered in Flanders.

At sea the year of 1626 was notable for the determination with which the Dutch pressed their blockade of the privateers and commerce raiders in Dunkirk. In that year they doubled their blockading force and strengthened their convoy protection with the result that losses of merchant shipping were negligible. However, in the next two years other calls on Dutch resources were so great that the navy was cut back. In consequence their merchant shipping losses rose alarmingly and, worse still, the success of the Dunkirk privateers induced many others in the same line of business to come to Dunkirk, thus increasing the burden on the United Provinces without any extra effort by Spain. This was certainly to Spain's advantage since her Flanders fleet was kept very short of funds during the Spanish financial crisis of 1629.

Some of the gloom in the United Provinces caused by these merchant shipping losses must have been dispersed by the capture of the entire Spanish treasure fleet off Cuba by Piet Heyn, a famous Dutch freebooter in 1628. Spain lost, and the Dutch gained a whole year's output of the silver mines – enough to pay two-thirds of the annual cost of the Dutch army. The effects of the cutback on the Spanish army and navy have already been noted, but the Dutch West India Company, whose ships had captured the silver, determined on expansion (as well as paying a 50 percent dividend). They chose Brazil as their target and sent a fleet of 67 ships to capture Pernambuco, one of the chief towns in north-east Brazil in 1630. The importance to Spain of the wealth of her American colonies is illustrated by the remarkably swift response to this Dutch invasion. A large expedition was sent out from Spain the next year and the Dutch were confined to a narrow bridgehead around Pernambuco where they were unable to exploit the resources of the region. A balance sheet of Dutch colonial expansion drawn up in 1633 would have shown that despite considerable efforts over the twelve years since the war with Spain was resumed, they had not reaped any commensurate reward in either the east or the west. They had made no impact on the Spanish Empire in the Caribbean or on the Pacific coast of America. Their only real gains were on Taiwan in the east and a narrow foothold in Brazil in the west.

STALEMATE

Both sides entered the next phase of the war (1634–40) having spent much with little to show for it, and exhausted by the blows of their adversaries. The most significant event in 1634 occurred on the land front. Philip IV of Spain decided on a partial reversal of his former strategy and over the next few years spent much more on his land forces than previously. He decided to send his brother Ferdinand the Cardinal-Infante (who proved a competent general despite his clerical title) north to the Netherlands from Italy up the Spanish Road through the Valtelline with 11 000 fresh troops in a final attempt to overcome the Dutch will to continue the war. On the way north the Cardinal-Infante combined his forces with those of the Holy Roman Emperor Ferdinand II to inflict a decisive defeat on the hitherto unbeaten Swedish army at Nordlingen. The incomparable infantry of the Army of Flanders (a courtesy title since they had not then reached Flanders, but the Army's traditions were with them) withstood no less than fifteen charges by the formidable Swedish army and then like the British infantry at Waterloo grimly moved forward to crush their enemy and drive him from the field. Nothing illustrates better than this battle in a German war the quality of the troops with whom the Dutch had to contend for more than 50 years. However Spain's final attempt to settle the war with the Dutch by a land campaign was thwarted by her old enemy, France. Alarmed by the Spanish success at Nordlingen and the probable collapse of the Swedish military effort Cardinal Richelieu, the chief minister of Louis XIII, realised that it would be necessary to turn the existing cold war into a hot one if Spain, in conjunction with the Hapsburg Austrian empire was to be stopped from dominating Europe. The Spanish response to the French declaration of war was to try and keep France from invading Spain by exerting pressure on her from the east with the help of the forces of the Catholic League in Germany. At the same time offensive operations against the Dutch were designed to force them to a separate peace. The first result of the new open French alliance was a joint invasion of the southern Netherlands in 1635, which initially threatened Brussels but then failed dismally. In the same year the Cardinal-Infante's troops seized the strategic fortress of Schenkenschans, which dominated the fork where the Rhine divides into the Rhine and the Waal giving direct access to the Dutch heartland. Frederick Henry was able to seal off this gap and thus prevent a Spanish breakthrough, and in the following year he re-captured this key fortress but was unable through lack of funds to carry his offensive further. In 1637 he re-captured Breda, lost to Spain in 1627, but the Spanish capture of Venlo and Roermond in the east re-dressed the balance and assisted in their long-term objective of recovering all territory on the present Dutch-German border lost to the Dutch. In 1638 Dutch attempts on Antwerp, and Geldern in the east, were repulsed with serious losses but the Cardinal-Infante was unable to follow these defensive successes in the following year because of pressure on the French front in Flanders. For their part the Dutch were inhibited from offensive action by the success of the Catholic forces in Germany and by the threat of further reinforcements reaching the Army of Flanders by sea. This threat was dispelled in 1639, but despite efforts on their eastern and southern fronts the Dutch achieved little and began to feel that increased expenditure on the land war did not bring commensurate results.

At sea, by contrast, Dutch fortunes revived dramatically during this period. Their navy showed increasing skill in blockading Dunkirk and in protecting merchant ship convoys. In the years up to 1639 their shipping losses were sharply reduced, though still far from negligible. Nonetheless in 1636 and 1637 the Spanish succeeded in sending troop convoys from the Biscay ports to Dunkirk. This was clearly hazardous but the alternative line of communications up the Spanish Road was becoming more and more difficult, owing to the progress of the war in Germany and in 1638 that route was closed by the fall of Breisach which controlled the point where the Road crossed the Rhine. The great risk of the sea route was brought home to the Spanish in 1639, when they suffered their worst defeat at sea since 1588. It was the climax of the naval war. Early in 1639 it became clear that the Spanish were assembling a large fleet of warships and transports in her Atlantic and Biscayan ports but the new Dutch admirals, the first of a brilliant band, were faced with a strategic dilemma; past experience suggested that the Spanish would brush aside the Dutch fleet unless all available Dutch ships were deployed well forward, preferably in the English Channel. If they did so then Dutch merchant ships would be at the mercy of the Dunkirk privateers. Fortunately for them they took the correct decision and Van Tromp was sent to patrol between Cap La Hogue and Portland Bill with about 18 warships (increased to about 30 during the first battle) where he met the Spanish fleet of 68 warships and 30 transports in September. He attacked all the way up the Channel, inflicting considerable losses (in contrast to the English experience in 1588), and forced the Spanish to shelter in the neutral English waters of the Downs, the roadstead off Deal. Van Tromp blockaded this Armada with his greatly outnumbered ships while the United Provinces made intense efforts to send him reinforcements. Within three weeks at most, Van Tromp had 96 warships of various sizes under command. If Nordlingen demonstrated the power of Spain on land the reinforcement of Van Tromp during the Battle of the Downs showed the maritime power of the Dutch. With this dramatic addition to his strength Van Tromp sailed into neutral waters and destroyed the Armada. Some of the troops got ashore and were eventually taken to Flanders in English ships but Spain's naval strength never recovered. The Dutch had to pay a price for their extraordinary effort in 1639. They could not afford to mount their blockade of Dunkirk early enough in 1640 and the privateers escaped to inflict very serious losses on Dutch merchant shipping. By 1640 both sides were feeling the strain. The Spanish had lost their battle fleet and the Dutch were facing crippling losses to the merchant fleet on which their wealth and power depended.

Despite the efforts of both sides to fight offensively by land and sea in the European theatre, the war was also fought fiercely in the colonies. The Dutch drive to acquire them centred on Brazil, the greatest prize for them and the largest potential loss for the Spanish. In 1634 they seized Curaçao and in the next year they broke out of their bridgehead around Pernambuco. By 1638 they had secured enough land to start sugar plantations. However, their colony could never be secure as long as Bahia was in enemy hands and two fierce assaults failed to take it. In the east the Dutch captured Malacca in Malaya and went on to secure much of Ceylon. This was the extent of their permanent gains in both hemispheres but they sent numerous raiding squadrons, especially to the Caribbean, and the Spanish were forced to spend more of their limited resources on fortifying ports and escorting merchant convoys. Then in 1638 a large Spanish fleet was sent to Brazil to eliminate the Dutch there. A hard-fought but indecisive naval battle took

The Rise and Decline of the Dutch Republic

place off Pernambuco but all hopes of Spanish victory were lost when their fleet was dispersed by a storm.

THE FINAL STRUGGLE AND PEACE

The final phase of the war opened in 1640, with Spain apparently on the point of collapse. An insurrection in Catalonia was followed by the loss of Artois to the French and in December Portugal seceded from the Spanish Empire. Philip IV tried to make peace with the Dutch to free resources for use against more immediate threats but they refused at a time of Spanish weakness. Despite reverses elsewhere morale remained good in the Army of Flanders and it was able, thanks to the fortifications which covered the land, to hold off both French and Dutch attacks on its Flanders base. In 1643, therefore, when the Dutch went on to the defensive the Army was free to go campaigning in northern France. There at Rocroi it met and was defeated by a French army under Condé. Owing possibly to a misunderstanding, no quarter was given and the infantry (by now a mixture of Spaniards, Italians and Germans, to name but the main nationalities) whose prowess had been shown at Nordlingen a few years before, was killed to the last man. It was the turning point of both the Thirty Years and the Eighty Years Wars. Spain never even attempted to reconstitute her Army of Flanders. The stone monument at Rocroi is both a memorial to one of the outstanding armies of modern times and the gravestone of Spanish hopes of dominating northern Europe. Though the war at sea saw no more dramatic victories (or defeats) like Rocroi or the Downs, there were in the final phase large efforts and heavy losses on both sides. Despite the serious cost to their merchant fleet in depriving it of convoy escorts, the Dutch launched a major amphibious expedition against Spain to take advantage of the Portuguese and Catalonian revolts. There was an inconclusive fight against a weak Spanish fleet off Cape St Vincent in 1641, but there was no landing in Portugal and no effective help given to the Portuguese. The Dutch merchant marine continued to suffer serious losses in 1645. In the following year when a French army besieged Dunkirk Dutch shipping losses were reduced, but Dutch trade was not really safe until the end of hostilities in 1647.

The closing years to 1648 also saw big changes in the colonial war. In 1641 Spanish troops in Brazil were disarmed by the Portuguese settlers as a result of Portuguese secession from Spain and the Dutch and Portuguese concluded a truce which gave the Dutch peace to exploit their possessions until 1645. In that year the Portuguese settlers in the Dutch colony of Brazil rebelled and by 1648 all Dutch footholds in Brazil and the Caribbean had gone. Their earlier attacks on the Spanish in this area may have weakened their enemies, but gave the United Provinces no large and lasting gains. There was to be no Dutch empire in America comparable to the one which they founded in the East, despite the effort expended. In the East, the Dutch continued to hem in the two Spanish forts remaining in the Moluccas and were able to monopolise the spice trade. They also extended their hold on Taiwan but failed to expel the Spanish from the Philippines. It is perhaps surprising that the Dutch did not make further gains in the East, but the Moluccas became the centre of the Dutch East Indies which they held until the twentieth century.

By 1647 both sides were ready for peace, and hostilities ceased while negotiations were carried on at Munster in Westphalia to conclude both the Dutch-Spanish (or Eighty Year) and the Thirty Years Wars. Spain was ready to concede much in order to be free to continue her war against France. The Treaty therefore recognised the independence of the United Provinces, including Dutch conquests in Flanders and Brabant such as s'Hertogenbosch and Maastricht. Dutch conquests in the colonies were also accepted, as was their right to trade with Spanish colonies in the East and West Indies. The Scheldt remained closed to Flemish shipping so that Antwerp's trade was throttled for years to come. Religion – one of the causes of the wars – played very little part in the final peace. Spain even failed to secure freedom of religion for Catholics in the parts of Brabant and Flanders which were ceded to the Dutch.

The years after 1648 were a golden age for the Dutch. They dominated the trade and commerce of northern Europe and were one of the principal centres for the arts and sciences. Despite this financial and cultural success, their naval and military power had declined by the beginning of the next century to such an extent that the United Provinces was no longer a first-class power. War with Britain had eroded both her navy and, as important, her merchant fleet to such an extent that in subsequent wars with France the Dutch economy was in no shape to defy the strongest land power in Europe. A very brief survey of these wars will show Dutch strengths and weaknesses which her former enemy, Spain, might have done well to note.

THE ANGLO-DUTCH WARS AND DECLINE

The three Anglo-Dutch wars between 1652 and 1672 were waged almost entirely at sea and were about trade; the British (the English and the Scots under one king) sought to wrest European trade from the Dutch. Therefore, in 1651, the British forbade the import of foreign goods into Britain unless carried in British ships or those of the country of origin. This would ruin the Dutch carrying trade and war began shortly afterwards, lasting until 1654. On balance the British won the naval war but each battle was exceptionally hard fought and only the slightly superior design of British ships and guns gave her the victory on most occasions. It was, however, Britain's strategic advantages which told in the long run. In the first place, Britain was still a mainly agricultural nation and could therefore endure for quite long periods the disruption of her seaborne trade. The United Provinces, however, depended on her merchant and fishing fleets for nearly all the necessities of life. Even a short blockade could be fatal. Britain had a second advantage, placed as she was across the exits from the North Sea to the Atlantic. It was relatively simple for the British Navy, so long as it was up to strength, to close the English Channel, the main route from Dutch ports to Iberia and the Levant, sources of much profitable trade.

The second war began in 1664 and ended in 1667. On balance the Dutch had the advantage at sea this time, but, rightly fearing the growing power of France on the mainland of Europe, sought a quick end to the war. The Dutch admiral De Ruyter therefore waited until the British fleet was laid up (to save costs) after the campaigning season of 1667 and then sailed up the Thames and Medway and destroyed much of the British fleet at its base at Chatham. Thereafter both sides agreed to end the war.

The third Anglo-Dutch war lasted from 1672 to 1674 and was the least justifiable of the three. Charles II was in effect suborned by secret payments from Louis XIV of France to join in a concerted attack on the United Provinces for reasons which were more cogent for France than for Britain. The British were generally worsted in the naval encounters and withdrew in 1674. On land, however, the Dutch faced a far more damaging war. The French launched a swift attack which took them as far as Utrecht, and the Dutch heartland was only saved from invasion by the ruinous expedient of flooding much land south of the Zuider Zee. Again the Dutch found a saviour in the House of Orange. William rallied the people and fought a shrewd defensive campaign. The threat from the Triple Alliance, (which the Dutch Republic had previously concluded with Spain and Hapsburg Austria) finally persuaded France to a temporary peace in 1678. William became king of Great Britain in 1688 and was therefore able to bring his second kingdom into two more wars with France, the first from 1688 to 1697, and the second, after his death, from 1702 to 1713. By the end of the second of these two coalition wars the Dutch, though economically strong, were outclassed in terms of military power by their allies and their wishes were virtually ignored at the final peace conference – a sure sign of second-class status.

CONCLUSIONS

In war both sides make mistakes and, as the saying goes, victory goes to the side which makes the fewest. It is small wonder that mistakes were made by those in the United Provinces, Spain, and England, who had to decide how to allocate war resources in two elements and three continents. It is surprising that the victors, the Dutch and the English, made so few errors. The main aim of Queen Elizabeth's foreign policy was to preserve a balance of power in Europe and thus prevent it being dominated by either France or Spain. She was lukewarm, to say the least, to the idea of an independent Dutch Republic; from her point of view the best solution was a united Netherlands under the loose control of the King of Spain and the worst outcome for England was to have a strong army under Spanish orders within easy reach of England by a short sea route. When this second alternative arose Elizabeth considered, not unreasonably, that France, which was more directly menaced by it, should undertake the task of removing it. When it became clear in 1585 that France was too distracted by civil war to tackle the Army of Flanders, Elizabeth was surely correct to send troops and money to the Dutch. For the same reasons when it seemed that France itself was likely to become a puppet of Spain in 1589 it was again correct to send aid to those in France who were fighting against Spain. Finally when, thanks to the timely conversion of Henry IV of France, the Spanish invaders were ejected she very properly withdrew her troops as quickly as possible. Since the situation in both France and the United Provinces turned out as England and not Spain wished, it is hard to argue that English aid was insufficient. The 20 000 troops sent to France between 1589 and 1594 were a heavy burden on English finances. It is even harder at this distance of time to suggest that Elizabeth's help was over generous, given her notorious propensity to disburse as few funds as possible as late as possible. England was a very small and poor country compared with the two continental rivals and she had no standing army. Consequently, Elizabeth, only gave English money or troops when she was sure that all of those who could and should contribute had done as much – a sound maxim in foreign policy. It is fair to conclude that Elizabeth's aid to the Dutch and the French was neither too little nor too much.

When we turn to England's maritime strategy, it is more difficult, even with hindsight, to tell exactly where the balance of advantage lay between all the available options. To begin with, hindsight itself causes problems, for some 'blue water' strategists may argue that more expenditure on the navy, instead of on the European commitment, could have provided a complete blockade of Spain, so that no silver bullion could have reached her from America. This would, the argument goes, have led to Spain's bankruptcy and surrender. The reply to this is quite simple. The fleets of 1588 were not capable of the type of blockade, so praised by Mahan and practised by the Royal Navy one hundred years later. Their ships did not have the sea-keeping qualities, their sea captains the discipline or their admirals the means of controlling other ships at a distance, these improvements were not fully effective until the wars with Revolutionary France. Experience with the elusive treasure fleets proves the point. Both the English and Dutch tried desperately to seize this prize and only once did they succeed, although there was an element of luck in Piet Heyn's success. The main criticism of the Elizabethan navy is that it was overly privatised. The nation's strategic needs were subordinated to private profit. Drake's 1589 expedition, which failed to reach the ports where the remnants of the Armada had taken shelter must go down as the worst blunder of the naval war; no exonerating facts have come to light. It has been suggested that after 1589 Elizabeth never trusted Drake again; if true, this was wise. It seems that the 1596 Armada was assembled hurriedly by Philip of Spain as a response to the sack of Cadiz earlier that year. The Cadiz expedition cannot be criticised for failing to destroy an Armada which had not assembled but the English should have considered attacking a more important base for the Spanish navy. The year 1597 marks the nadir of Queen Elizabeth's naval commanders. It was known that Philip was preparing another Armada and Elizabeth sent a strong fleet to destroy it in Ferrol where it was assembling. The commanders were persuaded by false intelligence that the Armada had gone to the Azores and sailed on there, hoping no doubt for treasure as well as the Spanish fleet. The Armada, which was in Ferrol all the time, then sailed to the Scilly Isles undisturbed on its way to Falmouth. It was dispersed off at the Scillies by a storm, surely one of the most providential in England's history, and had returned to Spain before the disorganised English fleet returned empty-handed. The fourth and final Armada reached Kinsale in southern Ireland after evading a small English squadron, but thereafter the English were reasonably successful in blockading the Spanish in Kinsale. The general conclusion is clear. The Elizabethan navy did not lack resources on really crucial occasions, but the tendency of its commanders once at sea to ignore their Queen's instructions was very costly in 1589 (when they failed to destroy the remnant of the first Armada) and could have been calamitous in 1597 (when they left England unprotected against another Armada). In sum Queen Elizabeth's land and maritime strategy were broadly correct but she and the nation were very nearly lost by the negligence of her naval commanders in the years after 1588.

The strategic problems and options facing Philip of Spain need a far larger canvas than those of his English adversary. As Paul Kennedy has so convincingly shown, the Hapsburg empire of Spain, by far the richest European power of the time was led into so many and such protracted wars to preserve its economic base, that its military and naval needs far outstripped the resources which that base could provide. In these circumstances it has been argued that the commitment to Flanders and the re-conquest, or the neutralisation of the United Provinces should have been abandoned, as it was strategically difficult and very expensive. Two facts illustrate this latter point very well. The Army of Flanders during the period under discussion required more than a quarter of the Spanish Crown's annual receipts to keep in the field, and this meant that between 1566 and 1654 it cost more than one and a half times as much as the Crown received from the Indies. If, however, Spain had evacuated Flanders, the penalties would probably have far outweighed the benefits, for those who would have profited would have been the two greatest enemies of Spain: France and the United Provinces. The former without the threat of the Army of Flanders on her northern frontier would almost certainly have tried to take control of northern Italy away from Spain and used the resources of that wealthy land to make more mischief for Spain. If the United Provinces had been freed of the threat by land at any time from 1590 onwards it seems almost certain that she would have redoubled her efforts to take Spain's colonies and her colonial trade away from her.

Granted that Flanders could not be amputated for fear of worse consequences, could Spain have won the war outright, without political concessions after the rebels had secured the Dutch heartland centred on the Provinces of Holland and Zeeland in 1572? It is hard to see how the war could have been won on land given the formidable defences of rampart and dyke built by the Dutch. Neither side ever made swift progress through these defences and had an outright breakthrough by the Army of Flanders seemed likely, then it is probable that other enemies such as England or France would have sent the relatively small amount of aid needed to continue a defensive war. At sea, however, the Dutch were far more vulnerable, as Philip seems to have realised when he launched the First Armada against England; this was surely intended not only to stop the flow of military assistance to the Dutch, but also to provide bases in England from which the Spanish fleet could dominate the North Sea. Two examples from the next century show how damaging such English bases could have been for the Dutch in the 1590s: the Spanish base at Dunkirk dealt severe blows to Dutch maritime trade between the 1620s and 1640s whenever the Dutch failed to blockade it properly; and the Anglo-Dutch wars of the later seventeenth century show how difficult, if not impossible, it was for the Dutch to mount an effective blockade of all English ports used for war or ocean-going merchant ships. If Spanish ships based in England had been free to prey on Dutch fishing and merchant vessels, the economic power of the United Provinces, which was just starting to grow, would have been crippled, and with it the power of the Dutch to make war.

It is not clear whether Philip II and his successors fully appreciated how vulnerable the Dutch would be to any lengthy interruption of their trade. They clearly had some ideas about this since, after the 12 year truce began in 1609, Philip's successor established the base for commerce raiders at Dunkirk which did so much damage to Dutch trade after the truce ended. However no one before Olivares, the brilliant but erratic chief minister to Philip IV, attempted to strike at the most valuable of all Dutch trade routes that ran between Danzig and Amsterdam. For the whole of the Eighty Years War the Baltic brought far more revenue to the Dutch than any other trading area; moreover the raw materials for shipbuilding, timber, hemp and tar also came almost exclusively from the Baltic. It is hard to imagine the Dutch being able to fight for long if their route to the Baltic had been cut. The plan which Olivares and Wallenstein devised in the late 1620s for the occupation of the German Baltic coast and the domination of the southern part of that sea would obviously have ended Dutch trade and possibly the war also, but it was so far-reaching that it was almost certain to invite a riposte from the Swedes. A more modest scheme to place naval bases on the North Sea coast of Germany could have cut the Dutch trade to the Baltic without necessarily exciting a counter-stroke by the Swedes. There is no doubt that the Dutch were very worried at the time by this possibility and took what steps they could to strengthen their forces in Friesland and Groningen to counter it. If (and it is a big 'if', bearing in mind the poor record of Spanish fleets in northern waters) the Spanish Army and Navy could have established themselves in the 1620s and 1630s on the North Sea coast of Germany and operated a raiding-base as they did at Dunkirk, they would have had a good chance of forcing the Dutch out of the war.

Any present-day student of strategy who studies a record of the Dutch decisions during the Eighty Years War must surely be amazed that a federated state such as the United Provinces, in which each Province had a veto over major policy decisions, should so often have chosen the correct strategic option before it was too late. Admittedly the Dutch were very fortunate that the House of Orange provided them during the war with one great statesman and two good generals when they were most needed; nevertheless the division of interests within the state was considerable. The inland provinces needed peace to develop manufacturing and trade with the German hinterland, whereas the coastal provinces could profit from a war which allowed the plunder of enemy ships and the riches which came from seizing his colonies. It is a wonder that together they so often chose correctly when deciding how to allocate resources between their army and navy. Admittedly they made mistakes, such as their over-ambitious campaigns in the southern Netherlands and their attempt to intervene in the war in Germany in the late 1620s, but looked at overall their choices between the land and the maritime option were usually right. At the start they had no choice but to build up an army and fortifications to defend their heartland. When England came to the aid of the United Provinces the war was automatically extended to the sea and the English, as the most threatened ally, had to fight it there. When the English naval effort was diminishing (or becoming less effective) in the late 1590s and early 1600s, the Dutch were ready to take over by sending fleets to cruise in Spanish waters and by attacking Spain's soft underbelly – her colonies. After the truce it required a nice strategic judgement to adjust spending priorities between the army in the Netherlands, the navy in home, or rather European waters, and finally the forces in the East and the West Indies and South America. Of course hindsight shows that the decision-making process could have been better, but one major decision adhered to for many years at considerable cost without immediate profits was to attack the enemy colonies in the Caribbean and South America in the 1620s and 1630s. It was partly the illusory hope of large profits which encouraged this persistance, but it paid off as a war strategy; forcing Spain to divert war resources into much useless defence work (e.g. the fortified ports of the Pacific coast of South America) and could be be seen as a true diversionary strategy – the first in a global war. The decline in the power of the Dutch people, when it came, was not due to imperial overstretch as with so many other European powers, but because the northern Netherlands was too small a base for the United Provinces to become a great power among the new European nation states. Two of these, Britain and France, which profited in different ways from the decline of the Spanish Hapsburg empire in the eighteenth century, are the subject of the next chapter. Britain had by the beginning of the century acquired the economic base and naval power on which a colonial empire could be founded. France had taken over from Spain as the predominant land power on the continent of Europe, thanks to the efforts of her king, Louis XIV. However, the tireless diplomacy and statecraft of William III, King of the

United Provinces and of England and Scotland, had before his death given Louis of France his first check, a fitting end to the period when the United Provinces played the role of a great power in Europe. Afterwards Britain succeeded her as the main bulwark against French expansion.

5 Britain and France: The Whale and the Elephant

With the accession of William of Orange and his wife Mary to the thrones of England and Scotland after the deposition of James II, Britain, (as it is correct to call her after the 1707 Act of Union) took over from the United Provinces the leadership of the coalition of powers resisting the expansion of France over the continent of Europe. This reflected a change in the relative strength of the two economies. The Dutch were finding the cost of maintaining land defences against their powerful neighbour an increasing strain and could not support so large a navy and so much colonial expansion as in the past. The British did not require expensive land defences and could therefore devote more resources to maritime war and colonial trade. The antagonism between Britain and France led to seven wars between 1688 and 1815. At the start, under Louis XIV, and at the end, under Napoleon, France reached a peak of military power and diplomatic prestige, though throughout the whole period she was arguably the strongest military power in Europe. By contrast, Britain did not raise armies comparable to those of other European powers, but her fleets became as large as those of her maritime rivals, France and Spain, together – and were certainly more effective. It would be fair to claim a reasonable measure of consistency for British foreign policy during the eighteenth century; it was, as it had been in Elizabeth's time, to prevent any one power from dominating the continent of Europe. The aims of French foreign policy were not so consistent, indeed there was a period of peace on the Continent from 1716 to 1740 as a result of cooperation between Britain and France, but the more normal pattern was of France and her allies fighting against a combination of other European powers who were militarily and, as time went on, financially, supported by Britain. The exception to this rule was the War of American Independence, of which there is more discussion later. The great interest of this period for the student of strategy lies in discovering the extent to which this series of wars provide the classic example of a conflict between a land and a maritime power; that is, between the whale and the elephant.

THE WAR OF THE LEAGUE OF AUGSBURG (1688–97) AND THE WAR OF THE SPANISH SUCCESSION (1702–14)

These two wars are best considered together since both are basically conflicts between France and a coalition of European powers brought together by the United Provinces and Britain. By 1685 the expansionist policy of Louis XIV of France had persuaded the United Provinces, Spain, Brandenburg Bavaria and Austria to form a defensive alliance (the League of Augsburg), and William of Orange was able, on his accession to the thrones of England and Scotland, to bring Britain into the alliance. Louis had sent his armies into the Rhineland in early 1688, but as soon as he realised that Britain had joined his enemies, he withdrew his troops from Germany and struck at Britain. He was able, thanks to the fine fleet created by his minister, Colbert, to seize the initiative and put Britain in greater danger than she had been since the four Spanish Armadas of the 1580s and 1590s. The French fleet landed the deposed English king, James II, in Ireland, and soon the whole country, except for the towns of Londonderry and Enniskillen, was under the control of the invaders. After their fleet had suffered a reverse at Bantry Bay, the French attack faltered. William III was able to land a considerable force in Ireland, defeat James's army at the Battle of the Boyne in 1690, and regain the whole country. As a diversion, the attack on Ireland had been most effective for the French, since William had to withdraw almost all British forces from the Continent and consequently the other allies were unable, or unwilling, to mount an offensive in Flanders. The recovery of the French fleet, after its reverse at Bantry Bay, was swift. Under the leadership of Tourville, one of the greatest French admirals it defeated the combined English and Dutch fleets off Beachy Head in 1690. As a result the French fleet controlled the English Channel, an objective which they attempted and failed to achieve many times in subsequent wars. Their control lasted only for the remainder of 1690, but Louis could not take advantage of his victory, since the amphibious forces for an invasion of England were not assembled.

By 1692 the English and Dutch fleets were strong enough to return to the offensive which was more than ever necessary as the French preparations for invasion were now well advanced. The French fleet was decisively defeated at La Hogue and the threat of invasion from across the Channel was removed for the rest of the war. The French now turned to commerce raiding under such skilled seamen as Jean Bart; this caused serious losses to the British merchant fleet but could not affect the outcome of the war. The threat in Ireland was lifted after hard fighting by 30 000 British and Dutch troops and William was able to send troops back to the

Continent. In due course the British contributed about half the Anglo-Dutch army in Flanders. It suffered a series of defeats at Fleurus (1690), Steenkirk (1692) and Neerwinden (1693), and was unable to break through the defended belt of fortified towns and fortresses which Vauban had built to cover northeastern France. Nevertheless, some of Louis best troops were casualties and as a final success William's army captured the strongly defended city of Namur in 1695. At sea the remainder of the war went less well for Britain. An important convoy of merchant ships bound for the Levant was intercepted and destroyed in 1693 by the revived French fleet from Brest. This emphasised the need to deal with the French fleet again but an amphibious expedition sent against Brest in 1694 with 7000 British troops aboard, was repulsed with heavy losses. Elsewhere the allied cause had some successes. Austria made gains in Italy and, as a result of the appearance of a strong allied fleet in the Mediterranean in 1694, a French invasion of Catalonia to capture Barcelona was turned back. However, the fleet was withdrawn in 1697 and the war became a stalemate. At immense cost France had held off attacks from most of the other European nations, but could not prevail against them. Peace terms agreed in 1697 gave neither side any real advantage, but the fleet which Colbert had created for France had been destroyed and was not replaced.

War broke out again in 1702 when Louis XIV tried to take the throne of Spain for his grandson, a move which was resisted by other European powers, notably Britain, Hapsburg Austria and the United Provinces. The war which followed was the only one in the series of Anglo-French wars in which Britain took a leading part in the land battles of the Continent. Thanks to the military genius of the Duke of Marlborough, Britain and her allies inflicted a series of defeats on the French at Blenheim (1704), Ramillies (1706), and Oudenarde (1708). Malplaquet in 1710 was a drawn battle in which both sides suffered heavy losses and the subsequent attempt by the allies to march on Paris was foiled by the French. As the allied cause in Spain never recovered from the defeat at Almanza in 1707, it was becoming clear by 1710 that there was a stalemate in the war on land.

At sea the British fleet was never seriously challenged in home waters since the French fleet had not been rebuilt after its losses in the previous war. The main part of the British fleet was therefore deployed on Marlborough's advice to the Mediterranean, in an attempt to influence the course of the war in Spain and Italy: Admiral Richmond writes of Marlborough that 'no statesman, not even Chatham, had a more comprehensive grasp of the problems of sea power and the interdepen-dence of the sea and land forces'. An attempt to capture Cadiz in 1702 as a base for Mediterranean operations failed, but a fleet was again sent south in 1704.

It captured Gibraltar and then met (off Malaga) a French fleet sent to recover that key point, Gibraltar. The battle at sea was tactically indecisive, but thereafter the French fleet remained bottled up in Toulon, and control of the western Mediterranean remained with the British fleet which retired every winter to its base at Lisbon, available thanks to a fortunate alliance with the Portuguese. The allies failed to exploit their mastery of the Mediterranean mainly because Austria, the main source of military manpower in the area, preferred to use her armies to conquer southern Italy rather than commit them to amphibious expeditions with the British fleet to strike at targets more vital to the main enemy, France. It was not until 1706 that she sent her best general, Prince Eugene, and his army with British ships to attack Toulon. It was thought that this fortress would be denuded of troops after the French losses at Ramilles, but Eugene found Toulon reinforced and strongly defended and was compelled to abandon the attempt. The only bonus was that the French destroyed their warships there to avoid capture by the British.

As a result of Austria's unwillingness to commit her forces again against the southern flank of France, the British and Dutch attempted to open a second front in Spain, but it became for them what it would become for France from 1808 to 1813, a sponge to absorb men and money with no commensurate reward. At one time more troops were allotted to Spain than to Marlborough in Flanders. The British fleet supported an expedition to capture Barcelona in 1705, and in 1706 the whole of Catalonia was in allied hands. A French attempt to re-take Barcelona in that year was foiled by the timely arrival of the British fleet from its winter base. Since the only effective supply line for the French was across the sea, they had to retire hastily to France. In 1707 the main allied forces were decisively beaten at Almanza in southern Spain and never recovered the initiative thereafter. The decision in 1708 to capture Port Mahon in Minorca, the ideal naval base from which to blockade Toulon, and control the coasts of southern France and Spain came too late. By then the allied cause in Spain was lost. The Spanish people were hostile to the allies' nominee for the Spanish throne and in favour of the French candidate. Without more indigenous support, or a far more effective use of the forces deployed there, the allies could not open their second front from which to invade southern France. After 1708 several small amphibious operations were attempted or launched against France itself but, as would be discovered in later wars, small amphibious attacks did not ever divert significant French forces.

In 1710 the Tory party, which was in favour of peace, gained power in the Parliamentary elections in Britain, and thereafter British forces steadily withdrew from the war. The Austrians, heavily dependent on British subsidies, and the Dutch were compelled to follow suit. The peace terms agreed in 1713 were less favourable than those which the French would have conceded in 1708/9. In particular, the French nominee for the Spanish throne, now enjoying strong popular support, retained his crown; but the Netherlands ports were removed from his (and therefore French) control and given to Austria which was not a maritime power and therefore no threat to Britain. The Bourbon alliance of France and Spain would undoubtedly prove a problem during the eighteenth century, but the main war aim of the allies was undoubtedly achieved; the attempt of Louis XIV to make himself the undisputed master of Europe was thwarted. Although she was the strongest power on the continent, France would not again threaten to dominate the whole continent until the advent of Napoleon.

In retrospect the first two wars between Britain and France in modern times can seen as part of one pattern. The same allies were engaged on the two sides and the area of conflict was much the same – western Europe – but whereas the first could be seen as a war of attrition, which wore down French resources without any spectacular results, the second showed decisive victories for the allies, even if these did not bring spectacular gains at the peace conference. This process of attrition is most apparent in the maritime war. The French fleet was not destroyed at La Hogue, only severely damaged: hence the insistence of William III that an attempt be made later to capture Brest. That operation failed with serious losses, but the French made no attempt to replace their battle fleet, built up with such care by Colbert. The fleet rotted in harbour, save for the squadrons sent to raid British and Dutch merchant shipping, and it was not ready for the next war when it came. Apart from the indecisive action off Malaga forced on it when it tried to recapture Gibraltar, the French fleet offered no serious challenge to the Royal Navy in the War of the Spanish Succession, which in this war had little help from the Dutch, who had to put most of their resources into their army to meet the threat from the French on land. The first of these two wars brought no dramatic victories to the allied armies under William III (save perhaps the capture of Namur in the closing stages), but in the words of Correlli Barnett, William 'had succeeded in permanently dulling the French cutting edge; and Marlborough was to draw the benefit'.

Less space has been given in this account of the War of the Spanish Succession to the great campaigns of Marlborough in Flanders and elsewhere, and more to the operations of the Royal Navy and to the allied armies in Spain and the Mediterranean because the main strategic problem facing the leaders of the alliance was how to use their naval superiority to help to bring about the defeat of France. After Austria had been saved by the

Battle of Blenheim, the main front for their offensive was clearly Flanders and the war was at one time nearly won there. If a second front directly threatening France had been opened elsewhere, so that French resources had to be diverted from Flanders, then obviously the chances of overall victory would have been increased. Two options for the use of the navy were rightly ignored. Britain did not then have the resources for mounting major attacks against French colonies overseas; nor had the Royal Navy the ships or the techniques to mount a close blockade of Brest – the main base for any maritime threat to southern England. Marlborough, following a view held by William III, correctly chose the Mediterranean as the main area of effort for the navy. It was, however, a mistake to commit so much manpower and treasure to central and southern Spain; this was done mainly to conciliate Portugal, an ally which provided facilities at Lisbon which were (initially) vital for operations in the Mediterranean. As has been seen, little progress was made by the armies sent there, the Portuguese were little help as allies and the Spanish were hostile to the allied candidate for their throne. Catalonia was a much more promising field for the allies since, as so often, the Catalonians were out of step with the rest of the country and accepted the allies as liberators. If available resources had been concentrated there, after the capture of Barcelona, an attack on southern France supported by the Royal Navy and possibly combined with an Austrian attack on Toulon, either from northern Italy or with naval support from the sea, could very well have created the required second front to support Marlborough in Flanders. Finally it should be noted that the efforts of both the French fleet and privateers to bring Britain to her knees by raiding her merchant shipping in both wars failed, although it caused great damage and pointed to the need for a growing commercial power to increase the naval resources devoted to protecting her trade.

The French, for their part, must have regretted their failure to use the fleet built up by Colbert to best advantage in 1690, when the Royal Navy was ill-prepared and at a strategic disadvantage because of the location of its bases. These had been established on the Thames and Medway, ideal for operations against the Dutch, but of little use when the enemy was France and the need was to watch Brest and intercept convoys of troops and supplies bound for England or Ireland. One of the reasons for the defeat at Beachy Head was the need to divide the fleet to attempt these tasks from distant bases on the east coast of England. If the French could have used their temporary advantage either to reinforce their initial success in Ireland, or to invade southern England, they could have knocked their main enemy out of the war and forced a separate peace on her. As it was, when they made the attempt to land 24 000 troops in England in 1692, the Royal Navy had some facilities on the south coast and won the victory at La Hogue. This damaged but did not destroy the French fleet, but no serious attempt was made thereafter, either in war or in the short peace which followed, to replace the losses or to build up a navy which could again mount a threat to the British in the English Channel.

It is hard nevertheless, to understand why the French did not do more to challenge the incursion of the British squadrons into the Mediterranean at the start of the War of the Spanish Succession. The British had to use Lisbon as an overwintering base for their ships deployed to the Mediterranean until they captured Port Mahon in Minorca quite late in the war, and therefore faced many problems both in supporting the British troops fighting in Catalonia and even in ensuring that Gibraltar was supplied with the men and munitions to resist the several serious attempts made by the Spanish and French to recover it. A stronger French fleet at Toulon at the start of 1702 might have prevented the fall of Gibraltar, or later turned the indecisive battle off Malaga into a French victory and thereby stopped the British from making their several attempts to open up a second front in southern France. The earlier French victory at Beachy Head had shown how a fleet with convenient bases could take advantage of an enemy forced to divide his forces because he was far from shore support. Admittedly French resources were fully stretched by the need to maintain large armies in north-western and central Europe, but if Louis XIV had been prepared to rely more on the belt of fortified cities and lines built on the eastern frontier of France, some resources could surely have been devoted to a Mediterranean navy. It must be admitted, however, that this would have been an unlikely course for Louis XIV to follow – whenever it was a straight choice between spending on the army or the navy he always chose the army.

THE WAR OF THE AUSTRIAN SUCCESSION (1739–1748)

For the quarter-century which followed the Peace of Utrecht in 1713, Britain and France were at peace with each other, though from time to time both engaged in wars with other countries. France needed time and peace to recover from the near bankruptcy which had faced her as a result of Louis XIV's attempt to dominate Europe. For her part, Britain was determined to prevent either France or Austria, the two strongest powers by land, from dominating the Continent, but she was not then the great colonial and commercial power which she was to become later in the century. Moreover, the Royal Navy was not yet capable of those battle-winning tactics de-

Britain and France: The Whale and the Elephant 93

veloped by Rodney at the Battle of the Saints or the technique of close blockade of French ports perfected by Collingwood later in the century. In consequence, Britain's performance can seem both dilatory and indecisive to those blessed with hindsight. The best correction for this is to bear these limitations in mind and discuss alternative strategies for Britain and France when the two subsequent wars have been considered.

There are really three distinct diplomatic and strategic phases to the War of the Austrian Succession. In the first and shortest, Britain fought Spain in 1739 to establish the right to trade in Spanish West Indian colonies. In 1740 this war merged into the European War of the Austrian Succession when Frederick the Great of Prussia seized Silesia from the newly crowned Empress of Austria, Maria Theresa. Britain sided with Austria but Prussia was joined in this attempt to dismember Austria by both Spain and Bavaria and was covertly supported by France. Finally in 1744 France declared war on Britain. Prussia left the war temporarily for two years in 1742 and concluded a final peace treaty with Austria in 1745. Britain's problem from 1740 onwards was to buttress Austria with subsidies so that she remained in the war against Prussia and France. In addition, she had the strategically unwelcome task of trying to defend George II's inheritance, the Electorate of Hanover, from French or Prussian attack. Both these tasks required money which could only come from the profits from overseas trade, so once again maritime supremacy was vital for Britain. By 1748 both Britain and France were ready for peace. Britain could find no way of curbing French expansion in Germany and the Netherlands whilst France was financially crippled by Britain's command of the sea and the consequent interruption of French overseas trade.

The largely naval war against Spain can be dealt with briefly. It started in the manner of Drake or Hawkins, with a British expedition to the West Indies to capture Spanish colonies and extinguish their trade. In 1740 it failed to take Cartagena and Cuba and, like other expeditions in later wars, suffered heavily from disease. French plans to support Spain in the West Indies were abandoned when war broke out in Europe, but despite this, British plans to extend operations in the Caribbean and South America failed and the war in these theatres gradually petered out. The cost of the abortive expedition of 1740 was soon apparent. The British Mediterranean fleet had not been reinforced and was consequently heavily outnumbered by the combined Franco-Spanish fleet, which was able to convoy a Spanish army to Genoa to attack the Austrian possessions in Italy.

By 1742 the Austrians were able to withstand the Spanish attack in Italy, thanks in large measure to a reinforced British fleet which from its base at Port Mahon was able to blockade the combined enemy fleet in Toulon and thus sever sea communications from Spain to Italy. The tedious and costly land route through France restricted Spanish efforts in Italy to the great benefit of the Austrians, who were facing far more serious threats elsewhere. By 1742 Austria had lost Silesia and Prague and the French were threatening Austrian rule in the Netherlands. Alarmed by the possibility of the French occupation of ports in Flanders, then under Austrian rule, Britain sent troops there in that year. In the following year British and German troops won a surprise victory over a French army at Dettingen. This removed the French threat to Germany but the victors did not follow up with an invasion of France because they feared an attack by the Prussians on Hanover. In the same year the French prepared a force to invade England, but it was discovered in time by the British, who quickly assembled a fleet to prevent this. The French expedition narrowly escaped destruction and was forced to take shelter in Brest. In 1744, the year in which France formally declared war on Austria and Britain, an indecisive action off Toulon was sufficient to give the British undisputed command of the Mediterranean for the rest of the war. The benefits of this were apparent in the following year, when the French landed Prince Charles Edward, the son of the Catholic claimant to the thrones of England and Scotland, in the latter country. The Jacobite rebellion which followed was a very successful diversion of British forces which had to be shipped back from Europe to defeat the rebel invasion of England, but it was no more than a distraction. If the French fleet had been able to land an army to support the rebellion, then Britain could well have been forced out of the war.

The year 1745 also saw the defeat of the British and German forces at Fontenoy and the capture by colonial forces of Cape Breton island off Canada. This was considered (because of the fortress of Louisburg) to be the key to Canada. In 1747 the British were able to reinforce their Atlantic fleet at the expense of their Mediterranean squadrons, with the result that they were able to destroy two very large convoys of French merchant ships, one bound for the West Indies and the other for the East. France was now seriously weakened; her overseas trade had practically ceased, a series of bad harvests had brought widespread famine and the British appeared to be about to overrun French colonies in Canada and the West Indies. In 1748 France accepted peace terms under which she gave up all her gains in Europe in exchange for the return of Louisburg and Cape Breton Island. The prospect of the complete loss of her colonies was undoubtedly more important to her than her recent gains in the Netherlands (notably the fortress of Bergen-op-Zoom) and the opportunity to seize Tuscany and perhaps more of Central Italy.

The War of the Austrian Succession bore some resemblance to the Anglo-French war which preceded it, the War of the Spanish Succession and some to the war which followed it, the Seven Years' War, but cannot really be compared to any of them. If one ignores the colonial war between Britain and Spain with which hostilities began (and most statesman engaged in the final peace negotiations did just that) then clearly the war began as a dynastic struggle between Austria and Prussia, with which neither Britain nor France had a direct concern. It ended as a war mainly, if not wholly, between Britain and France in which gains and losses in colonies and overseas trade were the key issues. At the start Britain had to relearn the lesson of the previous war: that effective support for an ally like Austria required maritime control of the western Mediterranean. A compromise peace stopped the fighting because Britain could not find a way to stop French armies overrunning northern Italy and the Low Countries and France could not accept the extinction of her overseas trade and the loss of her colonies in America, the Caribbean and possibly India as well. Britain stumbled on this war – winning strategy partly by chance, since the capture of Louisburg, which so alarmed the French government, was not the result of a strategic directive from London but arose from a local initiative in the colonies in New England. Her leaders could however claim credit for the decision to reinforce the Atlantic fleet at the expense of the Mediterranean fleet in 1747, which led to the destruction of French convoys bound for Canada and the Carribbean. This decision, which admittedly allowed the French to reinforce Genoa, was a belated recognition of the use of seapower in a colonial war. This would be fully exploited in the Seven Years' War which followed when the tactical skill and logistic support of the Royal Navy would be more fully developed.

The main lesson for both Britain and France was that they were both European and world powers. It was therefore no use winning a campaign in one theatre of operations if the benefits could be cancelled out by losses in another. If a war between Britain and France was to be won decisively it had to be won both in Europe and in the colonies, which meant at this time North and Central America. France would need to gain victories in the colonial wars to complement her gains in Europe, and Britain would have to try to ensure that expected gains at sea and in colonies overseas were not jeopardised by the defeat of her allies in Europe. A further lesson for France was that attacks on the British merchant fleet could inflict serious financial losses upon her enemy but could not bring victory in the war unless the French fleet could win supremacy in at least some key areas of the oceans of the world. Despite its losses, the British merchant marine was (according to later historians) larger at the end of the war than it was at the start.

THE SEVEN YEARS' WAR (1756–63)

Since both the main contestants had accepted a compromise peace with reluctance, it is not surprising that an unofficial war continued between them outside Europe, particularly in North America. The 60 000 French colonists in Canada, ably but not democratically ruled by a series of governors with ambitions to expand their territory, were faced by some two million British colonists settled in the relatively narrow strip of land between the Allegheny mountains and the sea. The French aim was to confine the British colonists within this area by linking Canada with their colony in Louisiana, using the Mississippi and Ohio rivers as their line of communication. To this end they began to build a series of forts along the route and the abortive attack on one of these, Fort Duquesne (now Pittsburgh), by a colonial force in 1755 led to the opening of the war one year later.

In Europe diplomatic blunders on the part of both Britain and Prussia enabled Austria to secure first France and then Russia as allies in an attempt to recover Silesia which she had lost to Prussia in the War of Austrian Succession. When the Franco-Austrian alliance was announced in 1756 Britain and Prussia hastily concluded an alliance, the former needing an ally to help to defend Hanover, the latter requiring above all financial support to maintain armies large enough to defend herself against the far more numerous armies of Austria, France and later Russia. In Europe at least, the odds were against Britain and Prussia; it is not too much to claim that without the military genius of Frederick the Great and his superb army, together with the strategic vision of William Pitt, the Earl of Chatham (who shortly assumed the supreme direction of the war for Britain) and the well-nigh invincible Royal Navy, France and her allies would have won the war. This had been called the first global war but this claim is surely unconvincing to the reader who has followed the story of the Ottoman assault on Christian nations financed by gold and silver from America, or the Dutch struggle for independence, which was fought not only in Europe but also in South America and the East Indies.

The war started badly for Britain when the government (not then controlled by Chatham) added military blunders to the diplomatic follies which had preceded the outbreak of war. As has already been mentioned the mixed force of British and colonial American troops sent to attack Fort Duquesne was almost annihilated on the river Monongahela and the Royal Navy failed to intercept a French convoy taking reinforcements to Canada. A French invasion threat across the Channel, probably a feint, persuaded the government to keep ships in home waters instead of reinforcing the Mediterranean, with the result that the weak British squadron there failed to stop a French expedition from sailing to Minorca and recapturing Port Mahon, an essential base if Toulon was to be effectively blockaded. Neglect of her fleet in peace was costing Britain dear. In America the British colonists were hemmed in by attacks by the French and their Indian allies. On the other side of the world a native prince, supported by the French, captured Calcutta, the main British base in northern India. This defeat was reversed in the following year by a victory at Plassey which secured the whole of northern India for Britain. Elsewhere, however, she faced failure and defeat, despite the fact that Chatham now directed war strategy. A British expedition sailed to capture Louisburg, the key to Canada, but was too weak to attack it. A British–German army was forced to surrender at Kloster Zeven, and Hanover seemed lost for good. It was Frederick the Great who saved the allies and made later victories possible. His victories at Rossbach and Leuthen in 1757 saved Hanover from further threat and, despite defeat at Hochkirchen (1758) he managed to keep his armies intact and to prevent the enemy from occupying for long any part of his kingdom, which now included Saxony. The year 1758 saw a further improvement in the British position in Germany when a new 'British' army (largely consisting of Hanoverians and German mercenaries paid for by Britain), was formed there. This had the task of protecting Hanover and also of guarding Frederick's western flank. Despite a series of French offensives it accomplished these two tasks for the rest of the war. This army of no more than 40 000 men ensured that Germany remained a heavy drain on the resources of France and her allies and must be seen as an essential part of Chatham's strategy for the war.

In 1758 this strategy began to bear fruit, but much credit for this must also go to Lord Anson, the First Lord of the Admiralty. Chatham, now the main architect of war strategy under the Duke of Newcastle as Prime Minister, had the responsibility for devising war plans (and the difficult task of persuading his colleagues and the voters to accept them and pay for them), but it was Anson who had transformed the Royal Navy, the essential tool for this strategy, into the near-invincible force which it soon became and remained with one significant interruption until 1815. Britain was well provided with the essential requirements for a major naval power at that time – a large merchant marine, excellent naval officers and ratings, numerous shipyards, and unhindered access to supplies of pitch, hemp, and spars, known collectively as naval stores. In all these areas Britain was better placed than her enemy, France, but Anson converted these strategic advantages into tactical superiority at sea. The first step was to gain complete mastery of the English Channel and the Western Approaches to it. All French ports on the Channel, but especially Brest, were to be subjected to what became known as close blockade. In the past the Royal Navy had blockaded enemy ports with cruisers, which would signal the exit of the enemy battle fleet to the main British battle fleet, sheltering in the nearest convenient anchorage. Anson now arranged for the cruisers, particularly those off Brest to have the close support of a detachment of the main battle fleet which could, in effect, stop the enemy fleet leaving port by engaging with superior numbers as the blockaded ships emerged one by one. In addition the enemy was unable to send troop convoys to his overseas colonies and his merchant ships and privateers were also kept in port. As a result, British maritime trade was freed from competition from a serious rival and its ships were far better protected by the reduction in French privateers.

The first results of Chatham's plans and Anson's innovations were seen in America. A force larger than that sent previously was despatched to Louisburg in 1758. The fortress was now more strongly defended than ever and the assault landing was at first repulsed, which seemed to herald the complete failure of the expedition. However, an undefended beach was found by two junior officers on their own initiative, the landing went ahead and Louisburg was taken. In the following year the expedition navigated the St Lawrence river to Quebec, a superb feat of seamanship, and landed troops opposite the city's defences. These were too strong for direct assault but just when it seemed that the British force would have to retreat before the coming of winter an unguarded path to the heights beside the city was found. British troops seized these heights and defeated the French army when it attacked. There was further fierce fighting before all Canada was in British hands, but the most important strategic gains were the capture of Louisburg and Quebec. Finally in 1760 a British force advancing up the Hudson River from New York captured Montreal and the last French army in America surrendered. In retrospect, a British victory seems inevitable, given the fact that the Royal Navy had command of the sea communications to France, but the early victories at Louisburg and Quebec were close – run affairs, with the British having all the luck on both occasions. At sea the tide of war flowed strongly against the French: the Mediterranean became again a British lake after a French fleet was defeated in 1759 at Lagos off Portugal. Even more important was the frustration in the same year of an invasion attempt covered by the French Atlantic Fleet which was mostly destroyed by the Royal Navy at Quiberon Bay. The obvious way to reap the benefit of these victories was, as Chatham realised, to take over France's remaining colonies and overseas bases. Senegal was taken in 1758 and Goree in west Africa a year later. After that Dominica and Martinique, the last French footholds in the West Indies, were lost to the British. In India forces of the British East India Company defeated the French and their allies at Wandiwash in 1760 and with the fall of their fortified port at Pondicherry in 1761 French resistance there virtually ceased. Chatham also attempted to relieve French pressure on Hanover and Prussia by a series of seaborne raids on France with a force of 13 000 British troops, a larger force than was sent to the allied army in Hanover at the time. In two separate raids in 1758, the docks at St Mâlo and Cherbourg were attacked and destroyed but they did not divert significant forces from the main battlefield in Germany, and must therefore be counted as a waste of scarce British troops. If these diversions were to be successful they would have to capture some vital objective (neither Cherbourg nor St Mâlo was vital) and hold it long enough for French troops to have arrive from Germany to retake it. Instead the British took ports of very minor importance and stayed only a few days.

The most valuable contribution Britain made to the Prussian war effort was undoubtedly her generous annual subsidy, but the help of the British subsidised army in Germany, now with nearly 80 000 men (including a small British contingent) should not be ignored. In 1759, after being defeated in an attempt to take Frankfurt-on-Main, it routed a French army at Minden and in the following year, won another victory at Warburg. In general the army suffered mixed fortunes in the field but, win or lose, it usually kept larger French forces engaged, and protected the Prussian armies from attacks from the west.

After 1760 as Britain achieved her main maritime and colonial objectives, and as costs mounted and were increasingly resented by the British tax-payer, the British global offensive began to peter out, but it flared up again when Spain unwisely joined the alliance against Britain and Prussia in late 1761. In the next year Britain sent expeditions to Portugal, Cuba, Brazil and the Philippines which were in the main successful; in a year Spain lost the benefit of her overseas empire. In eastern Europe, the war between Prussia and those not always well coordinated allies, Austria and Russia, continued with bitter fighting almost until the end. The Russians had defeated a Prussian army at Gross Jagersdorf in 1757 but Frederick reversed this with a victory at Zorndorf (1758). In the following year he himself suffered a crushing defeat at Kunersdorf, which led to the temporary loss of Berlin (1760) and Pomerania (1761). Despite these reverses the Prussian Army was rebuilt with British subsidies and Frederick won famous victories at Leignitz and Torgau (1760). The Prussian position was, however, still desperately serious, surrounded as she was by three continental enemies – France, Austria and Russia – but she was saved by the death of Frederick's implacable enemy, the Tzarina Elizabeth of Russia. In 1762 her successor withdrew Russia from the war. Fighting with Austria continued for another year but in 1763 both sets of adversaries (Prussia, Austria, and Russia in the east and Britain, France and Spain in the west), signed peace treaties to end the wars. In Britain, Chatham was no longer at the helm, as a peace party had come to power with the accession of George III and the peace treaty reflected this change of government. France regained her most profitable colonies in the West Indies and Britain secured the return of Port Mahon in Minorca. The true extent of Britain's victory, the most complete in any war which she fought, was emphasised by the fact that she remained the dominant power in India and North America, as well as being economically far stronger than her main enemy, France. Yet within 20 years the British Empire had sunk to its nadir and sustained the greatest defeat in its existence. The reasons for this reversal of fortune are best discussed after examining the war which caused this defeat – the American War of Independence.

THE AMERICAN WAR OF INDEPENDENCE (1775–83)

The causes of the rebellion of the British colonists in America are, to the author's relief, outside the scope of this study, but for the student of strategy two points immediately stand out. Firstly, there were at the time some four million colonists in what became the USA; not all of them supported the Revolution, but the rebels controlled the local administration and the militia, which were the levers of local power. Distributed as the colonists were in large numbers of nearly self-supporting communities, they represented an immense problem for administration and control if they were recalcitrant or even indifferent to the legitimate government. The second notable factor was the distances involved: the area of conflict stretched from Quebec to Charleston, South Carolina, (or even further) which is about as far as from London to Warsaw. No British general would have contemplated campaigning over those distances in Europe and yet the land communications on the American seaboard were far worse than those in continental Europe. Moreover the area of operations was 3000 miles away from Britain whence there had to come not only the strategic direction of the war, but every cannon, musket bullet and barrel of gunpowder with which it was to be fought, all supplied by sailing ships, which were slow and scarce. The British aim was to destroy the American field armies (the main one, commanded by Washington, numbered about 20 000) and occupy as much territory as possible to restore effective control to the British administrators and the loyalists. For this colossal task, comparable, as Correlli Barnett remarks, to invading Russia, the British could afford no more than 50 000 men (the same number as the force which took Canada from the 60 000 French colonists and troops defending it) and by no means all these served with the main field armies. Whatever the difficulties, one thing was certain – without command of the sea route to America and the coastal waters there, the task was impossible.

Open warfare started in 1775 with an invasion of Canada by an American army which captured Montreal and only just failed to take Quebec. At the beginning of 1776, the main British army in America which had been penned up in Boston by the revolutionary armies under Washington since the Battle of Bunker Hill, took advantage of seapower to move its base to New York with a view to an advance south from there to New Jersey and then to Philadelphia. The American Army, weakened by desertions, fell back before the advancing British and it looked as if the revolutionary cause was lost. In 1777 the British planned an ambitious strategy to end the war: New England would be cut off by the simultaneous advance of two armies – that of General Braddock, south from Canada along the line of the River Hudson, and another under General Howe, north up the same river from New York. Culpable carelessness on the part of the government in London allowed Braddock to advance south to Saratoga, even though Howe had abandoned the idea of a concentric offensive and instead advanced south to capture Philadelphia. Braddock, outnumbered and without supplies, was forced to surrender at Saratoga and the whole character of the war changed.

Since the end of the Seven Years' War France had succeeded in isolating Britain from potential allies on the Continent and planned, when she had built up her fleet, to renew the war and recover at least some of her colonies and trade. Possibly in the longer term France would have chosen, after recovering some colonial possessions, to have allied herself to Britain against the growing strength of the eastern European powers: Austria, Prussia and Russia, all of whom seemed to be growing more powerful in comparison to France and Britain. History took a different turn, however, and instead yet another Anglo-French conflict took place – but this time it was fought, thanks to French success in isolating Britain, at sea and in the colonies. France had been giving covert support to the American cause since the start of hostilities in 1775 but did not openly ally herself to the rebels until the British defeat at Saratoga showed that the Americans might succeed in expelling the British. A formal alliance was signed in 1778, and thereafter the crucial area of the conflict was the sea. Before the Franco-American alliance which Spain and the Dutch Republic joined later, Britain was faced with a war which she could not win. Now she was faced with a war in which she could be defeated.

From its beginning the American War had imposed a severe strain on the British fleet, whose ships were required in increasing numbers to blockade American ports, to support the amphibious operations of the British Army and to defend the British merchant fleet against the large number of well armed and skilful American privateers. All these tasks called for frigates (of which no navy ever seems to have had enough) and as usual in peacetime, the navy had been reduced. It was more difficult to re-equip the navy since the American colonies had been a major source of ships' stores and crews for the British Navy. This is well illustrated by the fact that, in the middle of the century, American shipyards built one-third of the British merchant fleet. In addition to the American challenge, the French Navy was far stronger than at the start of the three previous wars. Thanks to Choiseul, one of the best Ministers ever to serve a French king in war, the French Navy had been transformed. There were 65 ships of the line, backed by an adequate dockyard reserve of timber and other ships' stores, with a system of conscription for crews and worthwhile training for naval officers: all the essentials for a fighting navy, as Britain had discovered earlier in the century. Spain too could provide 60 ships of the line, though these were not so effective as those of the French. As a consequence of this peacetime build-up by her enemies and of her own practice of reducing the navy in times of peace, Britain found that her fleets were outnumbered on several crucial occasions when the French and Spanish fleets put to sea. The consequences of this weakness are illustrated by an indecisive engagement between equal numbers of British and French ships off Ushant in 1778. If the Royal Navy had been better prepared for war, with trained crews and perhaps a slight superiority in ships of the line, a decisive British victory, with serious losses for the French, might on past form have been expected. In that event the French would not have been able to send troops and ships to help the American colonists a few years later and American and British history might have been different.

As it was, the first serious French threat came a year later when 50 000 troops stood ready at St Mâlo and Le Havre to invade Britain when the Franco-Spanish fleet of 66 ships had overcome the 46 British ships opposed to them. Skilful handling of the British fleet enabled it to avoid a decisive action and at the same time remain as a barrier to an invasion fleet of troop-carrying ships. Elsewhere the outcome of the early engagements was far less favourable. British possessions in the West Indies fell to the French, and Gibraltar was put under a siege which lasted three years. Intense efforts were made by the Royal Navy on several occasions to deliver supplies, on one occasion in 1780 there was a major fleet action off Cape St Vincent. Somehow the garrison was reinforced and provisioned, but this entailed concentration of forces and the consequent neglect of other vital areas. Thus Minorca, with Port Mahon the base for blockading Toulon, was invested and fell in 1782, a year after the siege of Gibraltar was finally lifted, but an even more costly lapse was the failure to blockade Brest.

In 1781 a French fleet of 26 ships was able to leave Brest. It then split into two squadrons, one going to the East under the command of Admiral Suffren, one of the most energetic commanders ever produced by the French Navy. The other, under Admiral de Grasse, sailed westwards. The east-bound squadron first intercepted and destroyed a British convoy on its way to capture the Dutch colony at the Cape of Good Hope and then went on to secure that important strategic base from further British attack. Suffren then sailed on to his destination, southern India, where he was to support an Indian prince, Hyder Ali, who as a French ally was attempting to expel the British from the southern part of India.

On arrival Suffren's squadron had the best of an engagement with a smaller British force and was then able to capture Trincomalee in Ceylon, an invaluable base from which to threaten the British position in the southern part of India. This he succeeded in doing, fighting a series of hard-fought engagements with the British squadron until the end of the war in 1783. It is true that Suffren was never able to swing the war on land in France's favour, and he suffered from a lack of cooperation from the authorities at the main French base at Mauritius. Nevertheless, his squadron was a constant threat to the British supply line to India and with more good fortune he could have done far more damage to the British than he did.

The west-bound squadron was a great deal more successful, though its commander, Admiral de Grasse, was not cast in the mould of Suffren. It sailed first to the West Indies and might have been badly mauled or even destroyed when it arrived, battered and disorganised after its Atlantic voyage, if the British commanders on the spot, Admirals Rodney and Hood, had cooperated and concentrated their forces. Instead De Grasse was able to collect French merchant shipping and despatch it in convoy to France. Responding to urgent pleas from General Washington, he then sailed for the east coast of America and the decisive action of the war.

In 1778/9 the British again used their mastery of the American coastal waters to abandon Philadelphia, returning to New York to try to shift the weight of operations to the southern states of the colony, where they believed they had greater popular support. Charleston was captured and the British commander, Lord Cornwallis, became involved in a series of small battles which involved much marching and counter-marching in the up-country Carolinas. Finally, since he was not achieving effective control of the southern states, Cornwallis was ordered to take his much reduced army north by land to occupy Virginia, with reinforcements from New York and support from the navy. He received neither and by 1781 was besieged in Yorktown on Chesapeake Bay by an American army under Washington with a strong French contingent. More ominous was the presence in Chesapeake Bay of the French squadron under De Grasse. A British squadron under Admiral Graves tried twice, in March and September 1781, to dislodge the French ships without success and finally sailed back to New York leaving Cornwallis and his army to its fate. After a hard-fought siege Cornwallis surrendered and the war for America was virtually over.

The British avoided further disasters – if not outright defeat – by accepting American Independence and, with their resources freed, offering the French and their Spanish allies a compromise peace or a longer and bloodier war. France was facing severe financial difficulties and peace was agreed by the Treaty of Paris in 1783. The British threat of continued fighting was not an idle one, for they had begun to make an astonishing recovery, thanks to the huge resources which they were now devoting to the war. In 1782 Rodney and Hood made restitution, as it were, for their failure to intercept De Grasse on his arrival, and revenge for Graves' performance in Chesapeake Bay, by eliminating the French fleet under De Grasse at the Battle of the Saints. This was the first naval engagement when the Royal Navy used the tactic of breaking the enemy line of battle and overwhelming a portion of his fleet with superior numbers. The West Indies were saved from French domination. Meanwhile, despite the efforts of Suffren, the British and their Indian allies were able to defeat Hyder Ali and they went on to win victories in a series of hard campaigns against the Mahrattas in central southern India, eventually winning control of the whole area. However, it was the rapid growth of the British fleet in home waters which probably persuaded France and Spain to make peace.

The war against the American colonies had found the Royal Navy ill-prepared for war but no worse than in previous wars against the French; the needs of this war, however, were different. Frigates, rather than ships of the line (or battleships), were needed. Consequently, in the early part of the war frigates were produced quickly and in large numbers and all laid-up frigates were re-commissioned. However, no new ships of the line were built. The navy was kept short of funds because the government decided, when fighting broke out, to gamble on a military solution by sending as large a force as possible to America. In the end 50 000 troops, many of them German mercenaries (the same number that had won Canada for Britain), were sent to America to no avail and the decision to neglect the navy exposed Britain to very great danger. The unopposed passage of the Franco-Spanish fleet off the south coast of England in 1779 – which seemed at the time to be a real threat of invasion – spurred the government to an exceptionally large building programme, much of which did not bear fruit until the war was over. These extraordinary efforts came about because of Britain's strong economy and financial institutions, which provided a well-established system of public credit. It was therefore possible for Britain to cover over 80 percent of expenditure on the war by borrowing, leaving only 19 percent to be raised in taxes. France also borrowed heavily, and in the opinion of many historians, it was the mishandling of this debt which caused the crisis which started the French Revolution. Be that as it may, French government ministers were very doubtful in 1782 whether France's financial resources could stand the strain of a naval arms race with Britain. Even if funds had been available, it is doubtful whether France or Spain had enough of the resources, that is skilled shipwrights and seamen, well-equipped dockyards and assured access to naval stores (usually obtained from the Baltic or North America), to expand their navies much beyond their size at the time. They were wise to make peace when they did.

Of course, it does not follow that Britain could win a war of American Independence even if she could not be beaten by France and Spain. The magnitude of the task of conducting a war on a continental scale 3000 miles from home has already been stressed. It is possible that in 1777 the pincer-stroke by Howe and Braddock to cut off New England might, if coupled with the loss of Washington's army, have caused the leaders of the Revolution to lose heart and seek peace, but it would have almost certainly have required some political concessions from Britain: whether these would have been forthcoming is another question outside the scope of this study. What is clear, however, is that the military domination of the American colonies against the wishes of the inhabitants was out of the question for Britain. It could not be done with 50 000 men nor even twice that number. The experience of Cornwallis in the Carolinas shows how little could be achieved by an effective general and army in a countryside not actively hostile. When Cornwallis retreated north to Yorktown there was nothing to show for two years' hard campaigning. It is hard not to agree with the judgement of Correlli Barnett: 'It is probable that to restore British authority in America was a problem beyond the power of military means to solve, however perfectly applied.'

From the French point of view, the outcome of her three mid-century wars with Britain can have given her leaders little satisfaction. Although France had avoided Louis XIV's mistake of ranging all the European powers against her by attempting the military domination of the Continent, she had gained extraordinarily little in comparison with Britain. In the first of these wars (the War of the Austrian Succession) she had to give up her conquests in Europe to regain her colonies and overseas trade. In the second she lost her best hope of gaining a significant foothold in either America or India, and although she succeeded in the third in depriving her enemy of the main American colonies (Canada had not by then become highly regarded as a source of wealth) she had received nothing worthwhile for herself, despite the financially crippling burden of the war. Were there alternative strategies which France could have followed? The answer must surely be that she should have begun earlier to build the fleet which was created under the guidance of Choiseul after the Seven Years' War. Much of the infrastructure, such as dockyards and skilled designers and craftsmen and the resources, could surely have been found for a fleet, which if not as large as the Royal Navy, would have stood a good chance of securing sea mastery in one or more crucial areas of wartime operations. (French-built warships were as good as or better than their British counterparts). The Battle of Chesapeake Bay showed what could be achieved by this; with more support Suffren could possibly have achieved similar results off India and then France would have been able to keep the gains made by the French East India Company and its Indian allies. Nearer home there might have been a good chance of keeping the British out of the Mediterranean; even if Gibraltar could not have been retaken, the earlier recapture of Port Mahon on Minorca could have altered the course of the first two of the three wars significantly. Finally there was always the possibility of local mastery of the English Channel, as occurred soon after France entered the American War of Independence when France was unable to exploit her stroke of good fortune (if one may thus describe the heavy overseas commitments of the British Army and Navy at the time). These 'might-have-beens' may seem far-fetched to a modern reader, but these were the last of the wars in this series when the armies were small and professional. Small numbers of men gained or lost great continents overseas. The British Army losses at Saratoga and Yorktown numbered 5000 and 7000 respectively. The numbers of European troops engaged in India were even smaller. An adequate navy skilfully deployed might have enabled France to retain some significant footholds in America and India after 1783, even if the Americans were inevitably bound for freedom rather than French suzerainty.

THE FRENCH REVOLUTIONARY WAR (1792–1802)

After 1783 the nature of the Anglo-French wars changed again. The most obvious difference was that France again, as in the time of Louis XIV, had the other great powers of Europe ranged against her. At the start of the Revolutionary War they were trying to restore the Bourbon kings to the French throne; by its end they were trying to avoid defeat and serious loss of territory to France and the puppet states which she established with revolutionary credentials. Throughout the Napoleonic war which followed it, the other European powers were striving to avoid outright defeat and some form of subordination to France. The more far-reaching change was in the very nature of war itself. The new French armies had revolutionary fervour and great tactical initiative and flexibility but, above all, they were, in the words of Correlli Barnett:

> the vehicle of all the physical and emotional resources of the French nation. Ruthless leadership was to enlist these resources by means impossible to the ancien regime: conscription, requisition, central direction.

It could well be argued that these two wars, and not the American Civil War, were the first of the modern wars in which mass armies raised by conscription (or its near equivalent) and backed by something like complete industrial mobilisation could only be halted and defeated by a long series of battles in which both sides would suffer massive casualties. The British people did not adopt this method of waging war. Unmoved by revolutionary fervour and unwilling to put an army at the centre of national life they were not prepared to accept any form of impressment, except in a limited form for the navy. Indeed, although when threatened by invasion they would join local volunteer forces for home defence, they provided few volunteers for overseas service which, as they knew often, involved not glory or booty but death by disease in the West Indies.

The French revolutionary government declared war on Austria in 1792 and Prussia and the smaller German states joined Austria in a plan to invade France and restore the monarchy. In the following year France invaded the Austrian Netherlands (now Belgium) and the first encounter took place at Valmy in north-east France. It was not a pitched battle – there were only

500 casualties out of the 86 000 engaged on both sides, but the Prussian army retreated after a cannonade by both sides and the Revolution was saved. Most of the French units engaged were in fact from the old royal army but the myth of revolutionary valour was born and the new French Army gained much needed confidence and, equally valuable, time to reorganise. Britain entered the war against France in 1793. This was followed by a French attack on the Dutch Republic and in consequence Britain made her first strategic blunder. Mistaking the coming conflict for another of the mid-century maritime and colonial wars, the younger Pitt, who was Prime Minister, sent a large expedition to the West Indies to capture the French colonies there, rich sugar-producing islands which could produce immediate returns in increased trade. In the event the campaign in the Caribbean lasted until 1796 and cost 80 000 men of whom 40 000 died of disease and the rest were unfit for further service. It was a waste of scarce manpower on two counts; the French colonies could have been taken later on after a blockade and the troops were badly needed in Europe, the decisive theatre. However, the West Indies expeditions were not wholly inspired by greed and the desire for short-term gain, for it was sound strategy to deprive France of these islands as soon as possible. In the eighteenth century the West Indies represented enormous sources of wealth and it was wise to deprive France of this wealth as early in the war as possible. Unfortunately for Britain the wrong means were chose to achieve this end.

1793 was the year in which the allies probably had the best chance to extinguish the Revolution in France and they missed it. The Austrians freed the Netherlands from the French but failed to thrust at Paris and were driven back by a French counter-offensive. A Hanoverian and Hessian Army in British pay failed to take Dunkirk and a Royalist revolt in the Vendée was crushed while Britain debated about sending troops. Finally in the south an expedition of allied troops supported by the Royal Navy captured Toulon but was forced out by a counter-offensive. Rarely, if ever, were so many vital objectives in France available to Britain for the taking; none were secured in 1793. All Britain's available troops, up to 80 000, were or soon would be rotting in the West Indies. By 1794 the new French Army was ready, thanks to the genius of Carnot the War Minister, to undertake an offensive strategy. The British-paid army in Flanders was badly beaten at Tourcoing and retreated to defend Holland. It failed to do so in the face of repeated French attacks and the remnant was evacuated to Britain early in the next year. Meanwhile an Austrian army was defeated at Fleurus and retreated eastwards. The landward threat to France had disappeared. Prussia made peace but worse was to come for the remaining allies. In 1796 in his first campaign Napoleon swept the Austrians out of northern Italy and in the following year Austria made peace. Britain having started what she thought would be a limited colonial war against France in 1792, was left five years later without an ally on the Continent and in danger of invasion. The only British gain in the war so far were the Caribbean sugar islands, slowly captured at immense cost to the troops. By contrast, Revolutionary France had made gains in Europe which exceeded those obtained by Louis XIV after almost a lifetime of war. In 1794 the first major sea encounter took place in the Battle of the Glorious First of June. This was a tactical victory for Britain but a strategic reverse, since the grain convoy desperately needed to avert famine in France, and for the sake of which the French fleet had put to sea, was able to reach France unmolested. Thereafter the dominant position of Britain at sea to which she had become accustomed came increasingly under threat. The impending transfer of the Dutch and Spanish fleets to the ranks of her enemies forced her to evacuate the Mediterranean and soon the only foothold which the Royal Navy could protect in Europe was Lisbon. The bulk of British naval strength had to be withdrawn to home ports to protect the country from the very real threat of invasion. Then, in 1797, at the nadir of British fortunes, the Channel Fleet at Spithead and the Nore mutinied.

The same year, however, also saw the first signs of the turn of the tide. At the start, a Spanish fleet en route for Brest to support an invasion of Britain was decisively defeated and turned back off Cape St Vincent by a smaller British force. Later in the autumn the Dutch fleet was effectively put out of action at Camperdown by a British fleet of about the same strength. The Royal Navy was now free to concentrate against their main enemy, the French. The only invasion attempt made by the latter in 1797 was the landing of a small force in South Wales which was later rounded up by the local militia. In the following year there was a rebellion in Ireland, but this was put down before French troops could reach the scene. When 9000 French troops did arrive they were surrounded at Castlebar and forced to surrender. It might seem that stalemate had been reached between the two adversaries. Britain had no ally on the Continent to challenge the supremacy of France and she for her part could not find any means of striking a knockout blow at an enemy once more in full command of the seas around her coasts. This deadlock was, however, about to be broken.

In the early months of 1798 rumours began to reach Pitt and his colleagues in London that France was preparing a large fleet and expeditionary force in Toulon. Its destination was a mystery to the British government: it could have been Sicily, Portugal, or Ireland; but it was clear that it should if possible be intercepted and destroyed at sea. Pitt, having learned both wisdom and the need for boldness, decided that the navy was sufficiently strong in home waters to afford a detachment for duty in the Mediterranean again. This marked a turning point in the war and could indeed have ended Napoleon's career. For it was Napoleon, now a member of the ruling junta in France and its leading military commander, who was in command of the forces collecting at Toulon and their destination was Egypt – with the objective, it is suggested, of creating an overland route to India. Be that as it may, the danger of a French domination of the Near East, with the threat to Turkey and the south-eastern corner of Europe, was real enough and the British government was right to send Nelson and his squadron to the Mediterranean (although the final decision to divide his fleet was left to Nelson's superior in the fleet off Cadiz, Lord St Vincent, to whom much credit is also due). As is well known, Nelson narrowly missed catching the whole force (including Napoleon) at sea, but in the end, found the French fleet at Aboukir Bay after it had disembarked the troops. He destroyed it at the Battle of the Nile and left the French troops marooned in Egypt. The victorious British fleet took Minorca and its presence encouraged the Kingdom of the Two Sicilies to declare war on France. The news of the victory was enough to persuade Austria and Russia into the war again in the Second Coalition against France.

The alliance of Britain, Austria, Russia and Turkey started with some promising successes. In 1799 northern Italy was reconquered by Austria, while an Austrian and Russian army attacked French-held Switzerland and a Russian and British army landed on the Helder Peninsula in Holland, and was able to destroy the remnants of the Dutch fleet, which had escaped at Camperdown. However, Britain was again guilty of dispersing her resources, keeping no less than 80 000 troops in England for an amphibious attack on France, whilst discussion took place about the best objective. Walcheren, Belle Isle, Cadiz, Tenerife and Brest were all proposed and rejected. Finally two expeditions were sent: one to Ferrol and one to Cadiz, though without decisive results. After this promising start the Second Coalition began to fray. The Russian and British army in Holland was foiled by a skilful French defence making use of the water barriers and with Napoleon's return (without his army) from Egypt, France went over to the counter-offensive. Switzerland was retaken from the Russian general Suvorov, the Austrians were beaten by the French at Hohenlinden and in a very close-run battle Napoleon defeated another Austrian army at Marengo, recovering northern Italy. British seapower and a modest military force might have made all the difference if it had been applied to northern Italy. As it was, Malta was taken from the French, but Britain could not prevent Spain from overrunning Portugal and depriving Britain of another excellent base, Lisbon. Austria made peace with France in 1801 and the second Coalition was finished. Britain was again alone.

It was then that Britain's war leader, Pitt, recognising that this war was not for colonies and trade, but for the freedom of Europe, began to use the navy offensively in the main area of conflict and further afield. In 1801 the potentially hostile Danish fleet at Copenhagen was, to a large extent, put out of action by a British fleet, part of which went further into the Baltic, to threaten the same fate to a Russian fleet at Reval. This escaped to Kronstadt, which was heavily fortified, but a change of Czar served Britain's purpose just as well. Napoleon had been trying to close the Baltic to British trade by encouraging Russia, Denmark and other neutral states to boycott British goods and thus achieve a major French objective, which was to prevent her enemy from obtaining essential naval stores from the Baltic. With the change of Czar the so-called League of Armed Neutrality fell apart, but Britain's ever-present fear of losing access to naval stores, which caused the aggressive use of the navy at Copenhagen and after, remained. Britain's leaders must have wondered what would happen if France could dominate the whole of Europe, deny her enemy naval stores from the Baltic and, by monopolising all the shipyards in Europe, outbuild Britain and defeat the Royal Navy.

At the other end of what might be called the European battlefront (although the Near East was now a strategic backwater) Britain used her mastery of the Mediterranean to land an army in Egypt and defeat the French Army stranded there by Nelson's victory in Aboukir Bay in 1799 (the Battle of the Nile). Still, further away in India, seapower gave Britain more success. In 1798 the Sultan of Mysore, an ally of France, who had received very little material support, was defeated by the British and killed in the capture of Seringpatam. Thereafter the British Army – under the future Duke of Wellington – went on to defeat the Mahratta Confederacy (the dominant military power in central India) at the Battle of Assaye in 1803. The collapse of the Second Coalition did not force Britain on to the defensive; on the contrary she used her mastery of the sea to thwart enemy plans, to protect her own interests and to enlarge her own possessions. Both sides were feeling the strain and with the temporary fall of Pitt from power, peace was agreed in 1802.

THE NAPOLEONIC WAR (1803–1815)

After no more than a year of peace, mutual and probably well-founded distrust caused war to break out again. Britain, angered by French annexation of Holland and Switzerland, declared war in 1803. A year of purely defensive war followed, but with 172 ships of the line (battleships) compared to 33 French, 63 Spanish and 16 Dutch ships of similar power, Britain was able to impose a close blockade on enemy ports and steadily strengthen it. Napoleon directed all France's available efforts to building a fleet of transports and a battle fleet for the invasion of Britain.

The naval plan devised by the greatest military genius of the age paid no great regard to the hazards and peculiarities of the sea. The French squadron in Toulon was to break out and decoy the British blockading squadron to the West Indies by sailing there, but was itself to return to Europe at once. On its return it was to release the Spanish fleet from the ports in which it was being blockaded and perform a similar service for the French squadron in Brest. The combined fleets could thus establish local command of the English Channel while part of the British fleet was still in the West Indies, and therefore escort the invasion fleet to southern England and end the war. As is well known, this master plan failed, not least because the British commanders of individual Royal Navy squadrons collected in the Western Approaches to the English Channel, which was the vital area for the control of the sea approach to Britain. The French squadron left Toulon in 1805, but found itself, after its dash to the West Indies, forced to take refuge in Cadiz with the Spanish squadron which it was supposed to relieve. The 21 ships of the line in Brest never managed to beat the British blockade and as a result the threatened concentration planned by Napoleon never came near to being realised. A desperate sortie by the Franco-Spanish fleet from Cadiz in October 1805 ended in its complete defeat off Cape Trafalgar. The French and Spanish fleets never faced the Royal Navy in a major engagement for the rest of the war.

However, over a month before the Battle of Trafalgar, Napoleon had abandoned his invasion plans and had started his army marching towards a series of his most brilliant victories, in central Europe. Pitt, again Prime Minister, had been working throughout the summer to construct the Third Coalition against Napoleon. Russia was ready to join and, after hesitation, Austria too seemed prepared to declare war on France by the autumn, but Napoleon struck first. Before the end of that year he had forced the capitulation of one Austrian army at Ulm, entered Vienna, defeated an Austrian and Russian army at Austerlitz and made Austria sign a humiliating peace. The Third Coalition was over almost before it had begun. Pitt died at the start of 1806, but he had imbued his countrymen with a determination to continue the war with France and despite a succession of Prime Ministers in following years, British strategy remained remarkably consistent until the end of the war. In 1806 Prussia belatedly tried to stop the French advance into central Europe. She was punished by a shattering military defeat at Jena and Auerstadt. Then, in 1807, after two bloody battles at Eylau and Friedland, France imposed another humiliating peace, this time on Russia. She now dominated Europe as no state had since the Carolingian Empire of Charlemagne.

There was little that Britain could do with her navy to influence these awesome changes in the strategic map of central Europe so remote from the sea. However, during 1806 and 1807 she did her best to influence events on the Continent by a number of military operations, using sea power to seize the initiative. An amphibious force captured Copenhagen and destroyed the Danish fleet. In 1806 a small British army defending Sicily crossed into southern Italy and defeated a French army of about the same size at Maida, the first time that the British infantry in line had overcome French infantry attacking in column. A British fleet failed to force the Dardanelles and coerce Turkey and another took an army which eventually amounted to 12 000 men to seize Spain's South American empire (larger than Europe). It failed after initial success and by the effort Britain lost more than she gained.

The most productive use of sea power in this period was the despatch in 1808 of 16 ships of the line with supporting smaller craft and transports for 10 000 troops to the Baltic. The original idea was to support Sweden against coercion by France and Russia to join the French embargo against British trade. Eventually Sweden was forced to give in to French demands, but for the next five years a British squadron under Admiral Saumarez dominated the waters of the Baltic and secured, by a wise mixture of force and diplomacy, three important objectives. Firstly, Sweden, an unwilling ally of France, was able to evade controls on trade with Britain; secondly, Britain had continued access to those vital naval stores – timber, spars and pitch – which she needed to maintain her navy; and lastly, the presence of this squadron setting a clear limit to Napoleon's power surely encouraged Russia to resist French pressure and finally to join the coalition against her.

In 1808, the same year that this British squadron first sailed to the Baltic, another and even better opportunity presented itself to curb French power, this time at the other end of Europe, but the distance presented no problem for such a flexible weapon as a battle fleet. Spain rose against Napoleon. Spain had been a long-suffering ally of Revolutionary France for much of both the Revolutionary wars, and had suffered severe losses in ships and men, with little gain to show for it. However, Napoleon, now master of Europe, wanted a puppet state, not an independent ally, and by a shabby trick secured the throne of Spain for his brother Jerome. This foreign incursion was greeted with outrage by the great mass of Spanish people, who rose in a virtually spontaneous revolt against their new king without any clear lead or encouragement from their legitimate rulers or politicians. It was this popular uprising which gave the war in Spain its special character, for it was, as far as the Spanish share of the fighting was concerned, more than a sporadic guerilla war and and something less than a full-scale war between formed armies of regular troops with recognised bases and established supply lines, although it had some of the characteristics of both. The Spanish regular armies, which sometimes fought well but often badly, somehow managed to reform after their frequent appalling defeats; at the same time there were throughout Spain guerilla bands numbering from 50 to many thousands undertaking traditional tasks for such forces. They were so effective that towards the end of the war the French were forced, if they wished to ensure the safe passage of a courier, to send two squadrons of cavalry as escort. By one means or another the British and Spanish forces kept up to 325 000 French soldiers occupied in Spain but no more than a quarter of these could be concentrated against the British in 1810 for an invasion of Portugal. The rest were detained in other parts of Spain by the 100 000 or so regulars in the Spanish army, many of whom could not face the French in a set-piece battle, and the numerous guerilla bands. The indigenous armies did occasionally win clear-cut victories over the French as at Baylen, Tamames and Alcaniz, as well as defensive battles as at San Marcial in 1813; but it was the Anglo-Portuguese army under Wellington which, by inflicting successive defeats on the French, finally forced their evacuation of Spain, while the Spanish regular and irregular troops kept the bulk of French forces away from the main battles and in so doing bled them white. In four years the French lost 160 000 men not in pitched battles, but by guerilla raids and sickness.

There were two other reasons why Spain was an ideal location for Britain to engage a French army. In the first place, as Wellington noted at the outset, the countryside was so barren that no large French army could subsist on it long enough to overcome a determined adversary (as was shown by the ordeal of Massena's army before Torres Vedras) and the land communications with France were so poor that there was never any chance of the French reaching, say, the Portuguese border with enough troops to overwhelm Wellington's army. The second point, which was not recognised by Britain's rulers for some time, was that seapower gave Britain many advantages in a war on the Iberian Peninsula which she would not enjoy in most, if not all, other likely theatres for the war against Napoleon. Troops and all the gold, stores, food, arms and ammunition needed by the British, Spanish and Portuguese troops, regular and irregular, could be conveyed more cheaply and often more swiftly than the French could move equivalent quantities along the appalling Peninsular roads. Moreover, command of the sea enabled the British to rescue any allied army in difficulty, provided that it could reach the coast. The British army under Sir John Moore was picked up by the Navy at Corunna and lived to fight another day, unlike Cornwallis's army at Yorktown. By the same token, strongly defended ports could be held indefinitely against French attack, provided that the Royal Navy had unhindered access to supplies; the Spanish army held Cadiz throughout the war and kept their 20 000 French besiegers from more useful work. The French were in addition constantly under threat of attack from the sea. Thus two allied squadrons at Ferrol and Corunna in 1810 kept 20 000 French troops tied down on the Biscay coast by threatened landings; similar threats had corresponding results on the Andalusian coast. The defeat of a French army corps by a Spanish force of 12 000 at Barrosa in 1811 is another example and there are many more minor instances of this harassment. Although the British were a little slow in recognising the offensive value of such operations in Spain, they played an important role in tying down those French troops who were not directly engaged by the British army.

A brief survey of the British campaigns in the Peninsula will help to show when, and to what extent, they affected the main French campaigns in central Europe. The British Government responded to Spanish appeals for help by sending a small expeditionary force to French-occupied Portugal, with the objective of expelling all French troops from the Iberian Peninsula. It was commanded by the future Duke of Wellington, who won two small-scale victories which secured Lisbon as a base for supplies. When the army reached 40 000 Sir John Moore, one of Britain's ablest generals, assumed command and was ordered to advance into Spain to assist the Spanish army in ejecting the French from Spain. The prospects must have looked good to those in London, since one Spanish army had won the greatest of their victories by forcing the capitulation of a complete French army at Baylen. Moore was soon to learn that cooperation with the regular Spanish forces involved difficulty, frustration and real danger. He learned only just in time that Napoleon, who had entered Spain at the head of 250 000 men, was about to cut him off and that the Spanish armies with whom he was supposed to cooperate had vanished. After a swift and difficult retreat to Corunna in 1808/9 he repulsed the French army pursuing him in a battle in which he was killed, but his army re-embarked safely, and returned home, which was of vital importance, as it was the only British army in existence at the time. Napoleon left the mopping-up operation, as he saw it, to his marshals. Wellington returned to Portugal in 1809 to command the Anglo-Portuguese army (the latter trained, led and paid for by the British), and the pattern for the rest of the war was set. It was to be, as far as the British contribution was concerned, Wellington against a succession of French marshals, whom he defeated in turn.

For the next few years Wellington maintained his army in Portugal, defeating successive French armies sent against him. His view that British infantry in line, rigorously disciplined in drill to Prussian standards was capable of repulsing French infantry attacking in column, proved correct. In 1810 the French made their last and most determined effort to drive the British into the sea. An army of over 70 000 under Massena advanced into Portugal, but was held by a smaller British army ensconced in the Lines of Torres Vedras, stretching from the river Tagus to the sea outside Lisbon. These were, the French judged, impregnable and could not be outflanked, but Massena hung on in the scorched earth outside the Lines for six months until he was forced to retreat in early 1811 with the loss of 25 000 men from starvation and disease. Wellington maintained his army and the population of Lisbon with seaborne supplies, thanks to the Royal Navy. By 1812 Wellington was strong enough, with 45 000 men to carry his offensive into Spain. The French armies in Spain were reduced to 230 000 men, owing to Napoleon's need to concentrate all available troops for the attack on Russia. At Salamanca Wellington routed 40 000 French soldiers in 40 minutes, in one of the great encounter battles in history. He was compelled to retire to Portugal that winter, but in 1813 he finally drove the main French armies from Spain, securing, a notable victory at Vittoria and ending the year on the Pyrenees, with his shortened supply lines running to the Spanish ports on the Biscay coast instead of to Lisbon: this logistic switch being made possible by the British command of the sea. The British victory at Vittoria was the first of her Peninsular victories to have a significant effect on the main war in Europe and consequently on the policies of the great powers.

In 1809 Austria had once again declared war on France and her army, under the command of her best general, the Archduke Charles, had inflicted on Napoleon his first defeat, at Aspern-Essling. Shortly after, Napoleon recovered, defeated the Austrians at Wagram and once again forced Austria to peace, but the scale of these battles serves to put the Peninsular battles into perspective. The Austrian army at these battles numbered 80 000, Wellington's numbered 45 000; while the total of French casualties at Aspern-Essling were 20 000. Despite her many defeats, Austria can claim, in Correlli Barnett's words, to have 'throughout the War faced the main strength of France under the Emperor Napoleon himself and successively weakened it in great and bloody battles'. In 1812 Napoleon decided, surely correctly, that he could never dominate the continent of Europe unless he inflicted a decisive defeat on Russia. He marched on Moscow with an army of over 500 000 collected from France and her European satellites. He returned, with Russia unsubdued with fewer than 20 000 men. Prussia re-entered the war in 1813 but Russo-German armies were defeated at Lutzen and Bautzen. Nevertheless, the débâcle of the retreat from Moscow and the victory at Vittoria were having their effect, and Austria again entered the the war. At Leipzig the three European powers (Austria, Russia and Prussia) fought the French in the Battle of the Nations. Half a million troops took part in the series of battles lasting three days (one of the first battles of modern war in which mass conscription produced mass armies on one battlefield). Napoleon escaped but had to retreat to France where he held off the advancing allies until he was forced to abdicate in 1814. His return in 1815 to win two battles at Ligny and Quatre Bras and finally to lose at Waterloo to the British and Prussian armies (but less than half of the 'British' army came from Britain, the rest being German, Belgian or Dutch) ended the French attempt to dominate Europe. The clear victor was Britain, which finished the war with her home territory intact, her navy the strongest in the world and her economic and commercial strength unsurpassed for the next half-century.

Britain started the French Revolutionary War with a strong navy, thanks to the large building programme at the end of the American War of Independence. Perhaps it was this relative abundance of naval power which was one of the factors which persuaded Pitt to send the ill-fated expedition to capture the French sugar islands in the West Indies, but he also held the mistaken view that the war against the weak French Republic would be short, because of the nations ranged against her, and therefore decided that Britain could confine herself to a war on the French colonies. Whatever the reasoning, Pitt blundered in committing scarce and almost irreplaceable resources – British troops – to the West Indies. Any naval units lost could be replaced in reasonable time but the 80 000 troops could have been used to far better effect later and elsewhere. If they had been sent to Europe, for example to the Vendée, they could have helped to end the Revolution before Carnot had time to organise the French war machine.

Once Pitt realised his error, he had to decide how Britain's resources could best be used against a nation well prepared for a new kind of war on land. Clearly it was correct to make a strong navy the first priority, since it was the best, indeed the only effective defence of the home base, but it was far more difficult to devise a workable offensive strategy using naval power to defeat the French armies which were threatening and then defeating all France's enemies on land. Close blockade and convoy protection enabled Britain to grow wealthy enough to subsidise those European allies which were prepared to send armies into the field against the French, but successive defeats left them often unwilling or unable to do so. Victory at Trafalgar could not stop the defeats at Austerlitz and Jena. Gradually it became clear that the power of the Royal Navy could do much to confine French armies at the periphery of the European continent. Minorca was taken and held, and Sicily and Sardinia, protected by British land and sea forces, retained their independence throughout the two wars but, more remarkably, the British squadron in the Baltic protected British interests in the trade in naval stores from that region and prevented it from ever falling completely under French domination.

French power was therefore effectively confined, but Europe would still have been lost if the Russian steppes had not also proved an effective barrier to Napoleon's armies. It was therefore essential, if Russia was not to succumb either to French power or to her diplomacy, for Britain to intervene on land, not only to divert French troops from the potential allies in central Europe, but also to convince these allies-to-be that Britain was serious in wanting to continue the struggle. It was the victory at Vittoria which persuaded Austria to enter the war once again. As has already been seen, Spain proved an ideal point of entry for the British army, but there were earlier opportunities which Britain missed. For too long the British government and their military advisers seemed convinced that the coasts of France and Flanders were the best areas for amphibious attack; despite the failure of the expedition to the Helder Peninsula in 1799, another major and futile effort was made at Walcheren in 1809. At last the ideal theatre for British land and sea forces presented itself, in Spain, but even then Wellington was kept short of men and equipment. The earlier arrival of an effective siege train and at least some of the units wasted at Walcheren might have brought Wellington to the Pyrenees just as Napoleon was returning from Russia with no more than 20 000 men. The war could have ended at least a year earlier. Another possible theatre for British forces in 1800 was Italy. From a base such as Genoa it might have been possible to cooperate with the Austrian army and defeat Napoleon before France had time to recover from the reverses sustained in the Egyptian campaign. This is speculation, but it is clear that to maintain opposition to France among the other European powers, Britain had to commit land forces in a theatre where seapower could be used to the greatest advantage to support the army and, if necessary, to evacuate it. Provided that British forces could ultimately threaten important French targets, the fighting would inevitably divert French troops from other tasks in Europe but, almost as important, a British army on almost any part of the Continent would persuade other European powers that Britain was in earnest in the struggle against France. Vittoria is a long way from Vienna, but Wellington's victory there was enough to persuade Austria to declare war on France once more. Due to the military genius of their leader and the centrally directed resources of their nation, the French probably achieved as much with their armies during the Napoleonic War as was possible, given the logistics and communications of the time. It will be helpful to look back at the whole series of Anglo-French wars before considering what alternative strategies she might have adopted.

A RETROSPECT

When looked at together, the seven wars between Britain and France in the eighteenth century divide into two: the first two and the last two differ in important ways from the three which occurred between 1739 and 1748. The first and last pair were wars for the domination of Europe; in the middle three the acquisition of retention of colonies and overseas trade were the main objectives for Britain. Obviously the winning strategies for these two different kinds of war were likely to be different, but in either case Britain had to retain a navy strong enough to control the waters around the British Isles, including her Achilles Heel, Ireland. If she did this she provided the only effective defence of her home base and as the century wore on this defensive weapon became more and more successful in blockading French ports. This both throttled French overseas trade and prevented French reinforcements from reaching her colonies overseas, but at the same time provided a good defence against French attacks on the British merchant fleet. Since this strategy also freed Britain's trade from competition, it is little wonder that Chatham's conduct of the Seven Years' War, when the technique of close blockade was perfected, was extremely popular with mercantile interests in Britain. The great advantage which Britain gained from the desperate struggle waged by Frederick the Great was never recognised by Chatham or by British public opinion. The War of the Austrian Succession could reasonably be considered as a European war by the other contestants, but for Britain the colonial aspect was crucial, for it was her gains overseas, modest as these were by the standard of later wars, which enabled her to exchange some of her gains for assets lost on the continent of Europe.

French strategy in these colonial and maritime wars had, to some extent, to be the converse of that adopted by Britain. Potential allies of Britain in Europe had to be placated, so that all French efforts (if possible in concert with Spain) could be directed towards the navy. Given the start in the naval arms race which Britain had gained by 1739, together with the advantages which Britain enjoyed in facilities for building, crewing, and repairing ships, as well as access to naval stores in the Baltic and America, it was not realistic to envisage the Royal Navy being driven from the seas, but a strong French fleet built up and manned and trained over a number of years could well have gained local mastery of the sea in some key area. If this had been won by her enemy's neglect in the Channel or off Ireland, an invasion force prepared in advance for such an opportunity could have ended the war with a French invasion of Britain. If, as was more likely, the French fleet had gained sea mastery off India or America, there would have been a good chance of depriving Britain of one of her major colonies. It was France's misfortune that when she succeeded in achieving this, the colony which Britain lost, anglophone America, was the one possession which France could not acquire. If, however, Suffren had been better supported in the same war with more ships off India and a small expeditionary force energetically led, France and her Indian allies might have been able to expel Britain from India and make the recovery of it too costly for her enemy to contemplate. This would have involved a great effort by France and Spain, who ended the war because they feared that matching Britain's growing naval power would bankrupt them.

Turning to the two protracted attempts France made to dominate Europe between 1688 and 1713 and between 1793 and 1815, it is clear that her problems had multiplied. The two peripheral European states were always beyond her reach; Britain was protected by the sea and Russia by the vastness of her country. No modern European state from the time of the Hapsburgs to that of Hitler has ever dominated the whole of Europe. Ever since nation-states began to emerge at the end of the Middle Ages, Europe has been too fissiparous ever to accept the type of unification which for instance the rulers of China, India and the Ottoman Empire had been able to impose. Both Hapsburg Spain and the France of Louis XIV were defeated by a coalition of powers (excluding Russia, not then a European power) which had little in common except a determination not to be ruled by France or Spain.

If Napoleon was to succeed where Louis XIV had failed, he would have needed to send a larger army against Russia than he could have raised – and to have kept it there for years, rather than the few months of his advance to and retreat from Moscow. At the same time he would have needed a navy large enough to have secured mastery of European waters in order to ensure Britain's compliance with his design for a Europe subordinated to France. Despite the astonishing mobilisation of French resources, this double task was beyond the capacity of Revolutionary France. It was not inevitable that France would lose in a struggle with Britain; chance has often reversed the expected outcome in war, but it is difficult to see how France could have secured the domination of Europe with Britain and Russia against her. No strategist could plan on the assumption that she would. Moreover the grim resistance of Austria, whose many defeats and occasional victories served to bleed French armies from Austerlitz to Leipzig should not be forgotten. No alternative strategy could have saved French lives and yet given her a better chance of final victory.

One final intriguing question remains. Why was Britain, with twice the population of Napoleonic France, prepared to deploy only the same number of British troops (some 50 000) as she had over one century before in the War of the Spanish Succession? Whatever the complex reasons for this, the student of strategy can infer that this refusal to undertake a similar military burden to the other great powers in Europe enabled Britain to direct her manpower and industrial resources towards sea supremacy and the Industrial Revolution, which made her commercially and industrially dominant for the next half century and thus the greatest power in the world.

6 Before the First World War

In the fifty or so years after 1815 Great Britain was the most powerful state in Europe and indeed in the world, for she was the first power to be in a position to influence events in all five continents, or at any rate along their coasts, through her unchallenged command of the sea. As a result, she dominated world trade and finance and consequently acquired a larger overseas colonial empire than any other nation before or since. There were, however, limitations to this impressive achievement. She had a very small army in comparison with her continental neighbours, and never sought to emulate seventeenth-century Hapsburg Spain or eighteenth-century France by dominating the mainland of Europe. Instead she aimed to maintain a balance of power in Europe under which any power or coalition of powers which sought to dominate the Continent would be thwarted by an alliance between Britain and the remainder. In practice it must be admitted that this policy was only occasionally supported by active diplomacy and for long periods throughout the nineteenth century the British managed to ignore European events and concentrated instead on expanding their interests overseas. Thus major events such as the reunification of Germany and of Italy took place with Britain as a relatively passive onlooker. It is true that Britain played a leading part in forcing the Turkish retreat from Europe when with the support of allies she used her fleet to defeat the Turks at Navarino in 1827, but the Crimean War showed the limitations of seapower against a major land power such as Russia. Even when allied to France with the best army in Europe, it was extremely difficult to find a way to exercise effective restraints on a power which would in the following decades spread rapidly eastwards across northern Asia. No doubt the experience of the Crimean and Baltic campaigns of 1854 to 1856 was very much in the minds of Britain's military planners when in the closing years of the nineteenth century they began to try to find ways of resisting the supposed Russian military threat to India.

It is convenient to select 1860 as the year in which Britain reached the pinnacle of her economic and industrial power, always remembering the military limitations exposed by the Crimean War a few years earlier. At that time Britain imported half of the world output of cotton and subsequently exported enough goods made of cotton to make up half of the value of her exports. Two more statistical examples will suffice; they are for coal and iron, two commodities which were essential indicators for war potential in the nineteenth and early twentieth centuries. At this time Britain produced half of the world's iron and over half of its coal and lignite. In these years the Royal Navy was normally as strong as the next two largest navies combined. Britain's empire, like her navy, far outstripped those of her rivals and comprised both strategic bases such as Hong Kong, Singapore (though not yet fortified), Aden, Lagos, Gibraltar and the Falkland Islands, as well as India and vast tracts of land increasingly farmed by white settlers in Australia, New Zealand, South Africa and Canada. The third area of British predominance was finance. London was undeniably the financial capital of the world, directing investments which in 1870 brought in an income of £50 million a year.

However, as Paul Kennedy points out, we can with hindsight detect two structural weaknesses in what was then supposed to be Britain's impregnable position as the most powerful nation in the world. In the first place, she was alarmingly dependent for her wealth on international trade and finance. One-fifth of her wealth came from exports, a far higher proportion than in previous centuries. Seapower was therefore essential to Britain, not only to blockade an enemy to deny him food, raw materials and an export trade, but also (like Athens before her) to support her own national wealth by protecting her imports of food and raw materials and the exports on which her livelihood was based. Moreover, even if her navy was supreme, a global conflict might cut her off from her markets abroad. In short, as time was to prove, her wealth and power were far more vulnerable to war than the more basic economies of some of her European rivals which depended less on foreign trade and produced more of the food and raw materials which they required.

A second weakness was that the British devoted much of their wealth and skills in the field of finance to supporting the industrialisation of those countries which would, when industrialised, become her competitors. The British contributed much to the building of factories and, even more important, to the creation of those great inland communication systems (mainly railways) which would allow the continental powers such as Russia, the USA, and Germany with eastern Europe, to exploit their land-locked resources and large populations. These natural resources had, in past centuries of horse-drawn and river transport, been unavailable to economies based on such crude forms of transportation. Thus in Paul Kennedy's words, 'What industrialisation did was to equalise the chances to exploit one's own indigenous resources and thus to take away some of the advantages hitherto enjoyed by smaller peripheral naval-cum-commercial states.' Ironically, while Admiral Mahan was emphasising the importance of sea power it was being steadily undermined by the greatest of all maritime nations. Indeed Mackinder's theories, first propounded when the influence of Mahan was at its height, would be a far better guide to twentieth-century strategists than those of the navalist school. Seapower was, as Mackinder argued, waning in relation to land power and even if Mackinder's heartland of Eurasia has not yet become the fulcrum of the world there is little doubt that it was Germany's domination of much of eastern Europe which enabled her to withstand blockade in two world wars.

Railways were the key to the opening up of central and eastern Europe, but they were to have as dramatic an effect on strategy as they did on world trade. The use of railways enabled army commanders to eliminate the days and often weeks of marching needed to bring their whole force in contact with the enemy. In addition they could concentrate and supply far greater numbers of troops and this could be done without warning, often on the intended field of battle. In the eighteenth century limitations of supply fixed the maximum size of a field army in normal circumstances at about 80 000 men and the experiences of the 500 000 men who marched to Moscow under the command of Napoleon showed the limitations of horse-drawn and river transport, despite the care which their commander had taken beforehand to provide food and forage. After 1850, railways and careful staff work changed all this. France moved 120 000 troops to Italy in 11 days in 1859; if they had had to march it would have taken eight weeks. In 1870 Germany deployed an army of 1 200 000 men against France and in 1914 this number was more than doubled. However, the railways could not perform miracles all the time, and when the invading armies crossed into enemy territory the combination of limited and partially destroyed rail systems, together with horse-drawn transport often caused a severe shortage of supplies. As Martin van Creveld has pointed out, there are good grounds for believing that the German attack through Belgium on France in 1914 under the Schlieffen Plan would have failed through lack of supplies, whatever the outcome of the Battle of the Marne. Be that as it may, it is plain that a railway network vastly simplified the task of mobilising an army and deploying it at the frontier. The only limits on the size of the armies which could be so deployed were the number of fit men of military age and the economic and political constraints on conscription.

The advent of railways facilitated the growth of (perhaps even created) that other great late nineteenth-century invention, bureaucracy. The first true bureaucracy (using that term as precisely as a sociologist would) was the Prussian General Staff. It had been created before the advent of railways but it was Moltke's reorganisation of it after 1857 which transformed it into a true thinking machine whose members became professional advisers to their commanders. As Michael Howard has suggested, the Franco-Prussian war was as much a victory for Prussian bureaucratic method as for Prussian arms. It was a system which made war a matter of scientific calculation, administrative planning and professional expertise. After 1871 the three Prussian institutions – strategic railways, mobilisation techniques and, above all, the General Staff, were copied throughout the continent of Europe. For the first time sizeable groups of very intelligent men in more than one country were thinking about war long before it happened (or sometimes failed to happen), to ensure that their forces were mobilised on time, deployed to the correct frontier, armed with effective weapons and supplied with enough food and ammunition. Mistakes in any of their calculations might bring defeat very early in the war. As the cost of weapons and the time taken to develop and produce them increased, so preparation for war became more and more important, since major decisions about the allocation of resources, for instance between the army and the navy, could not always be quickly reversed if the test of war proved them to be wrong. The military (and naval) bureaucrats were available to offer advice to their political masters on these major decisions, but being bureaucrats, they were likely on almost all occasions to fight for their own service, trying to get the largest possible share of available resources for it, rather than giving dispassionate advice. Doubt and disagreement about the relative size and the tasks of the army and navy in any modern state were likely to become more prolonged and bitter when there were dedicated staff officers in each service providing facts and encouragement to the main adversaries. Although the most glaring examples of this aspect of inter-service rivalry occurred after the First World War, there was a notable failure by the staffs of the two services in both Britain and Germany to agree on plans to fight the First World War. The statesmen of the great powers, therefore, in the late nineteenth and early twentieth centuries often had to take major decisions about strategy without coordinated advice from their services.

The industrialisation of Europe also produced the technology to revolutionise naval warfare and, as on land, the changes were not to the advantage of Britain since the cost of any naval arms race tended to increase quickly at a time when her industrial lead over other European powers was fast diminishing. In the second half of the nineteenth century the ironclad warship driven by steam engines replaced the wooden-hulled sailing ship. Besides the obvious advantage of being freed from dependence on the wind, the ironclad provided a platform for large breech-loading guns with rifled barrels which by the end of the century could throw a shell 20 000 yards. The ironclad battleship and its more modern successors rapidly became a status symbol among industrial powers, even though the cost of building a squadron could be crippling. Moreover, as the defeat of the Russian fleet by a more modern Japanese opponent at Tsu Shima in 1905 showed, the penalty of relying on out-of-date status symbols could be disastrous. It was against this background of technological revolution in both land and sea warfare, when many familiar guidelines were no longer valid, that British statesmen had to try to solve the most difficult strategic problems facing their nation for some 80 years. The enemy this time was Germany.

GERMANY

By 1900 Germany, unified under Prussian leadership, rivalled Britain as an industrial and financial power and had the most modern and formidable army in the world. More disconcertingly, Imperial Germany was starting to build a modern fleet whose sole purpose appeared to Britain to be challenging the Royal Navy for command of the sea. Germany's real aims were probably rather different, but how they appeared to Britain would have important consequences for both nations. The diplomatic and military means by which Prussia came to lead a united Germany are not part of this study but an understanding of Germany's strategic position and her military power is essential. By her brilliant victories over the Danes (1864), the Austrian Empire (1866) and France (1870) Germany had established herself as the dominant power in central Europe and earned the bitter enmity of France, not least because of her seizure of the French provinces of Alsace and Lorraine. The weakening but still formidable Austro-Hungarian Empire was her ally, but diplomatic blunders and genuine conflicts of interest had set Russia against her and with the signing of an entente between France and Russia in 1891 (and even before then) the war planners in Berlin had to consider a war on two fronts, east and west.

At first Moltke the Elder, the architect of the recent German victories over Austria and France, had favoured an attack on Russia with a holding action in the west. However, an improvement in Russian mobilisation arrangements, thanks in part to new railways, and the reported increase in the fighting abilities of the Russian army rendered this option less attractive. The appointment of Alfred von Schlieffen as Chief of the General Staff in 1891 coincided with a more active search for a strategy which would give victory in the west before the still ponderous Russian mobilisation could deploy enough troops to overwhelm the Austro-Hungarian armies and the small number of covering troops which Germany would have to leave to delay a Russian advance into East Prussia. The thick belt of French fortresses along the Franco-German border between Switzerland and Belgium would prevent an early breakthrough on that front. In consequence of this staff appreciation the famous Schlieffen Plan was born.

This plan was in fact a memorandum prepared for his successor as Chief of Staff, Moltke the Younger. This, together with numerous subsequent appreciations and alterations was the basis for Germany's military strategy in 1914. It has also been the focus of much discussion and controversy ever since the end of the first World War. It envisaged in the event of war the maximum concentration possible of the German army on the western front so that it could sweep through Holland and Belgium, pivoting on Metz, thus outflanking the French army in its frontier fortifications. The German forces would then advance through northern France to reach a line from Abbeville, on the Channel coast, to Metz, by one month after the declaration of war. Thereafter, this immensely strong right wing of the German army was to outflank Paris, recognised as a strongly fortified position, and press the now much disorganised French army back against its own frontier defences on the Franco-German border. It was a breathtaking concept, but as the General Staff recognised at the outset, it would require every man the German war machine could press into military service. Harsher conscription laws in 1906 added six more divisions to the Army but, even so, Germany's leaders recognised that the margin for success was desperately narrow.

When he was appointed Chief of Staff, Moltke the Younger modified the plan in several important ways. First he decided that the offensive right wing should not cross southern Holland on the way to France. The change was not made on moral grounds concerned with the integrity of neutral nations but because it was considered that the Dutch army was so strong that a dangerously large number of German divisions from the all-important right wing would have to be left behind to contain it. As a result of this change, two German armies would have to crowd into the Liège gap before debouching on to the open countryside of Flanders. Moreover, since the railway system of southern Holland would not be available to support further German advances, the early capture of Liège and its associated railway system was essential. Moltke's solution to this problem was the early capture of Liège by a *coup de main* while the main Germany army was mobilising. This was clearly a risky move, but in the event it was successful in 1914. Next, Moltke altered the balance of forces planned by Schlieffen for the Western Front, making use of the extra divisions available after

1906. Moltke planned to deploy 23 divisions in Alsace-Lorraine, to resist the expected French attack there, instead of the nine proposed by Schlieffen. For the all-important sweep of his right wing through Belgium, Moltke allotted 55 divisions instead of the 59 proposed by his predecessor. Neither general set aside any forces to deal with any British expeditionary force sent to help the French in Flanders (although by 1912 Schlieffen recognised that the arrival of British troops might pose a threat to his plan), but, as has already been stressed, both Chiefs of Staff recognised that Germany had barely enough troops to carry it out. If on his deathbed in 1912 Schlieffen did not say 'Strengthen the right wing' he could well have done so. Before completing the story by describing the unfolding of the plan in 1914, it is natural to ask how the German Navy fitted into this potentially war–winning but clearly risky strategy. One would assume since the German Kaiser was the Supreme Commander of both services as well as head of the government, that land and maritime strategy would be closely linked. The answer may well surprise those unfamiliar with the results of uncontrolled rivalry between the services.

By the end of the nineteenth century the aspirations of the German middle class, particularly those with industrial or commercial interests, centred on a world policy rather than on the European hegemony at which Bismarck had aimed. In 1897 Germany turned decisively towards a 'world policy'. At that time tensions in Europe were temporarily eased by an agreement between Austria and Russia, as a result of which France sought to expand her possessions in Africa and Russia to exploit her position in the Far East. 'Most Germans', writes A. J. P. Taylor: 'had a sense of limitless strength and desired a world policy without reserve.' The conservative German government was happy to encourage this demand for external expansion to relieve internal pressure for social reform at home. The votes of social democrats in the Reichstag could be relied upon for expenditure on a large navy. This would, it was argued, safeguard Germany's food supplies; and there was also the feeling that naval power would help to establish her position on the world stage.

It was chance that brought Admiral Tirpitz to the highest post in the German navy at a time when German public opinion desired a great navy and was ready to pay for it, but had no clear strategic task in mind for it when it was built. Tirpitz himself was certainly endowed with superb political skills and had a great talent for organisation but was not necessarily a great strategist. With the eager support of the Kaiser, who had not previously been able to get the Reichstag to agree to vote money for a large navy, Tirpitz was able to produce a coherent naval development programme and, equally importantly, to persuade the Reichstag to agree to the necessary expenditure for it and for the subsequent extensions to the fleet. When the First Naval Law was submitted in 1898 Germany had seven battleships and Britain 38. Tirpitz proposed 19. The second Naval Law of 1900 planned a fleet of 38 and towards the end of his term of office in 1912 he was contemplating a fleet of 60 battleships, in response to the growing strength of the Royal Navy. None of these later developments were contemplated by the Reichstag when it voted for the First Naval Law.

In order to appreciate the force and attractiveness of the Tirpitz naval policy, it has to be contrasted with what it replaced. Hitherto, ever since the Germans began to build ironclads, their navy had consisted of a heterogeneous collection of battleships, cruisers and destroyers, dispersed at widely-scattered overseas bases as well as at home ports which could never mount a serious local threat to the Royal Navy, always seen as the main antagonist, in any part of the globe. In consequence, Germany had suffered a series of rebuffs on the international stage when attempting to intervene outside Europe. The most galling instance of this was the episode later known as the Kruger Telegram.

When in 1906 the Transvaal Republic in South Africa, independent but within the British sphere of influence, repelled the Jamieson Raid (an attempted *coup d'état*, unofficially mounted from British territory) the Kaiser sent a telegram of congratulation. He tried to involve Russia and France in this gesture of support, and at the same time secretly warned Britain that she would be faced with a continental league against her unless she agreed to a secret pact with Germany. The results were a total fiasco for the Kaiser. Russia and France did not agree to join Germany in support for the Transvaal and Britain refused to be frightened. Instead she invoked her naval power by ostentatiously forming a flying squadron for service anywhere in the world. Germany could do nothing to help the Transvaal and had been humiliated. The inability of the German people to use their unrivalled military power against the one nation which rivalled them in industrial and commercial power was naturally frustrating.

Against this background it is easy to see why the Tirpitz proposals were so readily accepted by the Reichstag, but it is also plain that there were no clear strategic plans as a basis for the use of the fleet. The proposal was for a modern fleet of 19 battleships based in Home Waters and the very mixed bag of warships at bases overseas in Africa and Asia would be withdrawn (and the bases closed) with considerable saving in costs. At no great extra cost (initially at any rate) the Germans would have a strong modern fleet able to threaten Britain's overall supremacy at sea. According to Tirpitz's 'Risk Theory', the German navy had to be able, if attacked by the Royal Navy, to inflict such damage that the presumably victorious Royal Navy would be weaker than the next strongest rival navy, (often thought likely in these circumstances to be a combined Franco-Russian fleet). Without assured command of the sea, Britain would be at the mercy of her European rivals and would then be deterred from attacking Germany or otherwise thwarting her after the first critical years of the build-up of the German navy. Once this initial danger zone of weakness at sea had been passed, it would be open to Germany to go on enlarging her fleet until it outnumbered the Royal Navy, since under the 'Risk Theory' Britain would be deterred from attacking the German fleet for fear of the consequences; but this exciting prospect of ultimate world domination was not part of the official argument put forward in support the First Navy Law.

The naval strategy underpinning the 'Risk Theory' rested in Paul Kennedy's view on four premises, all of which proved to be mistaken. Firstly it was assumed that, because of her vital overseas interests, Britain would be unable to withdraw her fleets from their overseas bases, such as those in the Pacific, Mediterranean and Caribbean, for fear of losing local naval mastery in those waters to her rivals: Russia, France, the US, or Japan. Secondly, the possibility that Britain had both the means and the will to outbuild Germany in a naval arms race does not seem to have entered into Tirpitz's calculations. Thirdly, the strategy postulated that, at the outset of any war, Britain would choose to attack the smaller German fleet, despite the risks, to dispose of the threat. Finally, there was always the expectation amongst Germany's rulers, that at some stage Britain would find that an alliance with Germany, or at least a tacit agreement to give her a free hand in Europe, was preferable to a naval arms race. None of these assumptions were valid, as will be seen when Britain's reaction to the threat from Germany is studied, but it worth emphasising again that the Tirpitz naval strategy, though flawed, was immensely successful as a means of persuading German public opinion to finance an ambitious and ultimately expensive programme of naval expansion, which might bring rewards in the long term, but had few if any immediate benefits. The intense desire to avoid rebuffs in foreign policy, such as that over the Kruger Telegram, the more generalised wish for a leading role on the world stage, the aspirations of the middle-class industrialists and merchants, were all satisfied by the growing strength of the German navy. In consequence, the Reichstag, the guardian of the public purse, rarely if ever carped as the bill for more and more warships rose higher and higher. As a political programme the Tirpitz naval strategy worked perfectly.

The true consequences of the Schlieffen Plan and the Tirpitz Risk Fleet will be discussed after the British reaction has been studied, but the question about the coordination of naval strategy with the Schlieffen Plan can be answered now, and quite briefly. There was no coordination or meaningful discussion whatever between the professional heads of the two services on a joint strategy, or a resolution of the policy differences between them. The Army General Staff and their political supporters in the Junker land-owning nobility and, to a certain extent, in the capitalist class, wanted a continental war against France and rejected the idea of a naval arms race with Britain. On the other side, Tirpitz and the political allies of the navy, largely the middle class in commerce and industry, deplored the idea of war with France and Russia; instead they wanted a naval conflict with Britain. The Kaiser, who should have brought the opposing sides together to resolve the argument which went to the heart of national strategy, made no move to settle the issue at all; indeed it is not clear that he or his chief minister recognised the seriousness of the disagreement. Consequently there was no attempt to allot resources sensibly between them. It may have been difficult for professional officers of either service to appreciate that there were financial and resource limitations, even in a fast-growing economy such as Germany's before 1914, but they should have recognised the difficult manpower position, especially after harsher conscription laws had to be introduced in 1906. The new German navy made calls on both money and manpower which the army needed if it was to carry out the Schlieffen Plan. The serious shortage of officer manpower was always a worry to the General Staff (partly owing to their strict criteria of birth and breeding) and the navy's demands for this resource were considerable. As Hajo Holborn writes,

> [It was even more surprising] that Schlieffen was unconcerned about the role of the German navy in a national program of defense. It could have no part in the type of war Schlieffen had planned for and the building of a navy of such size was, therefore, a waste of money and manpower. The army felt this all the time, for it was unable to procure enough funds and officer candidates for the formation of the new divisions which were needed for the implementation of the Schlieffen plan. Schlieffen did not complain however nor did he seem worried about the international aspects of the naval building program whose ultimate effect would be to bring a British army to the continent.

His successor, von Moltke, followed the same policy of silent disagreement and consequently the two services in the most military of the states in pre-1914 Europe, disagreed but ignored each other and went their separate ways.

GREAT BRITAIN

The 1897 naval review to mark Queen Victoria's diamond jubilee is often chosen as the best date to mark the zenith of British naval power and is certainly a convenient date as it is also the year in which Admiral Tirpitz was appointed State Secretary for the German Navy and outlined his plans for a new fleet. However, as Paul Kennedy points out, by 1897 Britain's lead over other naval powers had already begun to shrink. In 1883 Britain had 38 battleships and the rest of the world 40. In 1897 the comparable figures were Britain 62, the rest 96. British statesmen were coming to accept that local naval mastery in all parts of the world enjoyed in the middle of the century was now beyond Britain's reach. Reluctantly the British began to 'call their legions home'. The Admiralty were allowed by the government to accept for planning purposes that war with the United States was unthinkable and should not therefore be provided for in naval estimates of expenditure and then in 1902, alarmed by the possibility of a Franco-Russian fleet, dominating far eastern waters, Britain concluded the Anglo-Japanese Alliance. Two potential enemies were therefore deleted from the list.

When the Tirpitz expansion programme began to bear fruit it was treated with great suspicion both by the Admiralty planners and by the British public. This might seem unreasonable, since Germany, like other industrial nations (for instance, the US or Japan) which were anxious to expand their overseas markets and acquire colonies, could justifiably claim that they needed a navy, not to threaten Britain, but to protect their own overseas interests. However, the British were right to see German naval expansion as being different in type from the naval plans of other nations. The reason was simple: Germany was on Britain's doorstep and both had to use the same home waters: the North Sea, the English Channel, and the Western Atlantic. Neither could sensibly share control over their lifeline for trade, and hence economic power, with the other. Moreover, the facts of geography determined that the British Isles lay between German ports and the outside world (just as they had for the Dutch in the seventeenth century) and, unless Britain was prepared to surrender to blackmail, the Tirpitz 'Risk Fleet' would have to fight the Royal Navy if it was to justify itself and protect German interests overseas.

It was an accident of history, which neither Tirpitz nor his staffs could have foreseen, that Admiral Fisher should be appointed First Sea Lord and therefore professional head of the Royal Navy, just when the threat of the German naval building programme was being appreciated in Britain. Fisher was, like Tirpitz, a superb organiser with the knack of being able to persuade politicians to his point of view but, again like Tirpitz, he was less interested in grand strategy. This perhaps mattered less in Britain since the dangers of a close blockade of German ports in war had already been realised in the age of mines and torpedoes. The Admiralty had therefore drawn the correct conclusion, and when war came, operated a distant blockade at the exits from the North Sea and waited for the German High Seas Fleet to come out of port and challenge it. Fisher and the Royal Navy still expected a decisive encounter between the opposing battle fleets, and to that extent their plans for the coming war were at fault, but they were not prepared to risk the Grand Fleet close to German ports, in waters defended by mines and light craft with torpedoes in order to provoke a battle. In the event, Fisher's preparations for the war at sea did not have the serious flaws which marred German naval strategy. On other related matters of strategy his record was less admirable. The Committee of Imperial Defence (CID), consisting of politicians and service chiefs, which was set up to advise the government of the day on a coordinated naval and military strategy, naturally wished to have a naval view on the action to be taken in the event of war with Germany. Fisher was admantly opposed to the dispatch of an army expeditionary force to the continent of Europe, pressing instead for a series of amphibious expeditions to the Baltic to land troops in Pomerania to march on Berlin. When these ideas were (not surprisingly one feels) rejected, Fisher refused to take any further part in the deliberations of the Committee and withdrew from its meetings.

Nevertheless, his arrival as professional head of the Navy in 1904 galvanised the whole service. He reformed, reorganised and redeployed the navy to meet the threat from Germany in a remarkably short time. A new base had been made at Rossyth on the Firth of Forth in 1903. Fisher quickly found the ships for it. He gained more battleships for the Home Fleet by combining the three squadrons based on Hong Kong, Australia and the East Indies into one Far Eastern Fleet. He also withdrew ships from the Mediterranean station. As a result of these and other changes, nine battleships were added to the Home Fleet; a very significant reinforcement in relation to the German fleet at that time. Even more shattering, however, was the creation under Fisher's direction of the Dreadnought, the modern successor to the ironclad, which made every other battleship afloat, including those in the Royal Navy, obsolete overnight. The typical battleship of the time was a steel ship of some 17 000 tons with four 12-inch guns and about 40 small guns of little fighting value and a speed of 19 knots. In contrast the Dreadnought had ten 12-inch guns, twelve-inch armour, a displacement of 17 250 tons and a speed of 21 knots. No other battleship in the world could outfight or outsail her. When Fisher commissioned the first

Dreadnought in 1906, every other navy had to scrap as many of its existing battleships as it could afford to, and start again. The naval arms race was becoming far more costly for Germany than she would have anticipated as she had to increase the size of her fleet and modernise it before it was more than a few years old. Britain tried to moderate the arms race in 1907 by reducing her Dreadnought building programme, but the response from Germany was another naval law, projecting a large fleet of Dreadnoughts. Britain had to respond by increasing the naval programme in 1908 and in subsequent years. It was hard for the British government to see any other explanation for the accelerated German building programme of Dreadnoughts except a determination to wrest command of the sea from Britain. 'In reality', A. J. P. Taylor writes, 'there was no rational explanation. The Germans had drifted into naval expansion, partly for reasons of domestic politics, partly from a general desire for grandeur. They certainly hoped that a great navy would make the British respect and even fear them; they never understood that unless you could actually outbuild Great Britain, the only effect of this naval competition would be to estrange her.'

This point was brought home even more strongly in the final act of the Anglo-German arms race: the naval crisis of 1912. In that year the German government decided to increase the active fleet from 17 battleships and 4 battlecruisers to 25 battleships and 8 battlecruisers. This posed an almost intractable problem for the British, for they had only 22 battleships in Home Waters (and this figure included eight at Gibraltar.). There were three options, all most unpalatable, available to them: they could accept a reduced margin of superiority in the North Sea (or no margin at all), with all the dangers of diplomatic blackmail by Germany; they could abandon the Mediterranean (and redeploy the fleet there to Home Waters), possibly building a new fleet to send to the Mediterranean when it was ready in four years' time, at a cost of £15 million; or finally, they could come to an arrangement with France and rely on their old adversary's navy to provide a margin of superiority over the Austrian and Italian navies. In the end, after much debate and some despair, Britain chose the latter course. This meant that Britain had at last abandoned her long-held 'two fleet policy' of building a fleet which would outnumber the next two strongest fleets. For the remainder of the prewar period, Britain's sole aim in naval policy was to outnumber her presumed adversary across the North Sea. In 1914 Britain had 58 battleships, of which 19 were Dreadnoughts; Germany had 35 battleships, of which 13 were Dreadnoughts. The margin had been maintained.

The debate in Britain about military strategy in the years before 1914 was far less public than its naval counterpart, and yet the plans made, and the agreements reached by army staff officers behind closed doors were just as important for the war which was to come as the more public race of the battleships. It is true that in the early 1900s the British public was subjected to a number of 'invasion scares' in the shape of newspaper articles, plays, and novels (of which *The Riddle of the Sands*, written in 1903 by Erskine Childers, has lasted the best). All stressed the danger of a determined enemy across the North Sea with a large army and a growing navy. The anxieties provoked by these scares were mostly allayed by the construction of bases for the Royal Navy on the North Sea and the creation of the Territorial Army for home defence. It was left for the Committee of Imperial Defence to ponder in secret how to help France survive an attack by Germany.

In the last quarter of the nineteenth century the British Army lacked the confidence and status of the Royal Navy. The main reason for this probably lay in the difficulty of finding a believable and worthwhile role for the Army to undertake. Home defence was best left to the navy and most of the Empire was on continents or islands safe from land attack; there were, however, two exceptions: Canada and India. War with the US was barely conceivable and had been effectively ruled out by the naval planners. If it came there was little which the British Army could do to defend Canada at the 49th parallel. This left India, which became a more and more intractable problem for the British Army planners as the nineteenth century ended and the twentieth began.

Before the 1890s Britain's statesmen and strategists had assumed that the best way to foil Russian attack on India would be to force the Dardanelles, with Turkish acquiescence, enter the Black Sea and to land troops in Southern Russia. The army would use the threat of seaborne invasion to deter a Russian attack on India. As the 1890s wore on, the formation of the Dual Alliance between France and Russia and increasing Turkish hostility to Britain, made Britain's deterrent strategy less and less convincing. It looked as though India would have to be defended on its North West Frontier. When news came in 1904 that Russia was extending her railway to the Afghan border, the army's planners were almost in despair. Whatever the number of reinforcements required from Britain for India's defence, whether it was the 158 000 requested by the Commander-in-Chief of the army in India, or the 48 000 which the War office said was all it could supply, these troops could not reach India for months after the Russian invasion and when there they would face an army with three million reserves. The defence of India seemed impossible.

As so often happens to those faced with an insoluble problem, the army planners looked for a problem which they could solve, and started to work on that. This is not a surprising or unduly cynical view. It happens both to bureaucracies and to individuals, certainly the drawers of many a planner's desk in defence ministries and elsewhere in civilian bureaucracies are filled with insoluble and therefore neglected problems. What is certain is that when the menace of Germany in Europe was increasingly brought to the attention of the British Army staff in the early twentieth century, the records of the Committee of Imperial Defence and its related sub-committees were filled with discussion on how to deal with it, and the unsolved problem of how to defend India gradually faded from view. This was surely justified; Germany was an immediate threat, both in time and place, while that facing India was far distant, doubtful and if it arose, more long-term. There were other factors: the Foreign Office was, (and had been for a long time) anti-German and the War Office was eager to find a rational and sustainable role which would justify modernisation and expansion of its forces.

By 1905 the threat from the German fleet was well understood, but the decision to rely on the cooperation of the French fleet to defend British interests in the Mediterranean was some seven years into the future. Certainly in 1905 no thought had been given by the British government to sending an expeditionary force to France to support the French army. Nevertheless, in the spring of that year, the Director of Military Operations in the War Office ordered a war game to be played to see what the prospects were, in the event of a war between France and Germany, of the latter attempting an outflanking movement through Belgium, and what success this would be likely to have. The results were astonishing and would have a decisive influence on Britain's military strategy in the First World War. The conclusions of the study were as follows: if Germany were to attack France, they would sooner or later have to try an outflanking movement through Belgium, since the belt of frontier forts on the Franco-German border would be too strong for the Germans to penetrate; logistic difficulties would compel the Germans to keep their extreme right wing on the river Meuse; and any British help which was given would have to be prompt and in considerable strength. In the words of the War Office minute summing up the lessons of the game: 'An efficient army of 120 000 troops might just have the effect of preventing important German successes on the Franco-German Frontier'. The plan recommended was to put two British army corps into Antwerp within 23 days of the outbreak of war. It is surely very rare for a piece of operational analysis to be so prescient. Of course, many details were to be changed in the next ten years. In particular, Antwerp was rejected as the disembarkation point, in view of the danger of the force being boxed in, but in essentials the plan became the basis for Britain's military strategy in 1914. Equally surprising was the speedy acceptance of the planners' proposals by their political masters. Again, however, there was a proviso: the Committee of Imperial Defence accepted the proposals for planning purposes and for discussions with the French, but the British government as a whole was never committed to support France militarily until the outbreak of war. It was the Morocco crisis in the spring of 1905 which caused this abrupt change in the British attitude towards a military commitment to France.

The crisis was caused by a German attempt to humiliate France by publicly recognising the independence of Morocco which lay within the French sphere of influence. The reasons for this provocation are complex, but part of the German aim was to split the growing Anglo-French Entente. Britain was, for the first time, compelled to consider a common front with France and the Committee on Imperial Defence was asked to study the question with particular regard to the neutrality of Belgium, which the major European powers were pledged to maintain. The Admiralty proposed that if Britain were to go to war to uphold Belgian neutrality the correct response for the Army would be a series of raids on the German coast. The War Office proposal based on the war game already mentioned, was for an expeditionary force to land at the French Channel ports 12 days after the declaration of war and to operate thereafter on the left wing of the French Army. The Committee approved the War Office proposals and rejected those of the Admiralty. Thereafter the Admiralty virtually boycotted the Committee meetings and prepared its own war plans without consulting any other department. The Committee may have failed in its task of coordinating naval and military strategy for the defence of the realm, but this failure is surely offset by its success, first in calling for a new strategic plan for employing the Army in Europe and second, in endorsing what would be such a vital part of the allied response to the Schlieffen Plan.

The War Office was instructed to begin staff talks with their opposite numbers in France and these continued in the years up to 1914, thus implying a degree of commitment to speedy military aid by the British Government which was certainly not justified. The Cabinet was never consulted about this in the pre-war years and if they had been, some of its pacifist members would have had to resign, rather than accept it. Nevertheless, the CID continued to discuss and refine the army's plan in the years after 1905. Thus in 1908/9 a sub-committee endorsed the War Office proposal that the expeditionary force should consist of four divisions of infantry and one of cavalry to land in France and be ready for action within 20 days after the outbreak of war. Throughout the period between 1905 and 1914 the British Army, freed from the impossible task of defending India against a Russian attack, reshaped itself to meet its new continental commitment, with the happy result that the British Expeditionary Force sent to

France in 1914 was, many have claimed, the best equipped and trained army ever sent overseas by Britain at the start of a war.

THE CLASH IN 1914

Within two months of the outbreak of war in 1914, the pre-war strategies of all the combatant nations were tested and this was particularly true of the two nations which had to decide how to allocate their resources between their army and navy. The first to be tried was the Tirpitz naval strategy. His 'Risk Fleet' stayed close to harbour and never attempted to prevent the passage of the British Expeditionary Force to France. The whole German naval building programme had achieved nothing at the start of the war. Admittedly it put Britain to vast expense in maintaining her lead in battleship numbers but she still had sufficient resources to send a small but well-equipped army to France. On the diplomatic front, the Tirpitz naval strategy was a disaster. It drove Britain into a quasi-alliance with France and Russia, so that the Schlieffen-inspired invasion of Belgium, when it came, convinced British public opinion of the necessity of war and the British services were prepared for it. More than this, the German naval programme diverted resources (both men and industrial capacity) from the army which clearly needed them. There are two questions to be considered here: first, without the advantage of hindsight, how far did the German war planners succeed (within their own terms of reference) in preparing their country for war? On this criterion it would surely be agreed that they failed. The Army Chiefs of Staff were convinced that their forces were scarcely large enough for the task before them, yet they made no serious move to try to convince the Kaiser that his military strategy was being put in danger by the heavy drain on resources which were being increasingly diverted to the navy. Admittedly it might have been difficult to feed additional troops through the Liège gap into the front line wheeling through northern France. However, they should perhaps have thought of the possibility of providing more support for the frontline troops.

The second question, to be answered with hindsight, is whether it would have made any difference to the outcome of the German Army's offensive if it had had more reserves, or resources in some other form. Debate about the Schlieffen Plan has raged ever since the end of the First World War and will no doubt continue in the future, but Martin van Creveld's study of the logistics of this campaign has convinced many eminent historians that whatever the outcome of the Battle of the Marne in early September 1914, the German right wing would have ground to a halt through exhaustion and lack of supplies. Their infantry divisions on the right wing had marched all the way from the German frontier and depended on horse-drawn transport (which required large quantities of forage) to draw supplies from the railheads. Despite the best efforts of the German Army railway companies, the distance between these railheads (at the end of serviceable rail links back to Germany) and the advancing troops become longer and longer as the advance continued, and in some cases the advance would have had to be stopped if the small number of motor transport companies had not been able to keep supplies moving. In contrast, the French army was falling back on an undamaged rail and road network, which was also used to redeploy reinforcements along interior lines from their left wing after its disastrous offensive into Lorraine had been halted. It is certainly a moot point whether the German High Command would have put additional resources into the logistic system as motor and railway companies; the army had faced severe logistic problems in the 1870 campaign in France but there is little evidence from its successor in 1914 that they had learned from their previous mistakes in the field of logistics. Looking back at the Schlieffen Plan, it has the appearance of one more suited to the Napoleonic era, comparable indeed to the great sweep by the Grand Armée from Boulogne to Ulm, Vienna, and Austerlitz in 1805. It looks less formidable when one notes that the French Army, even when completely surprised by the direction of the attack, could use railways (and even the taxis of Paris) to redeploy to meet the threat. Moreover it was unwise to ignore the possible role of a British expeditionary force. This undoubtedly impeded the German advance, partly because its arrival was not expected. The British Expeditionary Force went on to play a very useful, if not decisive role, in the allied defensive victory of the counter-attack on the Marne. The odds were so finely balanced in the first few months of the war that few could argue that the part played by the small British force was irrelevant. The final verdict must surely be that German strategy for the initial (and, as she thought, the only) phase of the war, failed because her naval programme forced a nation which might have remained neutral (at any rate until it was too late), to prepare for and make a military contribution at the start of the war which disrupted, and was perhaps fatal, to the Schlieffen Plan, Germany's only hope of an early and victorious end to the war.

The judgement on Britain's pre-war plans turns largely on the point already discussed, namely the extent to which the initial German offensive was disrupted by the forces which Britain was able put in the field at the outset. On this criterion the 1904 military appreciation, and the preparations based on it, deserve high praise. The neglect by the Admiralty of the need to contribute to grand strategy by supporting the Army's plans is reprehensible, but had no adverse consequences, mainly because the admirals kept their eyes firmly fixed on the German High Seas Fleet and ensured that the Grand Fleet remained stronger by a safe margin. Admittedly, their partial neglect of the threat of the submarine, torpedo and mine caused some anxious moments at the start of hostilities when it looked as if the British anchorages on the North Sea planned for the Grand Fleet were not properly defended against attack by these weapons, but the Fleet hardly suffered from this lack of foresight, because the German navy was not equipped to take advantage of them at the start. It is also true that the Admiralty assumption that there would, as Mahan and his followers predicted, be a decisive battle between the two Fleets, leading to maritime supremacy for the victor, was never realised. The Royal Navy had appreciated, well before 1914, that mines and torpedoes had ensured that close blockade in the style which Anson had perfected was now too dangerous, but it had not foreseen that these weapons would also inhibit the bold use of capital ships in the open sea. With hindsight it is clear that the strategy which the British came to adopt under pressure of events was a success. A naval blockade was maintained, as planned, across the exits from the North Sea and the Grand Fleet challenged the German High Seas Fleet to come out of harbour and attack it, which was highly unlikely in view of its superiority. Germany had lost the war at sea, despite her vast expenditure on a battle fleet, until she belatedly put more resources into the submarine weapon.

By December 1914 almost all the expectations of war planners, not only in Germany and Britain, but in all combatant countries, had been proved wrong. It was going to be a long war, although almost everyone in authority (except Lord Kitchener who became War Minister in 1914) had thought it would be a short one. It was not going to be a war of manoeuvre on land with armies marching across Europe, as in Napoleon's time, but a static war of trenches and barbed wire, in which machine-guns and artillery would inflict horrifying casualties. At sea there would be no decisive clash between battle fleets in the style of Trafalgar, but instead a war of two blockades, conducted on one side with surface ships and on the other by submarines.

A full review of strategy for the remainder of the First World War has no place in a study of the strategic choices between land and sea, but it is important to note the extent to which the great powers involved were locked into the choices which they had made before the war began, by their heavy investment in men and materials. Thus Germany could not discard her fleet of capital ships and their very existence must surely have distracted her admirals and blinded them for some time to the importance of the submarine as a weapon for blockade. Under the inexorable pressure of events on the Western Front Britain created a mass army equivalent to the other European powers, on a scale unparalleled in her history. Yet even this could be fairly described, not as a change of strategy (which was to support France with land forces), but as a failure to foresee the consequences of that strategy. Be that as it may, it was for the British a traumatic change in the way they were accustomed to wage war. Even if with hindsight it is clear that intervention in the European land battle on a massive scale was the only possible way to avoid defeat, the huge casualties that this entailed (though also faced by other combatants) were nonetheless an abiding memory in the years after the First World War and this had a great and probably damaging influence on British strategy in the years before the Second World War.

7 Planning for the Second World War

Perhaps 'Lack of planning for the Second World War' would have been a better title for this chapter, since the remarkable thing about the start of the war was the lack of well-matured strategic plans like the Schlieffen Plan. Politicians and others had in a general way anticipated the coming war but almost no one, including Hitler, had been able to predict the time and place. In consequence it was difficult for the army, naval and air staffs to plan ahead; in any case the German and British army staffs had other reasons for lack of long range planning; neither were given instructions until very late in the day to expect a war in the west.

After the first few months the First World War made a mockery of all pre-war planning. The Schlieffen Plan failed and committed Germany to a two-front war. The French and Russian offensives failed disastrously with heavy losses. Perhaps the only pre-war army plan which worked well was the intervention of the British Expeditionary Force in the land battle in France which helped to prevent a French defeat. This, however, had the most profound strategic consequences which were not foreseen by the military planners. Britain was committed for the first time in modern war to a major military role on the continent of Europe and as a result suffered the massive casualties which have been a part of modern war on land as the Napoleonic and American Civil Wars had already shown. At sea Germany had to recast her strategy after the failure of the Tirpitz doctrine and by using the newly developed ocean-going submarine came as near as any other power in history to defeating Britain by sea blockade. The advent of the submarine and the aeroplane changed the terms of the war at sea permanently to the disadvantage of Britain.

The First World War was essentially a European, or at least a Eurocentred war, in which all the major offensives of the Allied Powers were aimed at the heartland of the Central Powers (that is, Germany, Austria-Hungary and the Turkish Empire). By 1917 one of the two world powers peripheral to Europe, namely Russia, was knocked out of the war but her place on the

Allied side was taken by the other peripheral power, the US. After the defeat of the Central Powers neither Russia nor the US, the Superpowers-to-be, played any significant part in European affairs in the 1920s and 1930s and it could be said that during this period the nations of Europe played at being great powers. Whatever their status, their strategic decisions in the 1930s set the pattern for the war which was to come. As before the First World War, both Britain and Germany had to decide how to allocate resources between land and sea forces, but there was now a new element in the strategic calculation – air power. Two other powers who would engage in the Second World War had to make similar strategic choices, but the remainder (which included both France and Russia) perceived the main threat against them, as being on land and the only strategic question that concerned them with regard to air power was to what extent air power would help them to meet the land threat. It was the pre-war planning (or lack of it) in Germany and Britain which had greatest effect on the early stages of the war and it will therefore be be convenient to discuss the plans of these two countries first. Japan and the USA had to face strategic choices after hostilities had begun (in Japan's case with the invasion of Manchuria in 1931, which in 1937 developed into a determined attempt to conquer China) and their choices can best be discussed as part of a narrative of the war itself. First, however, we must take account of some of the ideas about air power which were current in the 1920s and 1930s.

Powered aircraft had first been used in the First World War for reconnaissance over land and sea and then for the tactical support of engaged forces. By the end of the war, however, a new concept arose, largely inspired by the German Zeppelin and bomber raids on London, of an independent air force operating against the enemy heartland far behind the frontlines of the opposing armies, damaging essential parts of the enemy war machine such as factories, communications and even centres of government, to destroy the the enemy's will and his capacity to resist. The raids on London in 1917 were followed by the creation in 1918 of the first independent air force in the world, subordinate neither to the army nor the navy – the Royal Air Force (RAF). By the end of that year when peace came, the RAF was planning the creation of a strategic bomber force which would have attempted to destroy the Ruhr in 1919. After the war there was time to construct theories of air power, but it is as well to remember that the idea of strategic bombing came before the theories and those who planned the RAF strategic bomber force in the 1930s (or at least some of them) have denied that they were influenced in any way by the most important of the theorists, the Italian Guilo Douhet (1869–1930). Nonetheless, it is important to take some account of the theories of air power, of which that of

Douhet is perhaps the most comprehensive, because of the ultimate effect which they had on public opinion. David MacIsaac has summarised Douhet's theories as follows: 1) modern war allows for no distinction between combatant and non-combatant; 2) successful offensives by surface forces are no longer possible; 3) the advantages of speed and elevation in the three-dimensional arena of aerial warfare have made it impossible to take defensive measures against an offensive aerial strategy; 4) therefore a nation must be prepared at the outset to launch massive bombing attacks against the enemy centres of population, government, and industry – to hit first and hit hard to shatter enemy civilian morale, leaving the enemy government no option but to sue for peace; 5) to do this an independent air force armed with long range bombardment aircraft, maintained in a constant state of readiness is the primary requirement. This line of argument is familiar to, and has force for, a reader living in the present nuclear age, but the air-power theorists of the interwar years did not in the event provide a war-winning strategy for the Second World War. That war modified but did not overturn their thesis. It was true that in the air the advantage was with the offence and that targets could include government centres and industry as well as the armed forces of the enemy and that attacks on such targets could make an independent and significant contribution to victory. However, the 1930s prophecy of doom from the air overestimated the power of the offensive (the bomber did not always get through air defenses, or find its target) and underestimated the effect of bombing on civilian morale. None of this could be predicted with confidence in the 1930s and the interest for the student of strategy lies in trying to decide how far the advocates of air power persuaded their service colleagues and political masters to make what would turn out to be an unwise distribution of defence resources in favour of the air force.

GERMANY

Although it is convenient to begin a study of inter-war strategy with Germany, since it was the threat, actual or imagined, posed by that country which induced other European powers to rearm, it should not be forgotten that the first shots of the Second World War were fired when Japan invaded Manchuria in 1931, two years before Hitler's accession to power. Donald Watt has identified four major technological developments which produced overwhelming victories in the Second World War. These were firstly, the combination of tanks *en masse* with close air support, known as *Blitzkrieg*; secondly, radar, the ground-to-air communication link and the eight-gun all-metal-frame fighter, thirdly, the naval strike aircraft carrier, and fourthly the atom bomb. The first was nearly enough to win the war for Germany through her victories in Poland and France in 1939 and 1940, in the Balkans and Greece in 1941 and in Russia in 1941 and 1942, yet the surprising fact is that although the doctrine of Blitzkrieg was developed and perfected by German tank experts it was not worked into a comprehensive war-winning strategy (like the Schlieffen Plan) by the German General Staff in the years before the war. In fact, until the victories in Poland and France in 1939 and 1940, the German Higher Command did not really appreciate the war-winning weapon which its tank experts had developed. The story of Germany's preparations for war in the 1930s is essentially the story of Hitler's gradual domination of the professionals in the officer corps of the German army and of their reactions to his decisions on rearmament. They were horrified at the pace he set while he considered them insufficiently grateful for the opportunities he was providing and lacking the imagination to take advantage of them. The expansion of the German armed forces was indeed rapid. In late 1933 Germany withdrew from the League of Nations and the Disarmament Conference held under its auspices. In 1934 cadres for 24 army divisions were recruited, part of the cavalry was mechanised, and the build-up of the air force was begun. Universal conscription was re-introduced in early 1935 and an army of 36 divisions was projected. When war was declared in 1939 the Germans had 52 active divisions. This rapid march to war horrified the General Staff who had been preparing for a properly equipped and organised army to be ready by 1943 at the earliest. Hitler, however, dispensed with much that was considered important by the General Staff but was ready to spend lavishly on tanks and aircraft; it seems clear that he did not have any well thought out tactics for using these two weapons before war broke out but valued them for the terror they caused his foreign enemies when displayed.

Against this background the development of the doctrine of *Blitzkrieg* (the word itself hardly appeared in professional German military literature before the conquest of Poland in 1939) is all the more surprising. The theory of armoured warfare, involving deep penetration of enemy defences by tanks and motorised units freed from the need to protect and keep pace with infantry, was discussed in many armies after 1918. Two notable exponents in the 1920s and 1930s were General Fuller and Liddell Hart in Britain; the latter added two important concepts culled from German infantry tactics of 1918. These were the need for a heavy concentration of forces at the point of impact and the use of an 'expanding torrent' of force to be directed through the gap created by the initial attack to achieve deep penetration. These ideas found little favour in Britain although experimental armoured formations were created and tested on manoeuvres in Britain in the late 1920s and early 1930s. Similar ideas were being developed independently by Colonel (as he then was) Guderian in the Inspectorate of Motorised Units after 1931. Hitler's arrival in power in that year gave impetus to the development of tanks and aircraft, which he saw as terror weapons rather than as the spearhead of a new method of warfare. One gets the clear impression of a group of enthusiasts developing both the theory of, and the weapons needed for *Blitzkrieg*, without the encouragement of their professional seniors, but with the general support of the Head of State who did not appreciate the value of the weapon forged. Admittedly, the Germany General Staff had some excuse for their lack of interest. They were desperately worried by the acute shortage of raw materials and the danger that Germany would become embroiled in a long war for which she did not have the resources. However, the course of German strategy during the Third Reich was not determined by a set of rationally formulated grand objectives. Instead, as Michael Geyer points out, 'it was shaped by a series of gambles', that is, by the need to acquire one European country after another, the resources of each being needed to support the conquest of the next. Germany could only progress up the snakes and ladders board by landing on the ladder squares. From the arms factories of Czechoslovakia to the iron ore of Lorraine (to say nothing of the oil reserves found in France which kept the German Army mobile for two years) to the oil of Romania and the wheat of Ukraine, Germany was forced into continuous expansion and thus into the multiplication of her enemies by the needs of her economy and her armed forces. The General Staff foresaw some at least of this sombre picture and perhaps understandably neglected the technological development which would make Hitler's expansionary policy possible.

The invasion of Poland in 1939 was planned by General Manstein, the author of the first true *Blitzkrieg* in France in 1940, but the Polish campaign relied more on a series of encirclements of sections of the Polish Army near the German border than on deep penetrations by armoured forces, although these also occurred. Moreover if the attack on Holland, Belgium and France had taken place in autumn 1939 as originally planned, the German army would have advanced through Belgium towards Brussels with the intention of seizing as large a section of the Channel coast as possible as a basis for future operations. It might even have resulted in an eventual stalemate on the Western Front. However, General Manstein who was in late 1939 Chief of Staff to the southern of the two Army Groups assigned to this projected attack, saw the weakness of the plan, which was likely to run head-on into the French and British forces advancing to support the Belgians. He also realised that if the Panzer divisions could thread their way through the narrow valleys of the Ardennes and cross the River Meuse they would find flat open tank country, with few built-up areas all the way to the Channel coast. Moreover, a swift armoured attack would totally disorganise the supply lines of the French and British armies going to the assistance of Belgium, which would be cut off from their bases as soon as the German Panzer Divisions reached the Channel coast. Manstein argued for his plan at length with the German High Command, but to no avail. His persistence perhaps accounted for his next posting – to command an infantry corps in eastern Germany, well away from the scene of future action. At a routine luncheon with Hitler for newly promoted generals, Manstein was able to expound his plan again and reportedly obtained a sympathetic hearing from Hitler. Apparently a few days after this lunchtime meeting the Army High Command presented their version of the Manstein Plan to Hitler, who in due course accepted it. The High Command version deployed more troops for the thrust across the Meuse and generally placed more emphasis upon this aspect of the plan. It is very hard to be certain about the precise connection between the meeting of Hitler and Manstein and the conversion of the Army High Command to the Manstein Plan and their refusal to give any credit to the originator. Some points are, however, reasonably clear. The High Command plan was much more ambitious. It is hard to believe that the High Command would have put forward this revised plan if they had not been aware of Hitler's strong dislike of their original proposals. The existence of the Manstein Plan and the staggering success of the German campaign in the West on which it was based, owed everything to those tank enthusiasts who worked with General Guderian before the war to build up the weapons and the tactics essential for *Blitzkrieg*. The success of this, the first and most effective of the true *Blitzkrieg* campaigns, is too well known to need describing in any detail, but it should be stressed that it certainly exceeded the wildest hopes and plans of the German High Command. It may be unusual to find decisions on strategy depending on such chance happenings as a promotion and a lunch engagement, but certainly past strategic decisions which proved successful have depended on chance factors such as faulty intelligence. It was not chance, however, but sound reasoning that led Germany to place the main emphasis on her army when she rearmed in the 1930s, though it was only by chance that in 1940 she chose the correct strategy for the campaign in the West.

The other part of the Blitzkrieg formula was the responsibility of the German Air Force, the Luftwaffe. It provided the equivalent of mobile artillery, capable of keeping up with the fast cross-country advance of armoured divisions and available to attack strong points and troop concentrations which could hold up the advance of the Panzer divisions. It seems strange at first that the Luftwaffe commanded by Goering, the second most powerful man in the Third Reich, did not press for a larger share of the defence budget and a more independent role, especially since it was already a separate service, not under the control of the army or navy. The main advocate in the *Luftwaffe* for an independent strategic role was General Wever. However, he died in 1936, just as the Luftwaffe was learning important lessons from its participation in the Spanish Civil War. It became apparent to its commanders that modern bomber pilots found it extremely difficult to locate and hit any but the largest targets with any certainty. It also seemed clear that civilian morale under bombing was far less fragile than advocates of strategic bombing like Douhet supposed. Consequently, the dive bomber was developed from American experience in this field and the creation of a long-range heavy bomber force of four-engined air craft was abandoned. This may well have been because the prototypes of the four-engine bombers were relatively unsuccessful, but it was also realised that two-engine aircraft could be built more quickly and cheaply and the increased numbers available could make a greater impression on Germany's potential enemies. It was partly for this reason that the Luftwaffe tended to put the maximum possible numbers into front-line service and keep the minimum in reserve. There were other and perhaps sounder strategic reasons for these decisions. Germany's likely enemies at the time were Czechoslovakia and France, where likely targets could be reached by medium bombers such as the Heinkel and Dornier aircraft which were available in considerable numbers. Furthermore, Germany's step-by-step strategy of conquest depended, as has already been stressed, on the victors using to the full the resources of each conquered nation for the assault on the next. Wholesale destruction of enemy industry or communications by Luftwaffe bombers would not fit in with this strategy of plunder. The air force was therefore equipped and ready to cooperate with the army, always assuming that the enemy air force could be either neutralised or destroyed, as happened in most successful Blitzkrieg campaigns. Sometimes this was achieved by surprise attacks on enemy airfields at the start of the campaign but another effective Luftwaffe tactic was to overwhelm opposition by concentrating *en masse* over selected targets important to the army. The Luftwaffe did not operate close air support (which came to be practised later with such effect by the RAF and US Army Air Force) as it only had one aircraft type designed for this work, the Stuka dive bomber. This turned out to be an easy prey for opposing fighters. They were in any case a small part of the Luftwaffe bomber force and were used normally on targets some distance behind the front line. The two-engine bombers were, however, used most effectively on targets further behind the battle zone to assist the armoured advance, as the British army was able to confirm from the experience from its first few campaigns in the war.

Unlike its two sister services, the German Navy had no coherent strategy for its expansion in the 1930s. There was no equivalent to that propounded by Tirpitz before the First World War. That strategy may have been flawed, but it was at least clear and coherent. The Anglo-German Naval Treaty of 1935 was the outcome of an attempt by Britain to prevent the type of naval arms race which preceded the First World War. Under its terms Germany agreed to limit her navy to 35 per cent of the Royal Navy's surface ships and 45 per cent of submarines. In view of her success with the latter weapon in the previous war one would have expected the German Navy to have built additional submarines despite the treaty terms, possibly by clandestine methods. In fact both sides entered the war in 1939 with the number of submarines specified by the treaty although within a year or so Germany had added another 58 submarines to her fleet. This was paralleled by an ambitious plan in 1938 for the expansion of her surface fleet, designed to produce 13 battleships, 4 aircraft carriers and 33 cruisers as well as 250 U-Boats by 1945. It is very hard to see the justification for a fleet of this size, which would not be large enough to overwhelm the Royal Navy. Even if one were prepared to concede to the German Admiralty the foresight to predict the fall of France and the neutralisation of her fleet, Germany would still have needed the help of the Japanese Navy if she was to have any hope of victory at sea in a contest of capital ships. Yet if Germany were to count on Japan as an ally in a war in the mid 1940s, she would almost certainly have found the US with her powerful fleet among her enemies. On almost any reasonable assumption the German plan for a large surface fleet of capital ships was a waste of resources. It was in fact cancelled on the outbreak of war. She would have been far better served if resources had been concentrated sooner on submarines and surface commerce raiders, including perhaps some 'pocket battleships', in place of the very few 'super battleships' which she was able to complete.

GREAT BRITAIN

In contrast to Germany's rather haphazard system of allocating resources, with Hitler dealing with each service separately (and sometimes, as in the case of armoured warfare, dealing directly with subordinate branches of a service), the British rearmament programme after 1933 was at least well coordinated. The decisions which emerged from the bureaucratic machine were often wrong, sometimes disastrously so, but at least the needs of the three services were considered in one forum, the Defence Requirements Committee. This was set up in 1933 by the British Cabinet to coordinate the requirements of the three services and to advise on priorities. It was under the chairmanship of that outstanding service officer turned civil servant, Sir Maurice Hankey (as he then was), Secretary of the Cabinet, and had as members the civil service heads of the Foreign Office and the Treasury. The three Service Chiefs of Staff attended its meetings. From the outset the Treasury representative warned that the last war had impoverished Britain and that the next one if, or rather when it came, would bankrupt her. This point was not lost on the Government of the day which was both conscious of scarce resources and able to see enemies wherever it looked. Britain's former allies, the USA and Russia, had withdrawn from European affairs for different reasons and other former allies, Italy and Japan, were now potential enemies who seemed ready to dismember the British Empire at the first opportunity. However, after Hitler's seizure of power in 1933 it was Germany which was seen as the main potential enemy. Her growing army and air force awakened two of Britain's deepest fears. The German Army revived memories of massive casualties endured by the British Army in Flanders between 1914 and 1918, and the Luftwaffe inspired fears that Britain's cities and their inhabitants would be destroyed from the air at the outset of any future war. The Treasury predictions about future bankruptcy were all too correct, although that institution received little credit for it, but the fears about an immediate German air attack on cities were largely unfounded.

The German propaganda machine was used most skilfully by its creator Goebbels, to spread tales of the power of the Luftwaffe and its readiness to bomb the defenceless cities of its enemies. However, in 1939 the Luftwaffe lacked the capacity to obliterate British cities by bombing. The range from German bases was too great and even when bases in France became available after her defeat German bombers could not carry bomb loads of the weight routinely delivered by British bombers three years later. It will be necessary to return to this question when considering how far it would have been possible for Air Ministry intelligence experts to have divined the true position, but for the present one fact needs stressing. If one is to understand the fear which British Ministers felt at the prospect of raids by the Luftwaffe one has to realise that they expected at the outbreak of war the same sort of devastation as British bombers were to inflict on Hamburg and the Ruhr between 1942 and 1944. The fear of German bombers inspired much that was foolish and some that was good, indeed, vitally important, in Britain's pre-war planning.

Planning for the Second World War

Britain's policy towards her army in the 1930s illustrates all that was bad about her prewar strategic planning. In 1932 the repeated extension of the ten-year rule (under which the three services planned on the assumption that no major war would occur for at least ten years) was at last rescinded. The year 1918 saw some of the greatest achievements of the largest army which Britain had ever put in the field. Fifty-nine British divisions on the Western Front had defeated 99 German divisions in six major offensives and had captured nearly 200 000 prisoners. There were three-and-a-half million men under arms in 1918; by 1927 this had shrunk to about 207 000 out of which 105 battalions of infantry were formed, none of which were ready for action in fully organised divisions. The British Army had reverted to its Victorian role as a force for garrisoning India and the colonies. It had no settled doctrine for fighting modern war and the concept of armoured warfare was neglected by the nation which had invented the tank. Parsimony towards the army is part of a long British tradition and is perhaps understandable at a time when Britain faced economic difficulties and industrial weakness, but the record after 1933 when Hitler's intentions became apparent is less easy to forgive.

When the ten year rule was rescinded, the Chiefs of Staff reviewed the international situation and identified Germany as the main threat to Britain's security. They advised that no expeditionary force could be sent to the Continent until six months after the start of war and that the most that could be provided, after much expenditure on new equipment, would be four infantry divisions, one cavalry division and one tank brigade. In 1933 the British Government gave its special committee, the Defence Requirements Committee (DRC) the following order of priorities: 1) defence of the far eastern Empire; 2) a commitment to Europe; and 3) defence of India. The DRC considered that an expeditionary force would have to be sent to Europe in time of war, both to defend the Low Countries and to reassure France that Britain would fight. They costed this at £140 million (it included 12 reserve divisions in the Territorial Army) but the Army only asked for £40 million which was in fact half of the total sum allowed by the Government for all three services. The Cabinet cut the Army's share to £20 million and, fearful no doubt of the public reaction to any plans for another army expeditionary force for France, limited expenditure on that to £12 million. In 1935 when the international situation grew worse, the DRC argued that not only the five Regular but also the 12 Territorial divisions should be sent to France as soon as they had been made ready after the outbreak of war. Fearful of public reaction, the Cabinet would not agree, even in secret, to this proposal, although they allowed it to be used as a planning assumption. Many influential voices including that of Liddell Hart, the famous military commentator and strategist, were raised against Britain again assuming a Continental commitment, and even as late as 1937 there was still disagreement within the Government about the use of the Army in any future war with Germany, with the Minister responsible for the Army, advised by Liddell Hart, being against the despatch of an expeditionary force to the Continent. It is not surprising that in these circumstances the re-equipment of the army suffered. Throughout 1938 the British Cabinet's attitude towards a Continental commitment is best described in David Fraser's words as one of 'ambivalent hostility'. Even the Munich crisis, when 34 Czech divisions were sacrificed to gain time, did not spur the government to any immediate action regarding the Army's expeditionary force. Finally, in February 1939 (six months before it actually had to be sent to France), the Cabinet decided that five Regular divisions (4 infantry and 1 mobile division, the latter with some but not enough tanks) and 4 Territorial Army divisions should be sent to France as soon as possible after the outbreak of war. Subsequent events such as guarantees to Poland and Romania and the start of hostilities later the same year followed far too quickly for any effective use to be made of the Cabinet's belated change of heart. The British Expeditionary Force which sailed for France in the autumn of 1939 was surely the worst-equipped and least prepared for the enemy it was going to fight, of any sent overseas by Britain since Elizabethan times.

By contrast the Navy was better prepared, but not necessarily ready for the war which it would have to fight. The national revulsion against a large army committed to fighting in Europe did not affect the Navy, but the Washington Conference of 1921/22 banished any hope of a sensible re-equipment programme to replace the Royal Navy's fleet of ageing battleships. At the conference all naval powers (Britain, USA, France, Italy and Japan) agreed to build no new capital ships for ten years and thereafter to limit their fleets of these ships to the following tonnages: Britain and USA 525 000 tons each; Japan 315 000 and France and Italy 175 000 tons each; a similar agreement was reached on aircraft carriers, but no agreement was possible on limits for smaller surface ships and submarines. The Washington Treaty signalled the end of Britain's maritime supremacy. In effect she would find that war against Japan and Italy would be very hazardous, if not impossible without the help of the US, which was by no means a foregone conclusion in the 1920s and 1930s. When Germany began to rebuild her navy in the 1930s Britain's position became intolerable. The key to the defence of the British Empire in the Far East was the naval base at Singapore, constructed and defended at great expense after the First World War to house the main battle fleet of the Royal Navy. It was understood by friend and foe alike that if Japan attacked British possessions in the Far East, the Royal Navy would move in great strength to its base at Singapore, where it could thwart an invasion and pose a lethal threat to a nation as heavily dependent on maritime trade as Japan. The British threat became meaningless when Germany started to rearm, since the Royal Navy could not, so long as the Washington Treaty was in force, find the ships to guard home waters against the German and Italian fleets, and at the same time pose a credible threat to Japan from Singapore. Consequently in 1935 the Admiralty pressed on the British Government an Anglo-German Naval Treaty under which Germany agreed to limit her fleet to 35 percent of the Royal Navy with a higher limit, of 45 percent for submarines. The British negotiators assumed that they had achieved an effective cap on the German naval threat but it is clear that Hitler regarded the treaty as a license to build to the limit laid down – after which he could abrogate it. In any event after 1935 the Admiralty concentrated most of its attention and resources on the German threat in the North sea and the Atlantic, largely ignoring the threat from Italy in the Mediterranean, and Japan in the Far East. It was perhaps a fair assumption that in any war with Germany and Italy, France would be an ally of Britain and could take care of the Italian fleet, but reliance on the US to help Britain to counter a Japanese attack on the British Empire was a far more dangerous policy. The US gave no pledges of support in this area and consequently, for the first time in the history of her Empire, Britain was relying on another power to defend a large part of the British Empire without any supporting treaty. In effect, Great Britain had lost her centuries-old power to dominate any part of the world's oceans which were vital to her. This sad fact could not be blamed on the Royal Navy, since it was an aspect of Britain's weakness in relation to the growing economies of other industrial nations, but the inability of the Admiralty to foresee as accurately as some other navies the future of naval warfare was a serious error in naval strategy.

By the 1920s the application of air power should have become a significant factor in thinking about future battles on land or sea. In Britain little thought was given to either problem. The Royal Air Force spent the inter-war period fighting fiercely for its continued independence and for its strategic bombing role. It was reluctant to divert resources from this task either to tactical support of army operations or to long-range maritime reconnaissance and anti-submarine operations. In 1937 the Royal Navy took back control of the small Fleet Air Arm embarked on carriers but did not invest large resources in it. In pre-war naval planning it was relegated to the tasks of anti-submarine patrol and of scouting for enemy surface raiders. In 1939 the

Royal Navy had only one large purpose-built aircraft carrier in addition to its four converted carriers and one small carrier. Admirals (or generals or air marshals) cannot foretell the future, but the Admiralty should surely have paid some regard to the ships which the other two large navies were building in the 1930s. Both the US and Japan were developing large, fast carriers to attack enemy capital ships, with massed aircraft using bombs and torpedoes. In contrast the Admiralty favoured successive attacks by single flights of aircraft and these were, for much of the coming war, a generation older than American and Japanese naval aircraft. The Fleet Air Arm Fairey Swordfish achieved miracles, but their pilots deserved much better aircraft; had they had them, they could on several occasions have achieved even more startling results.

The results of this lack of foresight are well known. Off Crete in 1941, where the land-based Luftwaffe enjoyed complete air superiority, the Royal Navy lost three cruisers and six destroyers, while two battleships, one carrier, three cruisers and six destroyers were badly damaged. In the same year one battleship and one battle cruiser were sunk off Malaya and the aircraft carrier due to accompany them would undoubtedly have suffered the same fate if it had not been grounded in Durban on its way to the Far East. In the following year, after the fall of Singapore, the Far Eastern Fleet responsible for defending India and Ceylon was forced, through lack of air cover, to withdraw from the Bay of Bengal to African ports to avoid attack by Japanese carrier borne aircraft, losing two cruisers and having one small carrier damaged in the process. Fortunately for Britain, the Germany Navy never built aircraft carriers so the Royal Navy did not have to face any insuperable surface threat to its control of the Atlantic. If Germany's two powerful battleships, *Bismarck* and *Tirpitz* had the support of an aircraft carrier they could have proved to be a devastating combination against North Atlantic convoys. As it was air power played a crucial role in their destruction. Conversely, if the Royal Navy had possessed more fleet carriers and had equipped and trained its pilots for concentrated attacks on surface ships, it is hard to believe that they would not have been able to find and sink German surface raiders far more easily than was possible with surface ships and the limited carrier support available. The flying boats of RAF Coastal Command were invaluable for finding surface raiders but could not attack them with success. The great victory of the Fleet Air Arm was the crippling of the Italian Fleet at Taranto (this is said by some to have been the blueprint for Pearl Harbor) but in general the Mediterranean was not a satisfactory theatre for naval carrier operations since so much of the combat area was in range of German land-based aircraft with superior performance.

Another area in which the British Admiralty and Air Ministry neglected

Planning for the Second World War   155

the likely effects of air power was in the type of anti-submarine warfare which culminated in the Battle of the Atlantic. By the end of the war 246 German U-boats had been sunk by surface action and 288 by aircraft. Most of the latter fell victim to the long-range aircraft of RAF Coastal Command in a type of warfare which barely existed even in the planners' imagination before the war. This is no place to follow the twists and turns of the Battle of the Atlantic, which most historians would probably now admit was won by both the surface and air forces working together, (not forgetting the heroism of the merchant navy crews). However, the Admiralty and the Air Ministry should certainly share the blame for not realising earlier the crucial contribution of air power to the anti-submarine war and taking steps to put adequate resources into the production or purchase of the correct type of aircraft. This point will be considered later in the context of the US contribution to the Battle of the Atlantic; for the present it is enough to note that the Admiralty preferred to put its available resources into surface craft and the Air Ministry preferred to use the long-range four-engine aircraft as bombers to help the attack on the German homeland rather than quell the submarine menace.

As the 1930s passed the British Government became increasingly preoccupied by the threat from the air and the best means of countering it. This was reflected in the way the rearmament budget was shared out between the three services. In 1933 the RAF received £16.7m, the smallest of the service allocations but in 1938 (up to the outbreak of war) it received £133m, the largest of the three allocations. Over the whole period from 1933 to 1939, the Army received £464m, the Navy £582m and the RAF £433m. The increasing emphasis on the air force is not perhaps surprising in view of the growing fears of air attacks on the civilian population, but the air staff policy for the expansion of the RAF must with hindsight be a cause for some surprise and wonder. It is true that at the start of the rearmament programme, before it became clear that the RAF air defence system had a good chance of defeating the knock-out blow from the air, there was a sound case for trying to avert terror by counter-terror – by building a bomber force which equalled that of the Luftwaffe. However, this case for the bomber force as a deterrent was not the RAF's primary reason for strategic bombing. This had been seen as the main role of the RAF since the time of its founder, Trenchard, and during the 1930s rearmament this doctrine still held sway, as strongly as it had before the advent of Hitler and the Luftwaffe.

There seemed little or no hope in the early 1930s of destroying a bomber force attacking London, always assumed to be the main target for the Luftwaffe. The facts were thought to speak for themselves. Bombers approaching London at 15 000 feet could not be detected, even in clear weather, until they crossed the English coast; in consequence, by the time fighters had taken off and intercepted the attacking force it would be over London. The only way, therefore, so the argument ran, to avert such an attack was to threaten a counter-attack of equal savagery. The Prime Minister Baldwin described the dilemma even more starkly: 'you have to kill more women and children more quickly than the enemy if you want to survive'. The unstated dilemma from the RAF point of view lay in the question of what would happen if this deterrent worked and the enemy refrained from attacking civilian targets for fear of reprisals. A strategic bombing force built to carry heavy bomb loads over long distances would not necessarily be effective in other roles. As the experience of the Second World War showed, heavy bombers were not effective against submarines and the army needed medium bombers in large numbers working closely with the army rather than heavy bombers for area bombing. Some of the latter were certainly needed when the time came for precision attacks on special targets, such as oil refineries and the rail and road transport system, but (as will be seen) this was not possible for Bomber Command until later in the war, and did not require the very large numbers of four-engine bombers which were built at the expense of other aircraft types.

When it came to write its first report in 1934, the Defence Requirements Committee felt bound to keep strictly within its terms of reference which in effect required it to recommend ways of remedying the worst deficiencies of the three services without examining questions of policy or strategy. It therefore recommended the modernisation of the main Battle Fleet, the preparation of an expeditionary force similar to that sent to France in 1914 and, for the RAF, the completion of the plan for 52 home-based squadrons which had been the target since 1923 when the French air force had been considered to be the main threat. The Committee added that a further 25 squadrons would be required for the RAF but it considered that to recommend this would be outside its terms of reference, which were to remove the worst deficencies. The Cabinet decided on the basis of the DRC report to increase the Metropolitan Air Force from 52 to 80 squadrons by cutting the allocations to the navy and army.

Before tracing the subsequent development of what would soon be known as Bomber Command, it is salutary to try and discover what evidence was available to the air staff and others about the effectiveness of the knock-out blow from the air which Britain was trying so assiduously to prepare. As has already been mentioned, the German propaganda machine was always ready to threaten other countries with mass destruction from the air, and no doubt the Germans could have inflicted serious damage on defenceless countries near Germany's borders. The Spanish Civil War seemed to provide evidence to support German threats. Thus in two days bombing of Barcelona in 1938 the Italian Air Force killed some 1300 and wounded about 2000 civilians. Little attempt was apparently made to analyse or refine these figures at the time, although it should have been possible to get nearer to the correct figure. Recent studies suggest that deaths from air raids on both sides for the whole war amounted to more than 15 000 which is about 3 percent of the total killed. Rotterdam suffered 814 civilians killed in the first terror raid on the Western Front (propaganda pushed this figure up to 25 000) and in Coventry later the same year 514 were killed in one night raid. Shocking as these non-combatant casualties may be, they pale into insignificance beside those inflicted by Bomber Command raids later in the war. Thus single raids by mainly British bomber forces caused 5000 casualties in Dortmund, 40 000 in Hamburg in 1943 and 80 000 in Dresden in 1945. Neither these nor the earlier German and Italian raids so destroyed civilian morale that the governments concerned were forced to sue for peace. One is bound to question whether it was wise for Britain to to put so much of her scarce resources into bomber aircraft in the years before the war when better intelligence on the Luftwaffe's performance in Spain would have corrected the forecast of a knock-out blow. As Wesley Wark writes, 'By failing to collect and assess the sort of intelligence on German equipment, reserves, training and strategy that would have enabled it to make a decision on the true capabilities of the Luftwaffe, the Air Intelligence Directorate shared responsibility for the exaggeration of German air power that was widespread in the Air Ministry, Whitehall, the cabinet and the public mind.'

Moreover, an alternative to the counter-terror weapon was becoming available to the RAF after 1934. Late in that year a committee of scientists outside the Air Ministry was set up under the auspices of that Ministry's directorate of scientific research to consider scientific aids to air warfare. By early 1935 it became clear that radio direction-finding, now called radar, could detect aircraft far beyond the reach of the human eye or ear. As a result British fighters could be alerted and positioned in the air ready to attack enemy bombers even before they crossed the English coast on their way to bomb London or the Midlands. The Air Ministry pressed vigorously ahead with research into radar, and great credit is also due to Fighter Command, which cooperated closely with the scientists involved, to develop a fully functioning system with the radar stations linked by telephone to control headquarters, which themselves were linked by telephone to the fighter stations and to the fighter pilots in the air by radio. The whole system was in place just in time for its test in 1940 in the Battle of Britain, but victory was won by the narrowest of margins, for the number of fighter aircraft and of the trained pilots to man them, were only just enough to outlast the Luftwaffe. The Air Ministry policy of giving priority to bombers instead of fighters in the early part of the rearmament programme contributed to this state of affairs. It was not until 1938 that fighters received top priority. Indeed the numbers of fighters available in 1940 would have been considerably fewer if there had not been pressure from outside the Air Ministry. Donald Watt goes so far as to argue that the Air Ministry was forced to accept the development of fighter defences by the Treasury as the price of Treasury consent to their own bomber plans. The moving spirit in this was Sir Warren Fisher, the Treasury representative on the Defence Requirements Committee, and the results of his influence are apparent in the second and third reports of the DRC. Originally Fisher, like the rest of the DRC had been in favour of building up a deterrent bomber force, but the realisation in 1936/37 that Britain could not in the near future achieve parity in bombers with the Luftwaffe made Fisher change his views. He saw quite correctly that there was an alternative to the bombers, and that was to use radar and fighters to destroy the attacking bomber force. The later reports of the DRC reflected his views to some extent, but his influence on defence matters was greatly increased by the appointment of Sir Thomas Inskip, a Cabinet Minister. As Minister for the Coordination of Defence, Fisher acted, in effect, as Inskip's chief civil service adviser, and the Prime Minister, Neville Chamberlain, paid great attention to his views. Fisher and Inskip shared the prevailing apprehensions about bombing attacks, based as we now know on faulty intelligence, but the Cabinet decision in 1938 to give priority to fighters in the RAF budget owes much to these two men and was a far better preparation for the coming war than the Air Ministry alternative of counter-terror. By 1939 Fisher's influence with the Prime Minister was waning – he was due to retire shortly in any case – but by then his greatest service to Britain's preparations for war had been given. It would be wrong to see the resulting change in RAF priorities from bombers to fighters, as being solely due to Fisher. Clearly Inskip and Chamberlain were responsible for the final decision; Hankey the civil service (but ex-service) chairman of the DRC, frequently supported Fisher in committee, and he was admirably sustained by his colleagues in the Treasury. The best measure of Fisher's contribution is gained by imagining what Britain's preparations for war would have looked like if the Permanent Secretary of the Treasury at that time had been a man without Fisher's concern with strategy or his ability to convince others of the rightness of his views.

The 1938 decision to give fighters priority came just in time to take full advantage of the new eight-gun monoplane fighters coming into production. As it was, there were barely enough Spitfire and Hurricane fighters and pilots when the German bomber force, based not in Germany (as had been assumed before the war) but in France, started its attack on Britain. The fighter force was clearly going to be stretched to the limit but, even so, there was intense pressure on Fighter Command to disperse its scanty resources, first to defend the fleet anchorages in north Scotland, then to support the BEF in France and finally, after its evacuation from Dunkirk, to help the remaining British troops and the French armies still fighting in France. In May 1940 Fighter Command had only 39 fighter squadrons to defend the United Kingdom, while the estimated minimum number needed for the task was 46. The Commander-in-Chief, Sir Hugh Dowding, had expressed his concern about this drain on his resources on many occasions but had to accept it, as did the Air Minister. His reservations are well expressed in a note written in autumn 1939: 'I must put on record my point of view that the Home Defence Organisation must not be regarded as co-equal with other commands but that it should receive priority to all other claims until it is firmly secured, since the continued existence of the nation and all its services depends on the Royal Navy and Fighter Command.' The Air Ministry had sympathy for this point of view, but was bound, when allocating its resources, to pay some heed to other pressing needs, such as the British Expeditionary Force fighting to survive across the Channel. In the event, enough were left in the UK for the coming battle, but Dowding's note is a reminder of the difficult choices which had to be made about scarce resources in 1939 and 1940.

In addition to its air defence task, there were two other areas in which the RAF played a decisive and indeed war-winning role. Both of these were in support of another service, and therefore unpopular in pre-war days when the air force planners and commanders apparently thought (rightly or wrongly) that if their service were to concentrate its efforts on supporting either the Army or Navy, it would risk being dismembered by the other two services. The history of Coastal Command, (in which the RAF grouped all long-range aircraft available for maritime reconnaissance and for attacking submarines) illustrates this well. In the final tally, rather more submarines at sea were sunk by aircraft than by surface ships, but the maritime task was always at the back of the queue for new aircraft and had it not been for the purchase of a converted American civil airliner known as the Hudson in 1938, the Battle of the Atlantic might have been even more closely run. Even at the height of that battle in 1942 and 1943 it was extraordinarily difficult for Coastal Command to obtain long-range aircraft to help defeat U-boat attacks. It is not too much to claim that the weapon which turned the tide in the most desperate stage of the battle was the very long-range version

(VLR) of the Liberator bomber, developed for anti-submarine warfare, which alone could patrol the central area of the Atlantic, known as the mid-Atlantic gap, and prevent massed U-boat attacks on convoys. Yet it was extremely difficult to get the American Chiefs of Staff to release them, even though it was hard to claim – as they apparently did – that the small numbers involved would make a significant difference to the bombing offensive in other theatres. The RAF, however used few Liberators for any purpose except anti-submarine warfare until 1944.

The air staff in Britain were slow to appreciate the importance of air power to provide close air support for the army, although from 1939 onwards they realised the need to provide air protection for the Expeditionary Force and sent squadrons of scarce Hurricanes to France in 1939 and 1940, when they realised that they could be needed for the coming battle for Britain. There was a great shortage of suitable aircraft for ground-attack of targets in the battle zone and for longer-range interdiction bombing to stop supplies and reinforcements reaching the battle; this was made worse when it became plain that the Fairey Battle light bomber was a failure. Moreover, the concept of close air support was low on the list of RAF priorities and consequently developed slowly. This was partly because of the many other calls on its resources – and until 1938 there seemed no likelihood of a government decision to send the army to fight in Europe. The Army also failed to appreciate the importance of air power in the land battle, until chastened by defeats in Flanders, Greece and Crete in which the Luftwaffe played a notable part. The army commanders then pressed the RAF to provide dive-bombers, which the RAF, quite correctly as it turned out, rejected. This caused further delay in evolving the correct aircraft and tactics which could have been avoided if there had been fore-thought and inter-service consultation before the war.

Eventually the necessary techniques were developed in the Western Desert by the Desert Air Force under Air Marshal Tedder, which played an essential part in the defeat of the Afrika Korps. If the German and Italian forces there had received any significant part of the petrol and other supplies sent to them from Italy, the outcome of the battles from First Alamein onwards might have been different. As it was, the Afrika Korps and the Italian troops were virtually isolated in Africa by the RAF. Sadly, it took some time for the 21st Army Group and its Tactical Air Force to master the same techniques in 1944 in Normandy during the early stages of the battle, when the menace of the far superior German tanks had to be countered. Later arrangements were improved and the German armoured counter-attack at Mortain was badly mauled by ceaseless attacks from the air. Shortly after, the remnants of the German armies in the Falaise pocket were reduced, mainly by air attacks, to a crowd of disorganised men retreating with little or no transport towards the Seine. The pre-war Air Ministry cannot be criticised for failing to provide enough resources for Army Cooperation (as it was called then, a revealing phrase, since it implies a subordinate role for air power) or for Coastal Command, since there were not enough aircraft for all the tasks for which air power would be needed. The priority given by the Air Staff to the role of the strategic bomber seems to have blinded them to the need to consider the other tasks in which air craft might have an essential part to play. A study of the role of German and Italian air squadrons in the Spanish Civil War, and of the adoption of the bomber for attacks on ships by the Americans and the Japanese (as well as its use by the Luftwaffe against military targets after air superiority had been gained) might have alerted those concerned in Britain to the wider possibilities of the air weapon. Instead, the RAF, after a fierce struggle to maintain its independence in the 1920s, was imbued with the doctrine of its founding father, Lord Trenchard, that the task of the strategic bomber was all-important. It is now time to see how far the Trenchard doctrine stood the test of war.

The last and perhaps the most humiliating blow to the Air Ministry before the war was delivered by the Commander-in-Chief of Bomber Command. Sir Edgar Ludlow-Hewitt made a thorough inspection of his command on his appointment in 1937. Between then and 1939 he sent a series of damning reports which, in the sober words of the official history, *The Strategic Air Offensive against Germany*, showed that 'Bomber Command was not trained or equipped either to penetrate into enemy territory by day or to find its target areas, let alone its targets by night.' The history goes on to comment 'it is surely remarkable that it was less than a year before war broke out' that the air staff realised that Bomber Command was incapable 'of carrying out the operations of which the Air Ministry had based its strategy for the last four years'. In support of his conclusions the Commander-in-Chief pointed out that his crews were unable to operate except in fine weather and that their aircraft were extremely vulnerable both in the air and on the ground. In addition the air crews had neither the equipment, let alone the training, for accurate night flying or bomb aiming. This is no place to catalogue the defects in Bomber Command or the heroic efforts made by its crews to undertake their missions despite the handicaps. Even in 1941 when Britain was fighting alone and bombing was her sole means of striking at Germany, a report by D.M.B. Butt, a member of the War Cabinet Secretariat, based on air photos showed that, in 48 bombing operations carried out in a two-month period, only one-fifth of the bombers despatched actually reached the target area (which was defined as being within a radius of five miles of an aiming point). Intense efforts were made to improve on this, but it was clearly too late in the war for Britain to forge a completely new weapon. The Bomber Command offensive continued but it was in general confined to area-bombing of industrial targets, which in effect meant the wholesale destruction by night of cities which were centres of industry. There were many brilliant and gallant exceptions to this general rule, such as the raids on the Peenemunde rocket research station and on the Mohne and Eder dams, but the vast majority of raids were on cities.

With the entry of the United States into the war, the Bomber Command offensive was in due course strengthened by the heavy daylight bombers of the US Army Air Force, which could hit targets by day somewhat more accurately than the night bombers of the RAF. Nevertheless, by the middle of 1943 German defences were beginning to exact a heavy toll on both air forces. The German night fighters were inflicting unacceptably high losses on the RAF, and the crews of the US daylight bombers, mainly Flying Fortresses, were finding that their armament of numerous heavy machine-guns was no match for the German fighters armed mainly with cannon. Just when it seemed that both the day and the night bomber offensives against Germany itself would have to be called off, one of the few miracle weapons of the war appeared. This was the P-51 Mustang, an American fighter air frame which was so unsuccessful with its original American engine that on the initiative of the Air Ministry it was fitted with the British Merlin engine (first used on the Spitfire) instead. This transformed a rather in-different aircraft into something which no aircraft designer ever expected to achieve – an aeroplane with the performance of a fighter and the range of a bomber. When the new Mustangs began to come into service in the second half of 1943, daylight raids were resumed this time with Mustang escorts. They proved more than a match for the German fighters which intercepted them. As German losses mounted, the US bombers took as their targets aircraft factories and in 1944, synthetic oil plants, both essential for the survival of the Luftwaffe. As a result the German fighters were forced into the air to defend these vital objectives and were destroyed in the ensuing air battles. The first victory for the strategic bombing campaign was the destruction of the opposing air force, which was certainly not one of its original objectives. It was, however, an essential precursor to the land-ings in Normandy and the victory of the Allied Armies in north-west Europe. From D-Day onwards it would be hard to find occasions when the Luftwaffe made any significant impact on the battle. The effect of the attacks on what became known as the oil targets is best considered in the context of the Strategic Bombing Offensive as a whole.

Planning for the Second World War   163

No judgement of the effectiveness of Britain's preparations for the Second World War can be made without some assessment of the Bomber Command Offensive, which could be said to have started in 1942, after the problems of night navigation and bomb-aiming had been at least partially solved, and continued until the end of the war in 1945. Many books have been written on this subject and doubtless many more are to come. There will never be unanimity on this, but perhaps with the passage of time the following propositions will become more acceptable. The first concerns civilian morale; despite the horrific destruction of German cities, entailing very heavy loss of life, civilian morale did not crack. The second concerns oil; in the final months of the war both the day and the night bomber offensive had the 'oil targets' high on their list of priorities. In the final four months the German war machine was virtually immobilised for lack of oil. Special factors, such as the loss of the Romanian oilfields and the increasing vulnerability of Germany itself to air attack as she lost control of surrounding territories help to explain why this was only achieved in 1945, but it is clear that in that year the shortage of oil certainly hastened final defeat and helped to reduce casualties. The bomber offensive contributed to final victory, but did not of itself bring it about.

If strategic bombing alone could not defeat a major industrial power such as Germany in the 1940s, was it a wise strategy for Britain, alone of all the major powers, to invest so heavily in a strategic bomber force? Some of the reasons why this happened have already been mentioned briefly. In the 1920s, before large resources were invested, there was the fear, whether justified or not, amongst senior RAF officers that their service would be dismembered by the Army and the Navy unless it found some unique and war-winning role in which the other services could not share. In the 1930s it was thought that Germany had started to build a bomber force for the destruction of cities and would only be deterred from launching it against Britain if faced by an equally large force prepared to retaliate in a similar manner. Finally, after the defeat of France in 1940 there was the understandable desire to use the expanding bomber force to destroy as much as possible of Germany's capacity to wage war in the only way possible, while Britain stood alone against her. These explanations as to why the decisions were taken to invest resources in heavy bombers do not of course justify them as strategically sound. In any case, there were surely pointers before the war which might have suggested that these decisions were mistaken. It should have been possible with better intelligence to alert the British government to the fact that the Luftwaffe was not being built as a strategic bomber force. By the time that the defects of the bomber force became apparent, from the first reports of the new Commander-in-Chief in 1937, it was rather late to change plans radically. However, the record of air defence shows that the Air Ministry could change course and seize new opportunities when they presented themselves. The speedy adoption of radar by the RAF was the result of three separate and imaginative decisions. Firstly, the scientists in the Air Ministry enlisted the help of colleagues outside defence in tackling the problem of defence against air attack. Secondly the Air Staff, with the backing of the then Chief of Air Staff Sir Cyril Newall, pressed ahead with the construction of the chain of radar stations as soon as the technology had been proved. Finally, Fighter Command eagerly sought the help of the radar scientists and others in incorporating radar into the air defence system; indeed those concerned with the development of radar have stressed that from the start it was a cooperative venture, involving service officers and scientists on equal terms. As a result, Britain had a fully functioning system long before Germany and the US who had discovered the principle of radar at about the same time as Britain. In contrast, Bomber Command saw little need for help from the scientists, according to R.V. Jones, until their problems and casualties began to mount in 1941. One can only speculate about what would have happened if they had called in scientists who would have been familiar with the promise of radar, say in 1938 when their own C-in-C's reports were highlighting their deficiencies. The four-engined bombers were not then in mass production and it would have been possible to modify or reduce the construction programme if those concerned had been able to foresee the difficulties ahead. Certainly by the time the Butt report was produced in 1941 it was too late to make any but minor changes to the build-up of the strategic bombing programme and by then too many resources (and too many hopes) had been invested in it.

However, even when it is accepted that strategic bombing consumed too many of Britain's resources for the results achieved, it is still very hard to decide where those resources could have been more effectively invested, and yet the quantities are large. Between 50 per cent and 60 per cent of Britain's industrial production was devoted to the RAF, and Bomber Command received a significant proportion of this production. In 1944/45 there were about a million men in RAF uniform and again a fair proportion were in or supporting Bomber Command. One obvious proviso should be made; even if the resources allocated to the bombing offensive had been reduced, it would surely have been right to maintain a night bomber force with the means to strike at sensitive targets, such as oil refineries and aircraft factories, in conjunction with the US day bomber force of Flying Fortresses and other aircraft. Perhaps the air staff could have considered the diversion of say one-third of the resources allotted to strategic bombing. The obvious candidates for more air resources would have been the Commands supporting the other two services. The case for more Liberator aircraft being deployed, and deployed sooner, to Coastal Command for the Battle of the Atlantic is discussed later in this chapter in connection with US decisions on strategy. It is hard to see how additional RAF support would have averted the defeats of the British army in France in 1940 and in Greece in 1941, although additional air power might perhaps have saved Crete from capture. Thereafter, defeats might have been less costly and victories have come more quickly with more air support; but by 1943 it could be argued that the RAF Tactical Air Forces achieved in general all that could reasonably be asked of them. The final alternative to consider would be the transfer of RAF resources to one of the other Services. The first point to make is that additional resources by themselves would not have persuaded the Royal Navy to appreciate the potentialities of carrier-borne aircraft, nor would they have helped either the British or the US Army to procure a tank which would match those in the opposing Panzer divisions. Nor is it clear that industrial resources used for the production of aircraft and armament for the RAF could have been used by either of the other services, particularly the Navy, which needed ships, especially escort carriers, for the Battle of the Atlantic. The RAF, however, did have one resource which was desperately needed by both the British and US Armies in 1944 and 1945: men. In the autumn and winter of 1944/45 the British 21st Army Group in north-west Europe was forced to break up units and formations of good quality to provide reinforcements for the remainder. There was such a shortage of trained British and US infantry divisions that opportunities for earlier victory were perhaps lost. This also is discussed later in this chapter.

The expeditionary force which left for France in 1939 was so ill-equipped to face armoured warfare that its survival in 1940 was due as much to the failure of the enemy to press his advantage as to its own efforts. However, the blame for this does not rest mainly with the War Office. It is true that Britain's military leaders failed to foresee and arm against armoured warfare (it has to be remembered that, before the war the German High Command also discounted the ideas of their own tank enthusiasts), but, even if the British Army had been alive to the threat of *Blitzkrieg*, they would surely never have received the funds in time to equip the expeditionary force for this, since until early 1939 the government had decided not to send an expeditionary force to France in the event of war. The blame for the lateness of this decision must rest with Britain's politicians, rather than her military leaders or with the DRC.

In this context it is worth remembering that the two technological advances which brought victories in 1940 for Britain and Germany respectively – air defence with radar, and *Blitzkrieg* – were each supported and encouraged by civilians as well as service officers. In Britain radar was supported by the Treasury team led by Fisher, by Hankey, chairman of the DRC, and Inskip, the Cabinet Minister in charge of defence. In Germany the main supporter of *Blitzkrieg* was ex-corporal Hitler.

The Admiralty's concentration on battleships in preference to aircraft carriers was, in retrospect, a mistake, however, it did not entail catastrophic defeats. Losses of surface ships off Crete in 1941 were serious but were, to a considerable extent, redeemed by the naval air strikes at Taranto, which virtually incapacitated the Italian fleet. The naval defeat off Malaya was another matter. The loss of capital ships might possibly have been avoided if they had been accompanied by an aircraft carrier as originally intended, but it is very hard to see how the fall of Singapore could have been prevented by this small British squadron after the US Pacific Fleet had been so heavily damaged at Pearl Harbor. The Admiralty were right to judge in 1940 that with the loss of the French fleet to the Allied cause, Britain had no hope of combating threats from both the German and the Japanese Navies. In its long history the French Navy twice inflicted serious damage on its old enemy Britain. On both occasions another nation reaped the reward. On the first occasion the American colonists achieved their independence, on the second Britain lost her possessions in the Far East.

JAPAN

The Japanese conquest of South East Asia in 1941 showed what could be achieved, with the right weapons and tactics, by an island nation in a weak strategic position and without indigenous raw materials. Paul Kennedy has alluded to the tidal nature of the Pacific War. This started in 1941 when the Japanese poured over Asia until they reached a line from Burma to Singapore to the Aleutians within seven months of the start of the war. This tide was checked by the US Navy in epic battles (the phrase for once is apt) at the Coral Sea and Midway Island. Within 14 months the first retreat came at Guadalcanal and thereafter the tide receded steadily, until by 1945 the American tide lapped the shores of Japan itself. Nevertheless, Kennedy advises, it is far too simplistic to see the Pacific War as one between a weaker and a stronger economy in which the weaker gained initial victory by treachery and surprise and was ultimately overcome by the economically stronger power once resources had been mobilised for war. The true story is more complex and far more interesting, since the course of the war depended on a number of crucial strategic decisions and on the key battles

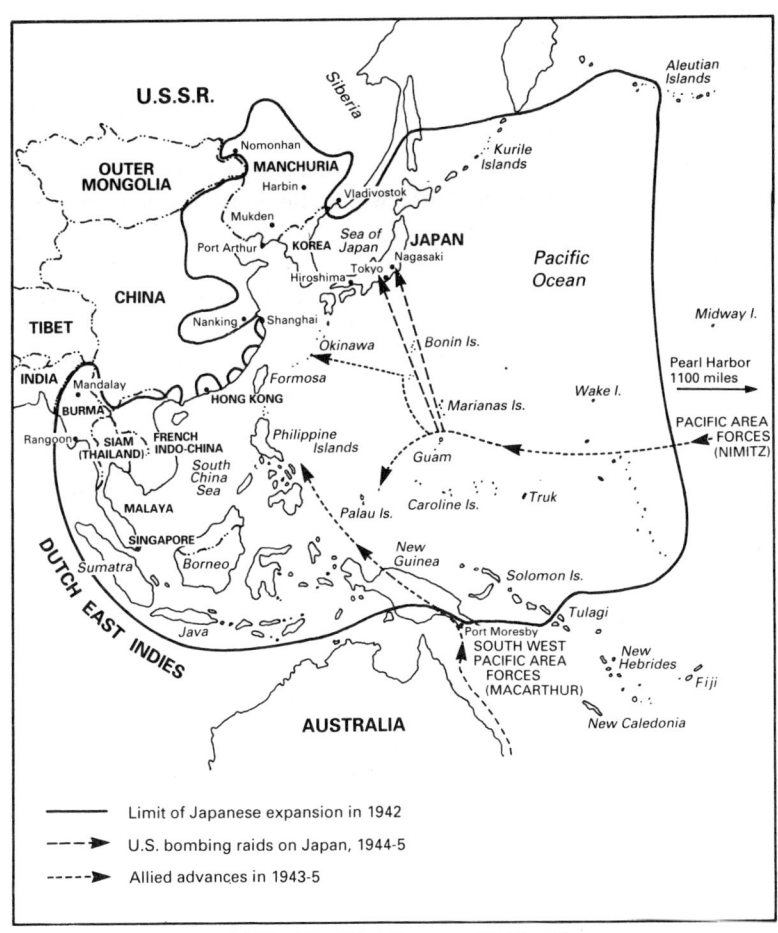

6. The Pacific Theatre 1941-45

fought as a consequence of these decisions. To put it another way, initial victory and ultimate defeat depended in this, as in so many wars, on strategic and tactical errors by both sides. Further interest is provided by a study of Japanese strategy, since its success depended on a careful balance of resources between the army and the navy. This balancing act was made no easier by the fact that the army was always the dominant influence in Japanese policy-making, yet it must have seemed to many that it was always the Imperial Navy which gained the most spectacular victories.

For Japan the war did not start with a string of victories in 1941; it started with her expansion on the mainland of Asia, where since 1931 the Japanese had seized great swathes of territory in China and Manchuria. Perhaps the best date for the 'start' of the Pacific war would be 1937, when Japan tried to seize the whole of China by a *coup de main*, and failed. Thereafter the war in China developed into a stalemate, tying down 22 divisions, from which the Japanese were desperate to extricate themselves. A solution to their problem in China was all the more important because of their anxiety about the intentions of the USSR. The brief, undeclared and local war with the Soviet Union in 1939, known as the Nomonhan incident, had given the Japanese a nasty shock. Their troops had been worsted in the fighting and the threat to the Japanese homeland from the forces in Russian Siberia seemed real and ever-present. Despite the conclusion of a non-aggression pact with the USSR in 1941, and Russian involvement in a life-or-death struggle with Germany, Japan maintained a garrison of 13 to 15 divisions in Manchuria throughout the war with the Allies. It is true that Russian forces in Siberia remained large, even in 1941 and 1942, but this was surely for fear of a Japanese attack; the war leaders in Tokyo can hardly have expected that the Russians would attack Manchuria when Russia was so hard-pressed in the west. Thus, commitments in China and Manchuria tied down the bulk of the Japanese army in circumstances which brought little advantage at heavy cost. It is not surprising, therefore, that by 1941 the two Chiefs of Staff agreed that the Chinese commitment must be eliminated as soon as possible. The occupation of French Indo-China by Japanese forces in 1941 was for the Japanese a useful first step in their plan to isolate China in order to deprive her of the military supplies needed to continue the fight against Japan. The Japanese government no doubt assumed that since the seizure of Indo-China followed the defeat of France by Germany it would be seen by the international community as a strategically logical and politically acceptable step. The French Empire would be regarded, they thought, as something ripe for dismemberment and so the occupation of French Indo-China would arouse the same sort of reaction as had followed their takeover of Manchuria some ten years before – protest but no retalia-

Planning for the Second World War   169

tion. This time the Japanese were wrong. The US, British and Dutch governments froze all Japanese assets within their jurisdiction, thus depriving Japan of the means to pay for all her oil imports, most of which came from the British and Dutch East Indies. Without oil the Japanese offensive in China would be halted and her forces there would be in real danger of defeat. If Japan was not to accept a humiliating climbdown she had to seize the oil-rich islands of the East Indies by force and, if possible, occupy Burma to cut the land route by which China received war supplies from the western powers. At a meeting in July 1941 the Japanese government decided to pursue their expansion south-eastwards, regardless of a potential war with Britain and the US.

The Japanese war leaders must have been fortified in their decision by a chance event, unforeseeable by any war planner or strategist and so incredible that a writer of fiction would reject it. After the fall of France in 1940, which subtracted the French fleet from the Allied total in the balance sheet of naval power, the British Chiefs of Staff reviewed the situation and came to the inevitable but gloomy conclusion that, in the event of war with Japan, it would be impossible to send a battle fleet to Singapore, which would have to rely for its defence on the Army and RAF units stationed there. Thus the long-held plan of 'the fleet to Singapore', the cornerstone of Britain's defence policy in the Far East, had to be scrapped. The millions of pounds sunk in Singapore's defences in the 1920s and 1930s when funds for the services were so short, were clearly going to be wasted; worse still these defences could be (and would in fact turn out to be) a trap for their garrison, since they were sited to resist attack from the sea and not from the landward side of the base. Nonetheless, the decision not to send a large fleet was surely correct. A copy of their appreciation was sent to the service Commanders-in-Chief in Singapore in the safe of a British merchant ship bound for Singapore. This was a fairly common practice but most unfortunately this document was not kept in the main safe in the bowels of the ship but in the smaller safe on the upper deck which was used for codes. By sheer chance this merchant ship was intercepted by a German surface raider, whose crew was able to rifle the code safe before the merchantman was sunk. The British Chiefs of Staff paper reached the Japanese war planners at about the time when the surprise attack on the US fleet at Pearl Harbor was being planned. It must have been clear to the Japanese Admiralty that, since there would be no British fleet to bar the southeastern advance of their fleet, the odds in favour of a surprise attack on the US fleet were much improved. Only one surprise attack instead of two (one at Pearl Harbor and one at Singapore) would have to succeed in order to give the Japanese mastery of the Pacific.

The strategic plan worked out in the autumn of 1941 envisaged three stages: 1) the destruction of the US fleet at Pearl Harbor by a surprise carrier aircraft attack, land offensives on Hong Kong, Thailand and Malaya with air raids and later landings on the Philippines and Borneo, and finally air raids to destroy US facilities on Guam and Wake Island; 2) when these offensives had achieved their objectives Japanese forces would occupy all Malaya, Singapore, the airfields of south Burma, the Bismarck Archipelago, and strategic points in the Dutch East Indies; 3) after occupying Java and Sumatra, Japanese forces would consolidate there and would also extend their control to the whole of Burma and capture the Nicobar and Andaman Islands in the Bay of Bengal. Six months were allowed for this ambitious plan of conquest. Thereafter the intention was for Japan to rest secure behind the ring of defensive outposts stretching from Burma to the Aleutian Islands, able to repel any amphibious counter-attacks which the USA could mount from her distant bases across the Pacific. From this position of strength Japan would be able to continue without interruption her subjugation of China, since the 'co-prosperity sphere of south Asia' would supply all the raw materials which she required.

The Japanese Army's ambition to conquer China had led the nation step by step into a war with the United States and other western powers in which her navy and its air force would have to play predominant roles. It was by no means clear, however, that these two services had in the past been allotted sufficient resources for the tasks which they were expected to undertake. The Japanese Navy had 10 battleships and 10 aircraft carriers as well as 36 cruisers, 113 destroyers and 59 submarines. It had studied and perfected the techniques of long-range air strikes by carrier-borne dive bombers and torpedo-carrying aircraft. In addition the battleship soon to come into service, the *Yamato*, would be the most powerful ship in the world, and sister ships were planned to follow. The Japanese Army and Navy air forces were not as large or as effective as they should have been for the task ahead. It is true that the Zero fighter was a good weapons system, but not as good as the best American aircraft available or just coming into service. The worst defect in the preparations for Japan's offensive strategy was the failure of the Army High Command to provide adequate forces to support it. Only 11 divisions were allocated to the new southern offensive, compared with 13 stationed in Manchuria and the 22 divisions bogged down in the war in China. There were, as will be seen shortly, other defects in Japan's preparations for the Pacific War, but the scanty military resources provided would be the most important influence on the initial offensive.

Planning for the Second World War 171

The opening attacks were as successful as even the most optimistic planners could have hoped. Nearly all the objectives were secured with minimum losses and maximum damage to the western allies. The US Fleet, except for the carrier element, was temporarily crippled at Pearl Harbor and the foolhardy British gesture of sending two capital ships without air cover to sea off Malaya was punished by the loss of both ships. When Japan's astonishing victories were complete her front line of defence stretched, as planned, from Burma through Singapore and the Dutch East Indies, then north to the Aleutian Islands. Her enemies were gravely weakened by their naval losses and the elimination of US forces in the Philippines and the British forces in Malaya and Singapore.

When they realised the extent of their success, the Japanese war leaders began to consider how these victories might be exploited. There seemed to be three obvious targets. 1) If Ceylon could be captured, the British fleet would be forced back to bases on the East African coast, and India itself would be open to amphibious attack. 2) If Australia could be occupied, the US would be denied the only practicable base from which to mount an offensive to retake the Philippines. 3) If Hawaii were captured, the US Pacific Fleet, however strongly reinforced, would be forced back to bases 3000 miles further away on the west coast of America. The Japanese Navy probably did not have the strength to mount all three offensives, but if Japan had attempted the third option and been successful, the conventional war against Japan would surely have lasted for one or perhaps two more years. Only the dropping of the atomic bombs on Hiroshima and Nagasaki, could have ended the war in 1945. If Ceylon had been captured and the Royal Navy forced back to bases in Africa, the course of the war against Germany might have been altered, since the supply route to British forces in the Middle East and a subsidiary route for supplies to Russia would have been in peril. It is fair to conclude that the results of further Japanese expansion beyond the limits set in her original plans could have had very significant effects on the war, though they would probably not have af-fected the final outcome.

As it was, the Army General Staff still dominated Japanese strategic thinking and their obsession with the war in China and the Russian threat from eastern Siberia prevented adequate military forces being released for any of these offensives. Instead the Japanese planned three, more modest, offensives and these were given inadequate army support and involved a dangerous dispersion of naval forces. The modified strategy involved: 1) an advance to Tulagi in the Solomon Islands and to Port Moresby in New Guinea, for which two of the available aircraft carriers were deployed; 2) the capture of Midway Island and the Aleutians and the elimination of the remaining American Pacific Fleet to which the last four serviceable carriers were allotted; and 3) further operations towards the New Hebrides Islands and Samoa, to cut communications between the US and Australia. These three simultaneous offensives required more troops than the Army was willing to deploy and worse still they entailed dividing their now limited carrier force. The dispersion of the carrier force was Japan's first fatal mistake.

The first of the three offensives, heading for northern Australia, was checked by a US fleet at the Battle of the Coral Sea. The second and probably more dangerous thrust, against Midway Island, was stopped by the main US Pacific Fleet in the desperately close-run Battle of Midway, in which the Japanese lost four carriers. All that was gained from this offensive to offset the loss were two of the Aleutian Islands. The offensive towards the New Hebrides was stopped in heavy fighting on and around the island of Guadalcanal. A larger force of Japanese troops could well have won the island; as it was they had to evacuate it. With their main carrier force shattered, the Japanese had no alternative after these checks to their amphibious offensives but to go on to the defensive. The tide was about to turn.

The American and the British counter-offensives, were equally inexorable; no ground which was regained (except in Burma) was ever lost again to the Japanese, although fierce resistance by the Japanese made every advance except the final one, a costly business. In the second half of 1942, two US offensives, one from Australia and one from Hawaii, began to get into their stride. With control of the air and the sea they could strike where they liked and the southern offensive from Australia developed the strategy of island-hopping, whereby the Japanese bases were neutralised, bypassed and left to 'wither on the vine', as the attacking US forces set up new bases further and further behind the intended perimeter defence of the Japanese 'Co-prosperity Sphere'. As the two American thrusts converged on the area of the Philippines, the Japanese suffered two more defeats; the first, the Battle of the Philippine Sea, lost the Marianas Islands to the Americans and after the second, at Leyte Gulf, the Philippines were lost as well. In 1944 the Japanese began a major offensive in China which succeeded in uniting their own forces in north and south China and cutting the area controlled by the Chinese into two halves. This success had no effect on the advances of the American forces which, after securing the Philippines, went on to capture Iwo Jima and Okinawa, the last two outposts before the Japanese islands themselves. The Japanese Army in China was redeployed along the coast of China to repel the expected American attacks, but the divisions in China could not be moved back to the homeland because the scale and variety of the US counter-offensive was showing up other weaknesses in Japanese preparations for war. Despite the fact that she depended more than any other country, even Great Britain, on the import of raw materials by sea, Japan's leaders had given little thought before her Pacific War to the defence either of the homeland or of the sea lanes leading to it. At sea the Japanese failed either to operate an efficient convoy system or to mount effective anti-submarine operations. In the air they had inadequate air defences and no force of bombers with the range to strike back at the bases from which the US were attacking the main cities of Japan. In consequence, by late 1944, the Japanese merchant navy had almost ceased to exist and her cities and industries were being devastated by US air attacks. Her leaders saw that continued resistance would bring ruin and were apparently ready to negotiate a surrender even before the two atom bombs were dropped. Japan was brought to defeat in 1945 by two strategic errors, for which the Army General Staff, the dominant force in Japanese strategic planning, should take the blame. First and most fundamentally, Japan ignored her most vulnerable point, her open maritime flank to the east, and failed to provide a balanced navy and air force to defend herself against attacks from that quarter. Her second mistake, once the war with the US and Britain had begun, was to fail to exploit her initial success by reaching out to Ceylon, Australia and Hawaii. Whatever her pre-war preparations, and however brilliant and foolproof her wartime strategy, Japan could not outfight the US and the other allied powers. A better pre-war strategic plan for her forces might have delayed the end for a year or two and perhaps have reduced Japanese losses, always assuming that atomic weapons had not been used against Japan.

THE UNITED STATES

The Japanese attack on Pearl Harbor and the almost simultaneous start of the war against Germany obviously posed a major strategic problem for the United States. As Maurice Matloff stresses, the early adoption in Allied discussions on strategy of the principle of beating Germany first was the most significant and controlling decision in Anglo-American policies in the Second World War. It was, in the light of what was known at the time, undoubtedly the correct decision to take in 1941–2, and hindsight provides no reason to alter that judgement. It was in effect a decision to give the US Army priority in the allocation of resources and one could not therefore expect the US Navy, burning to avenge defeats at the hands of the Japanese, to welcome it. If the war against Japan had been first priority the navy would have undoubtedly secured more of the available resources.

The 'Germany first' decision had in fact been discussed by the American and British Chiefs of Staff in early 1941, almost a year before Pearl Harbor; they took the view that in the event of the United States entering the war, Germany was likely to be the predominant member of any hostile coalition and that therefore the main Anglo-American effort should be directed against her. The combined Chiefs of Staff went on to advise that if Japan entered the war, the United States should remain on the strategic defensive in the Pacific until Germany had been defeated. After Pearl Harbor, Roosevelt and Churchill confirmed this strategy. For the former this was a politically courageous decision since the American public was likely to demand the early defeat of the nation whose stunning victories in the Pacific had humiliated the US armed forces. Had it been adopted, the risks of a 'Pacific first' strategy, would have been great: either or both of the European allies might have succumbed to Germany. The Soviet Union was still under tremendous pressure from the German Army and even if the Russian people survived this, their leaders might well have been prepared to negotiate a separate peace with Germany if they had realised that the US would not be coming to the rescue until Japan had been defeated. Great Britain was certainly not going to desert the United States and seek a separate peace but there was a real danger in early 1942 that she might be starved into submission by the U-boat attack on her Atlantic lifeline. There was another danger in leaving Germany until last. On past experience, it seemed likely to be Germany, rather than Japan, which would be most likely to make some scientific or technological discovery which might alter the course of the war. Hindsight would support this. Although it seems clear that German scientists were not about to produce an atomic bomb in 1945, the guided missiles and rockets which they did produce by then could have been far more destructive if there had been more time for their development. Finally a Russian assault on Japan from her bases in eastern Siberia might well prove to be a vital part of the final combined assault on the islands of Japan. It was inconceivable that the Soviet Union would agree to enter the war against Japan whilst she was still engaged in a life-and-death struggle against Germany. Nor for that matter could Great Britain disengage from the fight against Germany during 1942 and 1943 and turn her forces against Japan. Apart from the severe limitations on shipping, imposed by the need to keep the UK itself and her Middle East base in Egypt supplied, there was a real danger that if she relaxed her grip, Germany could inflict serious defeats upon her either in the Atlantic or in the Middle East.

Planning for the Second World War 175

It was one thing to decide on the correct strategy, but quite another to find unanimity within the service establishment about how it should be interpreted and implemented. The US Navy had to take second place under the 'Germany first' strategy and her commanders were constantly arguing for more resources and being tardy to release for service in Europe those ships and aircraft whose production or allocation they controlled. The whole debate about what goes where was complicated by the fact that early Japanese victories in the Pacific had to be curbed. Indeed from the end of 1941 until mid-1943 the bulk of servicemen and supplies sent overseas went to the Pacific theatre. Thereafter shipments to Europe predominated but even as late as December 1943, two years after Pearl Harbor, America's military and naval strength was almost equally divided between the European and the Pacific theatres. There were several reasons for this; the most important has already been mentioned. The Japanese tide seemed about to overwhelm both Australia and the Hawaiian Islands, both essential bases from which the United States would have to launch its counter-offensive. Naval and military reinforcements had to be despatched to protect these bases, and even if this had not been justified on military grounds there is little doubt that American public opinion, perhaps discreetly encouraged by the naval lobby, would have forced some such step on her leaders. Another argument for further support for the Pacific which greatly impressed President Roosevelt was the need to prevent the military collapse of China. The US had always had great sympathy for China, even before the Japanese attack, and naturally desired to help the innocent victim of unprovoked aggression. Quite apart from this understandable sentiment was the conviction that, properly supported, China could play a key role in the final assault on Japan. This chimera of China emerging as a great power obsessed many in America, not least the President himself. Nothing came of it and the Allies got a poor return for all the military supplies which they sent at great cost and effort to China. The Chinese Nationalist leaders were more concerned to buttress their position against their Communist rivals than to win victories over the Japanese. The war in China admittedly embroiled much of the Japanese Army, but this was due more to the nature of the country itself and the relatively disorganised resistance of the Chinese forces (both nationalist and Communist) than to regular set-piece offensives by the Nationalist army supplied with American weapons.

These early reinforcements of the Pacific theatre succeeded in stemming the Japanese advance, with notable victories being won at Midway Island, on Guadalcanal and elsewhere. These successes inevitably brought pressure for more reinforcements to exploit what had already been achieved. The arguments of a victorious commander pressing for the means to achieve yet more victories are some of the most difficult for a civilian politician to resist and Admiral Nimitz and General MacArthur were not commanders who would let their case go by default. It had always been assumed by the planners in Washington that the bulk of the US Navy and Marines would be deployed in the Pacific, but in the event many more troops and aircraft and more specialised equipment were committed there than were originally intended. Consequently, despite the immense superiority of Allied armaments production (a reliable estimate made later by Wagenfuhr and quoted by Paul Kennedy puts it at three times larger than that of the Axis powers), the pull of the war in the Pacific led to shortages of shipping, amphibious landing craft, long-range maritime aircraft and troops for the European theatre. These shortages were not crippling in their overall effect but we must now consider whether the war in Europe could have been won in 1944 if these deficiencies had not existed.

It was clear to all concerned that the Battle of the Atlantic had to be won by the Allies before US troops and their supplies could be moved to Europe in sufficient quantities to invade the Continent and finish the war against Germany. The Battle itself could have been said to have started in 1939 with the outbreak of war between Britain and Germany. The attempt to blockade Britain using submarines to sink merchant shipping had been made in the First World War when it nearly succeeded. In the Second World War the battle was even more intense, and after 1940 the U-boat fleet had the great advantage of bases in French ports on the Atlantic coast. The advantage in the battle went first to one side and then to the other, but the heaviest shipping losses and the real crisis came after the United States had entered the war. The initial increase in the number of ships sunk was mainly due to the reluctance of the US Navy Department to introduce a convoy system off the east coast of the US. Shipping losses reached alarming levels before the Navy Department changed its mind, with the inevitable result that the build-up in Europe was delayed.

However, the more serious long-term threat to the main Allied supply route came from the new U-boat tactics in operation in the mid-Atlantic in 1942. Thanks to the breaking of the Royal Navy's convoy code by German signals experts, 'wolf-packs' of U-boats were able to locate escorted convoys, pursue them on the surface where the U-boat was faster than the convoy and then attack with torpedoes when submerged. As the crisis approached in November 1942, 120 U-boats sank 50 000 tons of shipping. Exceptionally bad weather in the Atlantic halved sinkings in the following two months but in February 1943 300 000 tons were sunk and in March 476 000 tons, most of the losses being of ships in convoy. It looked as though wolf-pack tactics aided by the deciphering of the convoy codes had beaten the well-tried system of convoy protection. The British Admiralty were seriously considering the possibility of dispensing with convoys and reverting to individual sailings. The apparent U-boat victory was, however, illusory.

An essential part of any victory over the U-boat had to be the shipping replacement rate and by the start of 1943 it was rising to meet losses so that by the end of the year all ships lost since 1939 would have been replaced by larger and better craft. However, it was becoming clear that the most effective way of combating the U-boat menace was by using air power. Aircraft could reconnoitre the sea around the convoys and attack the U-boat wolf-packs when sighted on the surface. Successful attacks reduced the U-boat fleet, but even if the attacks failed they forced the U-boats to submerge and their reduced underwater speed made it impossible for the U-boats to catch up with a convoy. The complementary surface weapon for aircraft was the Support Group, a small flotilla of anti-submarine craft. These were not tied to convoy-escort duties and were therefore able to seek out the wolf-packs of U-boats and continue attacks long after the aircraft had had to return to base for lack of fuel. These groups were immensely valuable, yet such was the shortage of suitable ships for them that one group had to be disbanded after only two months in action.

The supply of anti-submarine aircraft was equally discouraging for those admirals and air marshals fighting the U-boats. Escort carriers built to carry 20 anti-submarine aircraft were becoming available in 1943 but not in 1942 when the crisis began. The main requirement for the anti-submarine campaign was undoubtedly the long-range four-engine aircraft with radar, searchlights and effective depth charges, capable of long-range patrols and of finding and attacking submarines in all possible weathers. Of these only one, the Very Long Range Liberator, could reach mid-Atlantic and thus close the 'mid-Atlantic gap' where the U-boats operated most freely. Admiral King, the US Chief of Naval Staff was intensely reluctant to release Liberators for this work. One former Commander-in-Chief of Coastal Command, speaking more generally after the event, is quoted as saying, 'Admiral King's obsession with the Pacific cost us dear in the Battle of the Atlantic.' VLR Liberator squadrons were at last deployed in Newfoundland in March 1943 and escort carriers were allotted to convoys. The number of the same aircraft type available to RAF Coastal Command in the UK was also increased from five in August 1942 to 14 in February in 1943. The Atlantic gap in air cover for convoys was finally closed and by May the results were apparent. U-boat losses in that month were 43, inflicted at a ratio of about 3:2 between aircraft and surface escorts. These losses exceeded the replacement rate by more than twice and Admiral Dönitz, the German Naval Chief of Staff, withdrew his U-boats from the Atlantic, conceding in his memoirs that this marked defeat in the Battle of the Atlantic.

There is a strong case for thinking that the Battle of the Atlantic could have been won earlier if more of the right resources had been allocated to it. The key items were few, Very Long Range Liberator Aircraft, escort carriers, destroyers and corvettes. Only a few more were needed in each category. The Liberators provided the most crucial assistance and the C-in-C of RAF Coastal Command at the time has stated that the battle was won by the middle of 1943 with less than 50 of these aircraft, all in RAF squadrons except for six in a Royal Canadian Air Force squadron in Newfoundland. At the start of 1943, when the situation was desperate, the US Navy had 52 of these aircraft (the US Army also had some), but even by February only the 18 under RAF command or control, were deployed to fight U-boats in the Atlantic. In the absence of any other role as crucial as the commitment to the Atlantic battle, the deployment of US Navy Liberators (available towards the end of 1942) could have thwarted the U-boat attack earlier in 1943.

If victory in the Battle of the Atlantic had come six months earlier than mid-1943, men and materials for the invasion of Europe could have arrived in Britain and North Africa that much sooner, but it is certainly not self-evident that this would have advanced the defeat of Germany, say to the autumn of 1944. Indeed, the earlier arrival of the forces earmarked for the invasion could have been disastrous if it had tempted American commanders to insist on the invasion taking place in late 1943. There is no reason to believe that it would have been easier if it had been attempted then; the troops would have been less well trained; the air attacks against the so-called invasion targets would have been less well advanced; and the logistic preparations in Britain would not have been complete. However, there may be a case for saying that if the Allied commanders in Europe had more resources at their disposal, both because the Atlantic battle had been won sooner (and the build-up of resources for the invasion had started sooner), and because the priority of the European theatre had been recognised more consistently in the allocation of scarce resources (such as infantry divisions and landing craft for amphibious operations), the war in Europe could have been won in 1944. This would have been possible, so the argument would run, because the Allies would have been able to take advantage of one of the two so-called 'missed opportunities' in the European theatre in 1944.

The most well-known of these is probably General Eisenhower's refusal in August 1944 to sanction the proposal by General Montgomery for a single thrust from France to the Ruhr by 21st Army Group with some reinforcement of US troops in order to take advantage of the complete defeat of the German armies in France. Eisenhower judged that Montgomery's plan was ruled out on logistic grounds until German troops had been cleared from the mouth of the River Scheldt so that the sea approaches to Antwerp would be cleared and the port there available for use. In the light of the recent study by Martin van Creveld it seems fairly clear that an advance to the Ruhr, with supply lines stretching back to the Normandy beaches, would have been likely to fail for lack of supplies. If Antwerp had been available as a port the problem of supply would have been soluble but the sea approaches were not cleared until Walcheren island was taken in November 1944, by which time the chance of a single thrust to the Ruhr was long gone. In any case, the merits and demerits of Montgomery's proposal are not really relevant to the present discussion. It is plain that the resources and manpower needed were available either on the Continent or in Britain. The plan was not implemented because American troops and supplies were being sent to the Pacific theatre rather than Europe.

The second so-called lost opportunity of the war in the west arose during the Italian campaign. The US Chiefs of Staff and the President agreed with great reluctance to the invasion of the mainland of Italy in September 1943 because they feared that it would divert resources from the all-important cross-Channel assault on France planned for 1944. Just as the Allies landed in Normandy in 1944, the Allied armies in Italy broke the German front, captured Rome, and drove the opposing German forces north in great disorder. Finally, German troops stabilised a line in the Appennines covering the Po valley. Allied attacks on it during September failed to break through before winter stopped further progress. The offensive was resumed in April 1945 and within three weeks the line was broken and all German forces in Italy surrendered.

The achievement of the Allied armies is all the more remarkable when one realises that after the capture of Rome they lost seven divisions (four French and three American) and numerous landing craft which were required for the invasion of southern France in August 1944. This subsidiary in-vasion had long been planned as support for the Normandy landings when the outcome of these could not be known. In the event the southern invasion had no effect on the battle in the north where the breakout from Normandy was already assured. However the departure of these divisions drastically altered the situation in Italy. When the German army started its retreat north from Rome it numbered 14 divisions as against 21 Allied divisions in pursuit. When the Germans reached their defences in the Appennines they had 26 divisions whereas the Allies had only 21. It is true that many of the German divisions were under strength and short of equipment but they were in strong defensive positions and the chance of an Allied break-through was much reduced by the transfer of seven divisions to southern France. Of course the agreed strategic objective for the Italian campaign was to divert as many German divisions from the main front, in north-west Europe, but strategy should be adapted to take advantage of any opportunity. If some of the troops and landing craft destined for southern France could have been retained in Italy and further divisions deployed there instead of to South East Asia or the Pacific, there would have been an excellent chance for the Allied armies in Italy to defeat the German armies opposed to them before they reached their defences in the Appennines. An amphibious landing on the Istrian Peninsula to seize Trieste might then have opened the way for a thrust through the Ljubljana gap, with Vienna as the ultimate objective.

It would still be open to question whether victory on this scale would have ended the war in Europe in 1944. A comparison with the Salonika campaign in the First World War may prove helpful. An Allied army had landed in Salonika in 1915 but for three years it failed to make any headway against the defences manned by the army of the Central Powers in the mountains between Greece and Serbia. Finally in 1918 the Allied army broke through these mountain defences and their subsequent advance, which was virtually unopposed, was only halted by the Armistice in November of that year. As Sir Winston Churchill later wrote, referring to arguments during the war about the value of the Salonika campaign, 'The controversies were silenced by the remarkable fact that it was upon this much abused front that the collapse of the Central Empires first began.' An encircled nation down to its last few reserves may find that a break anywhere in the front line, nor necessarily in one of the most important sectors, can bring total collapse. The parallel with Italy seems close.

In August 1944 General Maitland Wilson, the Supreme Commander in the Mediterranean, proposed that the seven Divisions destined for southern France should be retained in Italy for a thrust into the Po valley supported by an amphibious landing on the Istrian Peninsula. With hindsight it is plain that such a move – reinforced in the way suggested – could well have exploited the very favourable situation created by the Russian victories in the Balkans. By early September Russian troops had occupied Romania and moved into Bulgaria. By mid-October they had joined Tito's partisans in Belgrade. By this time, not surprisingly, they had outstripped their supply lines, and obvious logistic difficulties dictated that the next Russian offensive should be on their central front, directed at Berlin. If an Allied offensive from north-eastern Italy based on Trietse could have moved through the Ljubljana gap it would have found its advance into southern Austria and Hungary facing very weak resistance, a re-run of the Salonika campaign. A strategic prize of great value, including many arms factories could have been taken. Maitland Wilson's proposals were rejected. As has already been mentioned they were certainly contrary to the strategic aim of the Italian campaign and there was a severe shortage of trained infantry divisions, to say nothing of landing-craft, so the rejection may not have surprised the Allied commanders in Italy. Underlying these objections were political reasons. The American leaders were determined not to get mixed up in Balkan campaigns and Balkan politics. The Russians for their part were determined to liberate and occupy the Balkans themselves; Allied troops in possession of part of them would be an inconvenience, to say the least. Apart from those on the spot, military opinion has not favoured this extension of the Italian campaign, either at the time or since, and its British official historian has produced strong arguments against the 'Trieste option', but they tend to take the strength of the Allied forces in the European theatre as given and on this basis the arguments could be sound. However, if the resources for both the European and the Pacific, including the South East Asian theatres of war are taken together, there is at least a good case for arguing that if extra divisions and landing-craft had been deployed in Italy, a thrust through the Ljubljana gap could have ended the war in the west in 1944.

Such a transfer of resources need not have delayed the defeat of Japan (with or without the use of atomic bombs) for, as John Ellis argues in *Brute Force*, the bitter rivalry between the US Army and Navy forced the United States and its allies to accept two major offensives across the Pacific where one would have been enough. Neither Service would agree to a Pacific strategy in which the other would predominate and hence secure the overall command. Consequently President Roosevelt had to agree that General MacArthur and his army forces should attack from Australia towards the Philippines while the US Navy and Marine Corps advanced island by island across the central Pacific. Either offensive would have been enough to secure the defeat of the Japanese whose air, naval, and merchant marine losses were so serious by 1944 that they would have been unable to re-deploy their scattered forces to meet the US attack. Ellis considers that the southern offensive under MacArthur should have been chosen, but others might argue that a thrust across the central Pacific would have been the better option as it would have secured bases from which US bombers could reach Japan. There is clearly room for debate here which should also question whether the troops and landing craft assembled in India in 1944 for the invasion of Malaya in the following year could not have been better employed in Europe. If it is accepted that amphibious ships and troops in India and the Pacific could have been spared for Europe in 1943–44, the theory that they would have been better deployed on the Italian front may be well founded. Bearing in mind the communications and logistics available on the various Allied fronts in the second half of 1944, it was the only place where with more forces the Allies might have ended the war against Germany.

IN RETROSPECT

It is now clear that in the Second World War Germany, Britain and Japan all made serious mistakes in the allocation of resources between land, sea and air forces Since it has normally taken many years to develop and manufacture new weapons systems in the twentieth century, it was not always possible for nations at war to rectify the mistakes made in peace. In previous centuries it had been possible to re-equip a neglected navy, as Britain did during the later years of the American War of Independence, but it might have been impossible, even if those concerned had wished it, to re-shape RAF Bomber Command into a tactical or a daylight bomber force in time, when its limitations as a precision bomber force became apparent in 1941. If the weapons had been available, they could have been used for different purposes to those originally contemplated. Some of the excellent fighters produced by both sides for air superiority operations became with modification long-range bomber escorts or ground-attack aircraft, with excellent results. Similarly, the Liberator bomber, when modified for the anti-submarine role, became the mainstay of the Allies in the Battle of the Atlantic. Not all the combatant nations were able to make up for lost time in all areas of tactics and technology. Britain and the US always seemed to be a generation behind the Germans in the design of tanks and the Japanese never mastered the problems of anti-submarine warfare.

It is remarkable how many of the victory-winning ideas and equipment were not supported at the outset by the High Commands of the services which produced them. The British Air Ministry was admirably quick to perfect radar and combine it into an effective air defence system, but was undoubtedly slow to draw the further conclusion that effective air defence based on radar might (as it eventually did) limit the effectiveness of the bomber force which they were building. The Imperial Japanese Navy Command were not wholly wedded to the concept of the fleet aircraft carriers until after Pearl Harbor and consequently wasted resources on super-battle-ships like the *Yamato*, which never fired its main armament against enemy ships and was sunk by enemy aircraft. A similar fate awaited the *Tirpitz*, a monument to the German Admiralty's fascination with battle-ships when resources should have been concentrated on building U-boats. Dönitz, the German commander, required 300 U-boats to maintain an effective attack at all times on the North Atlantic shipping routes. Fortunately for the Allies he was not able to deploy a force of this size until July 1942. The Luftwaffe was well prepared with aircraft for obtaining air superiority over the battlefield and was ready thereafter to support the army but it was not so well served at Command and staff levels at the outset. It was perhaps for this reason that in July 1940 when it had the best opportunity for independent action (delivering a knock-out blow from the air against Britain) which any air force was ever to have before the coming of nuclear weapons, it had neither the doctrine nor the techniques to take advantage of it. The chance of total and swift victory over France was not foreseen and in any case if the Luftwaffe had been trained for the knock-out blow it might not have been so effective in its role of supporting Blitzkrieg. The prewar planning of the Luftwaffe is marred by one serious failure. Practically no thought was given to cooperation with the navy largely because, it is said, Goering, Head of the Luftwaffe and Raeder, his opposite number in the German Navy, were hardly on speaking terms.

Another feature of the pre-war planning is the lack of clear guidance which the service planners received on their country's political objectives or strategic aims. The German services had expected the coming war to be fought in the east and they were not ready for a long war in 1939 against the western powers, France and Great Britain. The British services chiefs were prepared from the start of rearmament to regard Germany as the main enemy but emphasised that it was beyond Britain's capacity to fight Italy and Japan as well. This advice was no doubt heeded but it was certainly hard to act upon. However, the British government should surely have accepted much sooner that if France was to be Britain's ally (and there was no one else) Britain would surely have to promise to commit troops to the Continent of Europe to secure a French alliance. The leaders of the Japanese army and navy were so politically influential that they could reasonably be regarded as the government. In that case they have only themselves to blame for getting so entangled in China that they could neither withdraw or disengage without loss of face, nor even find the additional resources to secure the nearby sources of raw materials for continuing the war. In some ways the US might seem to have been the least prepared of all the combatant nations, since she lost the use of a major part of her fleet in the first few minutes of the surprise attack which brought her into the war. However, even if her tactical surprise was complete, the pre-December 1941 discussions between the American and British Chiefs of Staff about strategy meant that when war came to the US her leaders had good advice and followed it. Germany was defeated first and the decline and defeat of Japan followed quickly after, partly because of the final technological surprise of the war, the atom bomb. The effect which this would have on all future strategic choices is the subject of the next chapter.

8 The Cold War – and After?

When atomic bombs were dropped on Hiroshima and Nagasaki the map of strategic choices was changed for all time. The knock-out blow from the air that Britain and other countries had feared in the 1930s and which Britain above all others had tried to deliver during the war that followed was now undoubtedly possible. The third strategic choice, 'air' was clearly now an option in its own right as an offensive weapon for some nations while many others would have to consider whether potential enemies possessed a nuclear capability and if so how they could be deterred from using it. The two strongest powers to emerge from the Second World War, the US and the USSR, could not realistically reject the nuclear option. Each felt that it had to have nuclear weapons to be secure from the other. Another group of powers, which could call on the necessary knowledge and skills, acquired these weapons because of their distrust of one or other of the Superpowers, as the US and the USSR came to be called. This group included Britain, France and China. As time went on a further, less definable group of powers, involved in various regional conflicts, have considered the nuclear option as a final weapon to avoid defeat at the hands of their opponents. Israel, India, Pakistan, Iraq and South Africa come into this category, but the extent to which any of them have produced nuclear weapons has been kept secret by the nations concerned.

AFTER THE SECOND WORLD WAR

All of this was unimaginable in 1945 when even the concept of a Cold War between Superpowers armed with nuclear weapons was unknown. Now in the 1990s, when one by one of the states of Eastern Europe, which have been more or less under Russian control since 1945, are apparently rejecting Communism and trying to reassert their independence, the Cold War may indeed be over, as even Russia herself appears to be rejecting Marxism and seeking a new relationship with the West. Whatever the outcome of these almost incredible and wholly unforeseen events, it is surely a good time to study some of the strategic choices made by one of the Superpowers during the nuclear age, that is since the Second World War. Inevitably, the US is the subject of this study, as apart from anything else, the Russian archives are not available to historians to anything like the same extent. There is another good reason for studying the US rather than the USSR, and that is that the former faced a strategic dilemma which did not trouble the latter. In 1946 and 1947 when the US leaders confronted the fact that their country faced a threat from the Soviet Union and its allies they realised that they could not afford to let Europe outside the Communist bloc, or Japan fall under Soviet control and that US strategy could not in consequence be confined to the defence of North and South America. The defence of Japan posed fewer problems for the US since the sea imposes a barrier to the Soviet army but in Europe no such water barrier exists (at least until the English Channel is reached) and US security policy had, for the last 40 years of the Cold War, to combine the security of the North American continent with maintaining the integrity of that tip of the Eurasian land mass known as Western Europe.

At the end of the Second World War the US had three simple foreign policy objectives: 1) to work through the United Nations to solve international problems; 2) to reach some sort of understanding with the USSR in order to establish some sort of *modus vivendi*; 3) to rely on Britain to resume her pre-war role as peacekeeper in those areas of the world where she was strong and the US weak. These would include the Eastern Mediterranean, the Middle East, the Indian Ocean and parts of South East Asia. By 1947 all three objectives were proving inadequate as a basis for foreign policy. The UN was already showing that as an organisation it could not succeed where the League of Nations had failed, and the USSR seemed to be unwilling to limit her territorial expansion. It was Britain, the third leg of US policy, which gave way first. In early 1947 Britain had to tell her ally that she was unable, in view of her desperate financial position, to continue to provide the resources which Greece and Turkey needed to resist pressure from the Soviet Union. It was high time for the United States to reassess her foreign policy. The foundation for this had been prepared by George Kennan, a US diplomat with experience of Russia, who was serving in 1946 with the US Embassy in Moscow. From there he sent the 'Long Telegram' (as it was later dubbed) which reminded the State Department of the continued and deep-seated hostility of the Communist USSR towards the capitalist US and warned of the dangers of 'chumming up' to the Soviet Union. Later Kennan wrote an article based on the telegram, stressing the need for 'a long-term, patient but firm and vigilant containment of Russian expansive tendencies' and thereafter 'containment' has been used to describe this doctrine, which despite apparent differences between the attitudes and actions of succeeding US Presidents, has been the cornerstone of the foreign policy and national strategy towards the USSR in the years between Stalin's expansion in 1947 and after to until Gorbachev's more conciliatory stance.

THE COLD WAR

A change of policy along the lines which Kennan proposed was established when President Truman asked Congress to vote funds to support Greece and Turkey. His address to Congress contained the following: 'I believe that it must be the policy of the United States to support free peoples who are resisting attempted subjugation by armed minorities or outside pressures', and this became the basis of the Truman Doctrine. There are several important points to note about the interrelationship of containment and the Truman Doctrine. First, neither could be described as military strategies directing preparations for war. Kennan himself believed at the time that the Soviet Union had no intention of starting another general war and that military force was not a proper instrument for containment. In 1947 US leaders believed that the main danger was that Western Europe, which was on the verge of economic collapse, would fall to Russian – directed communist subversion, rather than to military invasion. Secondly, containment was not seen as a universal strategy. Kennan had suggested that there were only five regions of the world where the sinews of modern military strength could be produced in quantity. These were the US, the UK, the USSR, the industrial area of the Rhine Valley, and Japan. Only one of these, he pointed out, was under Soviet control, and the main task of containment was to ensure that none of the others fell into Russian hands. However, to secure Congressional approval to the novel policy of US aid to distant countries in time of peace, Truman felt it necessary to preach a crusade against Communism. A 'particularist' foreign policy, designed to ensure that no one country, or group of countries, could become strong enough to threaten the US, was eventually transformed, despite Kennan, into a 'universalist' policy which seemed occasionally in later years to be based on the premise that the US could not be secure unless she controlled the world. President Truman's espousal of containment undoubtedly saved Europe from collapse, but his own Truman Doctrine must bear some responsibility for US involvement in Vietnam. Finally, and most remarkably, the strategy of containment was based, in the author's mind, on the conviction that the Soviet Union would not be able in the long term to hold down Eastern Europe and that Soviet Communism carried within itself the seeds of its own decay. Kennan identified nationalism as one of the main forces which would destroy Soviet hegemony in Eastern Europe and the events of 1989 seem to have proved him right. It is less clear that he foresaw the inherent weakness of the economic system which would force Soviet Communism to relax its grip on its Warsaw Pact allies in the first place. However, few can claim to have read the future of Soviet Communism so successfully as the original author of the containment strategy.

The first fruits of containment were economic and military aid to Greece and Turkey, as a result of which the former was able eventually to crush the Communist-inspired revolt, and the latter was encouraged to resist Soviet pressure for greater naval access to the Mediterranean. This was followed in 1947/48 by the Marshall Plan, which created the conditions for the dramatic recovery of Western Europe. However, growing fears in Western Europe about the military strength of Soviet Russia made it inevitable that containment would require a military as well as an economic strategy. These fears were not unreasonable after the communist coup in Czechoslovakia in 1948 and the Soviet Union's attempt to expel the Western Allies from Berlin by a blockade lasting 324 days. The nations of Western Europe, whose economies were now recovering, began to consider re-arming for collective defence. Eventually, in 1949, the North Atlantic Treaty was signed, bringing the US and the Western European nations, including West Germany, into formal alliance. It had been thought that the European Allies would provide the bulk of the conventional forces to defend Western Europe against attack from the east, with the US atomic bomb in the background as a weapon of last resort. The explosion of the first Russian atomic bomb in 1949 destroyed this strategy overnight. US military leaders had advised that the US monopoly was safe for five or more years; now they had to accept that within a short time the Soviet Union could secure something like parity with the US in atomic weapons. The United States decided that the best use she could make of her temporary advantage would be to build up NATO conventional forces, so that by the time there was nuclear parity between the US and the USSR, NATO would be able to resist conventional attack from the Soviet Union. The only means of delivering atom bombs to their targets at the time was by aircraft: the US, with bases available in Europe, was better placed than the USSR to threaten nuclear war. Two further events destroyed this assumption. The announcement of the first Russian H-bomb in 1953 (a year after the US H-bomb) showed that an incomparably more destructive weapon would shortly be available and by the next year it was becoming clear that the USSR was creating a force of heavy bombers with which to launch nuclear strikes directly at the US itself. The current NATO strategy was failing for another reason; Western

Europe was unwilling, or perhaps unable, to mount the effort to produce and equip conventional forces large enough to deter a conventional attack by the Soviet bloc. It was clearly time to re-think US and NATO strategy and the incoming US President and his Secretary of State were ready and willing to do this.

The US Joint Chiefs of Staff developed the New Look strategy in 1953, with an initial contribution from the British Chief of Air Staff, who had been one of the air staff planning the RAF bomber offensive before the Second World War. The new strategy stemmed from a growing realisation in both Britain and the US that it was going to be too expensive for the democratic countries of the West to match the conventional forces of the totalitarian countries of the Eastern bloc in peacetime. It also owed something to the realisation that an essentially defensive and reactive strategy put the West at a disadvantage against an aggressive Soviet Union. The new policy, looking to the long term, stressed that it was essential to maintain 1) a strong military position with the capability of inflicting massive retaliatory damage by offensive striking power; 2) US and Allied forces in readiness to move rapidly to counter Soviet aggression and to defend vital areas; 3) a mobilisation base protected against crippling damage. The Chiefs of Staff policy paper used the phrase 'massive retaliation' which became well-known later in connection with deterring a general war including an assault on Western Europe. Part at least of the retaliatory damage inflicted on the aggressor was to be achieved by using nuclear weapons tactically to offset the smaller number of NATO divisions in the battle zone. Whatever the original intentions of the Chiefs of Staff, repeated pronouncements by US leaders, particularly by President Eisenhower's Secretary of State, J. F. Dulles, shaped NATO strategy somewhat differently. All concerned became convinced that NATO could never match the conventional forces of the USSR and her Warsaw Pact allies and consequently the US troops in Europe were there not as a shield with a nuclear capability to be used in the last resort, but as a trip-wire to trigger a nuclear response. The budgetary effects of the New Look strategy were welcomed in the US. The growth in expenditure on conventional army and naval forces was stopped but there was a continued build-up of the US Air Force.

The New Look remained official doctrine from 1953 until the Kennedy administration took over in 1961. By 1957 it had become clear from monitoring by the US of Soviet missile tests, as well as the appearance of the *Sputnik* rocket over the US, that the USSR had intercontinental rockets which could reach America. The cost of massive retaliation by the US against Soviet aggression was likely to be an equally devastating counter-strike by the aggressor. A number of different influences came together to persuade the incoming administration that it was time for a change. The European Allies and NATO Commanders were becoming sceptical about the willingness of the US to risk total destruction from nuclear armed rockets as a result of mounting a nuclear response to a minor incursion, or series of incursions, by Warsaw Pact forces in Europe. These doubts were taken up by the US Army and Navy, who were becoming alarmed as the Air Force continued to receive the major share of the defence budget and all roles for conventional forces seemed to have become peripheral. In addition, a number of scholars, such as Robert Osgood, Henry Kissinger and Bernard Brodie, were analysing nuclear war, which led them to question the New Look and examine the possibilities of limited nuclear war. As a result, US nuclear strategy was revised to accept that the most stable balance of terror in the nuclear age was likely to be based on a recognition by both sides of Mutual Assured Destruction once nuclear weapons were used. The evolution of nuclear strategy and continuing progress towards a measure of nuclear disarmament need not be discussed here, but the changes to NATO doctrine are all important for this chapter, which aims to show how the US balanced nuclear and conventional forces in the defence of Europe. The strategy of Flexible Response was put forward by US Army Chiefs of Staff Ridgeway and Maxwell Taylor and after acceptance by the US became official NATO policy in 1967. It has remained so until the present. When it was adopted it was stated that there would be a 'flexible and balanced range of appropriate responses, conventional and nuclear, to all levels of aggression and threats of aggression'. The statement went on to promise that 'should aggression occur, these responses would maintain the security of the North Atlantic Treaty Area within the concept of forward defence'. Perhaps this is not so much a strategy for war as a catch-all formula for reconciling opposing and probably irreconcilable objectives, but it has stood the test of time (if not that of war) and is worth more attention for that reason alone.

 When tactical nuclear weapons became available between 1953 and 1955 for delivery by either artillery, aircraft or guided missiles it became necessary for NATO to agree a military doctrine for their use. This became all the more urgent when it became clear that the US was prepared to make them available, with suitable safeguards, to certain European members of NATO to support their conventional forces. The weapons were assimilated, into the New Look strategy, as they were seen as a useful means of inflicting massive retaliation on the conventional forces of an aggressor, but the arrival of the strategy of Flexible Response gave a far more important role to tactical nuclear weapons. They were seen as a vitally important first step on the ladder of escalation, punishing the aggressor by inflicting heavy losses on his conventional forces without going to the ultimate step of destroying his cities. The difficulties soon began to present themselves. From the military point of view there was the objection that if the conventionally weaker side resorted to tactical nuclear weapons, when its own forces were struggling in the conventional battle, it would risk their complete destruction by the tactical nuclear weapons of the enemy without any countervailing advantage. From the political point of view the German reaction had to be considered most carefully. For the Germans any tactical nuclear weapon could be seen as strategic, since it would almost certainly land on German soil and was likely to kill or maim many German civilians. As time went on, NATO reached some consensus that tactical nuclear weapons were indeed a useful additional rung on the ladder of escalation and would certainly complicate the calculations of a Soviet aggressor about the consequences of an attack on NATO territory. Some within NATO thought that one weapon could be exploded as a warning that, unless the conventional attack was halted, all-out nuclear war would begin. Others argued that if the first use of nuclear weapons was a small tactical weapon it would not be seriously regarded as a warning by an aggressor, indeed in the confusion of a battle it might not be distinguishable from conventional weapons. There could be no public resolution of this argument over use, since the essence of Flexible Response as a strategy is to conceal from a potential aggressor what particular response would be made to any aggressive act.

Tactical nuclear weapons therefore became part of the nuclear armoury of NATO and were made available by the US under a 'two-key' arrangement to other NATO allies, all of whom no doubt recognised tacitly that possession of them was a relatively inexpensive means of redressing some of the imbalance between the conventional forces of NATO and the Warsaw Pact. It became clear in time that the number available in Europe far exceeded what could sensibly be used under any recognised NATO strategy and in the 1980s moves were made to secure some reduction, by both sides if possible.

It has to be accepted that the US has always had a particular difficulty in adapting a deterrent strategy to her foreign policy goals, a difficulty which was not faced by her adversary, the USSR. Since one of the principal objectives of containment was (and is) to keep Western Europe free from Soviet control, the United States has had to operate a policy of extended deterrence; that is, the threat of nuclear retaliation had to cover both incursions into her own territory and also those of her European allies thousands of miles away across the Atlantic. When the New Look trip-wire strategy failed to reassure the European part of the NATO alliance, the US had to change to a new strategy of which Flexible Response was, and is, a part. Since this NATO strategy has remained in force for more than 20 years during which there has been peace in Europe, it could perhaps be counted a success. It does, however, embrace, without concealing them, at least two contradictions. First, as Laurence Freedman points out, with regard to nuclear strategy as a whole, we have now reached a position where 'stability depends on something that is more the antithesis of strategy than its apotheosis – on threats that things will get out of hand, that we might act irrationally, that inadvertently we could set in motion a process that in its development and conclusion would be beyond human control and comprehension'. With this paradox in mind we can still ask whether Flexible Response represents a wise allocation of defence resources in the context of Superpower confrontation.

This brings us to the second contradiction in the strategy. As the policy statement already quoted makes clear, NATO threatens to operate a range of responses within the concept of forward defence. In other words, in order to limit any Soviet incursion into the territory of its German ally to the very minimum, NATO is prepared to forgo the advantage, familiar to military strategists throughout history, of giving up space to exhaust an attacker before launching a counter-attack. This is the price paid by the US for an alliance with Germany which provides the largest and most readily available army in Western Europe. Despite the abandonment of the trip-wire strategy, the US has had to change to something with some of the same features in order to obtain the conventional forces to operate the strategy of Flexible Response.

It seems, then, that the US has to risk the destruction of her homeland (and no doubt the planet) to contain Soviet expansion. Yet it is hard to see an alternative, credible strategy which would have stilled European doubts about the US commitment to European defence. If Europe could or would not produce sufficient conventional forces to ward off a conventional Soviet attack, sooner or later the US would have had to introduce nuclear weapons into the balance.

This is not to argue, however, that the United States made the correct distribution of her resources to maintain extended deterrence. If in 1989 both Superpowers were prepared to reduce their arsenals of intercontinental nuclear missiles by about half, subject to satisfactory verification, then one is bound to ask why stocks of these weapons were so large in the first place. The overprovision can be explained – at least in part – without plunging too far into the detail of US nuclear strategy. One obvious factor was the missile race between the two Superpowers, each trying to outbuild the other on the basis of previous arms races (such as the Anglo-German naval race before 1914), convinced that superiority meant security. The analogy was and is false on two counts. First and most obviously, missiles are not so public as battleships; they can be (and were) concealed, so that even with intelligence from satellites there were doubts as to how many nuclear missiles the enemy had. There have been at least two occasions when public opinion in the US has been misled into believing that the USSR had secured a dangerous lead in either bombers or intercontinental missiles over the US. In both cases the belief in US inferiority was false, but the effort to close the non-existent gap lead to increased US efforts which the USSR felt bound to match; the increases in missile numbers on either side did not bring increased security.

There was also another and deeper problem in the matter of nuclear security which is best illustrated by the US approach to the question 'How much is enough?' As Laurence Freedman writes, 'No single public figure has influenced the way we think about nuclear weapons quite so much as Robert S. McNamara', who was Secretary of Defense under Presidents Kennedy and Johnson. Not only did he introduce many new concepts about nuclear strategy but he set the overall numbers of intercontinental and submarine-launched missiles at levels (ICBM 1054 and SLBM 656) which lasted until 1980. It is interesting to see how this was done, according to Alain Enthoven, one of his systems analysts. An early study based on the approach of Systems Analysis, which McNamara introduced at the Department of Defense, was the Hickey study of 1961. This started by calculating scientifically how many of the planned weapons systems would be needed to destroy 75 per cent and 90 per cent of all strategic targets. This estimate was then combined with the objective laid down by McNamara that the US strategic deterrent should be able to destroy 50 per cent of the industry and 25 per cent of the population of the Soviet Union. As a result, the systems analysts could restate the problem 'how much is enough deterrence?' in such a way that all the component parts – missiles, bombers, anti-ballistic missiles, and civil defence – fell into place and could be put into a numerically-based system in which alternative hypotheses could be tested. McNamara's achievement in using one inter-service model to consider funding for US strategic retaliatory forces from the Air Force and Navy, continental air and missile defence and civil defence should not be underestimated, and the fact that the levels which he set lasted so long after his departure, show that the reasoning behind these calculations commanded general assent. However, in restrospect this way of tackling a strategic problem must cause some unease. One gets the impression of planners to whom figures had become all-important and who, like engineers designing a bridge, would double the maximum planned load for the bridge to be on the safe side. Surely it would have been wiser, as some have argued then and since, to look more at Soviet intentions and ask whether past evidence showed a nation or a government willing to sacrifice half its industry and a quarter of its population to secure an area of Western Europe devastated by nuclear fall-out. Some regard to Soviet intentions would surely have set lower limits for strategic missiles at this early stage of the missile race with considerable subsequent benefits.

The evident willingness of the two Superpowers to reduce their nuclear arsenals so dramatically in 1989 is an indication that fears fostered by the Cold War persuaded both to acquire more nuclear weapons than were needed for security. It is far more difficult (without a war, of course) to assess the adequacy of US strategy for her conventional forces, but the tensions generated by the Cold War create one particular difficulty for those responsible for allocating defence resources, which is especially difficult in the US where public expenditure decisions are shared between two separate bodies within the state: the Executive and the Legislature. As weapons systems and other equipment for war become more and more complex and expensive each service needs more and more of the defence budget to meet its needs. Moreover each will tend to see its prestige and even its survival as an independent service as being bound up with its success in the battle with the other services for a bigger share of the defence budget. This is particularly true of the Navy and Air Force, both of which see their task as being the manning of weapons systems rather than, like the Army, being equipped with weapons. It is also true that both of these services in the US have, since the Second World War, tended to concentrate on weapons systems which now seem more relevant to that war rather than the next (if there is one during their lifetime). The concentration of the USAF on the heavy bomber was entirely correct in the 1950s before intercontinental missiles were perfected, but to expend resources on the obsolescent B-1 bomber in the 1980s when manned aircraft are increasingly vulnerable seems wasteful, to say the least. The emphasis which the US Navy places on large nuclear powered aircraft carriers is puzzling to many. The Soviet Navy has never posed a surface threat for which carriers would be the answer. One would have expected that strategists in the US Department of Defense would have identified the main Soviet conventional threats and then allocated the resources to deal with them. In that case the two most serious threats to the US commitment to Europe would have been the

The Cold War – and After?

Warsaw Pact armies on the mainland and the Soviet submarine fleet in the Atlantic. An appropriate allocation of resources to deal with these threats would have given the US Army greater priority for tanks and other armoured vehicles and reserve stocks and arranged for the Air Force to concentrate on support for the land forces of the NATO alliance, partly with guided weapons and cruise missiles. The US Navy would be directed to concentrate more on the less glamorous problem of anti-submarine warfare, which would require support from the Air Force and less on expensive and vulnerable carrier task groups. A number of sophisticated arguments have been advanced by proponents of aircraft carriers to the effect that the only, or at least the best, way to defeat enemy submarines is by striking at their bases with aircraft from carriers. This is not the place to pursue these and other arguments for a large carrier fleet, but it has to be said that these arguments do not command general assent among those who have tried to weigh the needs of one service against another.

Michael Dockerill has offered the following definition of the Cold War: 'a state of extreme tension between the Superpowers, stopping short of all-out war but characterised by mutual hostility and involvement in covert warfare and war by proxy as a means of upholding the interests of one against the other'. On this basis it is reasonable to suggest an end or at least a definite hiatus in the Cold War in 1989, in which case the worth of the US policy of extended deterrence (including the military strategy of Flexible Response) can be judged in relation to the more than twenty years since it was adopted by NATO for the defence of Europe. Ignoring in this context the overprovision of strategic and tactical nuclear missiles, the strategy can be counted a success despite some doubts about the way in which resources were allocated during some of the time for conventional weapons. It has to be said, however, that although the threat of covert action by the Soviet Union to take over Western Europe was probably considerable between say 1946 and 1949, thereafter (with the creation of the NATO Alliance) the only way in which the Soviet Union could dominate Western Europe would have been by direct military attack and this, with hindsight and better knowledge, does not seem to have been a likely or credible Soviet move. However, for so long as a Soviet attack seemed possible to the European members of NATO, and they have been able to point to the large Soviet armies within easy reach of their borders, then the firm promise of US support was essential to give Europe the self-confidence to develop economically and to resist Soviet pressure for political, strategic or economic advantages. If US support was to be given to Europe for this purpose, then inevitably it had to include the threat to use nuclear weapons.

AFTER THE COLD WAR

However, even if the Cold War is really over, no responsible statesman is yet predicting general and complete disarmament. Western Europe, a prosperous but vulnerable community, will still for some time to come have to consider her security. Whatever the long-term future of East and West Germany, whether or not they are unified and whether or not they are neutralised or wholly or partially demilitarised, it seems reasonably certain that the European Community with a Germany as a major, perhaps a predominant partner, will continue to exist; it has been too economically successful to be abolished for political reasons. If this prediction is correct, some Western European nations will have to maintain land and air forces for their own, and perhaps for the Community's protection from continental neighbours, and no doubt from other nations further afield. They may well decide to retain a European nuclear deterrent as a relatively inexpensive method (in terms of both money and manpower) of dissuading potential enemies with either nuclear or large conventional forces from hostile action. If the EC as an economic unit grows too large to be an effective political unit with integrated defence forces used for common aims, one can see a smaller grouping of Western European nations, with or possibly without Germany, forming a military alliance. The United States will almost certainly continue to be interested in retaining the friendship of, and having influence over, Europe (both as a wider economic and, if it comes about, a smaller political grouping). If as is more than likely, this wish is reciprocated, both parties will have to consider some form of protection for sea-borne traffic in both peace and war. It would seem therefore that decisions about the allocation of defence resources between land, sea and air (including nuclear weapons, however delivered) will still have to be taken both in the US and in Western Europe for some time.

In addition, the United States must consider her widespread interests in other parts of the world in relation to potentially hostile powers with or without nuclear weapons: provided that the US takes the lead, as she did in the Gulf crisis of 1990, a group of European nations is likely to cooperate in any military initiative to preserve western interests outside Europe. This may not be an easy or inexpensive task in years to come. The US Department of Defense (admittedly an interested party) predicts that by the end of the century fifteen nations will possess nuclear weapons. Some experts are convinced that in 1990 twenty-seven states in the Third World have guided missiles which could carry nuclear warheads and if these are not available then many of these states could acquire chemical warheads instead. Bearing in mind the devastation caused by industrial accidents in chemical plants such as those at Seveso and Bhopal, it is quite possible that surprise attacks on undefended cities with chemical weapons could prove as destructive as mass bomber raids on cities in the Second World War. It is sobering to realise that probably the only practical and lasting defence against large-scale chemical attack is the threat to reply in kind.

Even if it is assumed that for some years to come the USSR will be ready to cooperate with the US in maintaining the status quo world-wide, and that China remains unable or unwilling to project military power far outside her borders, it is clear that there are a number of so-called middle-rank powers whose armed forces are strong enough to cause major problems for any nation seeking to be a world power. The days of 'gunboat diplomacy' are gone and light air mobile forces are not sufficiently powerful to repel armoured attack or to expel aggressor states for territory seized in a surprise attack. States aspiring to a peacekeeping role or interested in broadly maintaining the status quo in the world will have to be prepared to send sophisticated forces from all three services for long distances from their home base and to keep them there for a long time. Given the simmering regional conflicts in many parts of the world, caused or exacerbated by nationalism or religion, it is safe to predict that well into the next century there will be nations in every continent (except perhaps Australasia) having to make strategic choices between land, sea and air.

Bibliography

A study such as this which attempts to cover almost 2500 years of warfare and strategy must rely on many standard histories for the factual record. It would be tedious and pointless to list them all. Instead I have, under each chapter heading below, listed those books and articles which offer new and useful interpretations of past events or provide a fairly detailed account of periods where the historical record in English is sparse. When an author is quoted verbatim the relevant book is listed, and in brackets after it, the number of the page in that book from which the quotation is taken.

1 Strategic Choices

President Truman's remarks about strategy come from his message to Congress about defence reorganisation reprinted in *Public Papers of Presidents of the USA; Harry S. Truman 1945* (Washington, DC: US Government Printing Office, 1961). Michael Howard's 'Use and Abuse of Military History' is reprinted in *The Causes of Wars* (London: Temple Smith, 1983). David Henderson's Reith Lectures are published in *Innocence and Design* (Oxford: Basil Blackwell, 1986). Three other books which have influenced this chapter and those that follow are Michael Howard, *War in European History* (London: Oxford University Press, 1976); W. H. McNeill, *The Pursuit of Power* (Oxford: Basil Blackwell, 1983); and R. E. Neustadt and E. R. May, *Thinking in Time* (New York: Free Press, 1986). The evolution of the staff officer discussed in this chapter and in Chapter 5 relates to those who would now be called planning staffs concerned before and during a war with planning the correct strategy for it. Martin van Creveld, *Command in War* (Cambridge, Mass.: Harvard University Press, 1985) chooses a wider definition, covering also those serving in the headquarters of a commander in the field. The evolutionary stages proposed here would not of course apply in the wider context.

2 The Ancient World

The dilemma for Athenian strategy is admirably discussed in Peter Green, *Armada from Athens* (London: Hodder & Stoughton, 1971). H. H. Scullard, *A History of the Roman World*, Fourth Edition (London: Methuen, 1980) is very helpful on those periods of the Second Punic War on which contemporary records are scanty. The quotation is from page 219.

3 The Ottoman Assault on the West

Sir Charles Oman, *History of the Art of War in the 16th Century*, reprinted (London: Greenhill Books, 1989) still provides an excellent account of the Turkish assault on

Christendom. It would be very hard to make sense of the naval strategy of the opposing powers in the Mediterranean without reference to J. F. Guilmartin, *Gunpowder and Galleys; Changing Technology and Mediterranean Warfare at Sea in the 16th Century* (Cambridge: Cambridge University Press, 1974).

4 The Rise and Decline of the Dutch Republic

For this and the next three chapters, Michael Howard, *War in European History*, W. H. McNeill, *The Pursuit of Power*, already referred to and Paul Kennedy, *The Rise and Fall of the Great Powers* (London: Unwin Hyman, 1988) give essential background on the problems faced by the Spanish, French and British Empires at their zeniths and when they declined. Admiral Sir Herbert Richmond, *Statesmen and Seapower* (Oxford: Oxford University Press, 1946) and E. H. Jenkins, *A History of the French Navy* (London: Macdonald and Janes, 1973) discuss naval strategy over the period up to 1945. Britain's problems with military strategy during the same time are well discussed in Correlli Barnett, *Britain and her Army, 1509–1970* (London: Allen Lane, 1970). The struggle between Elizabethan England and Spain and the strategic issues are convincingly described in two books by R. B. Wernham: *Before the Armada* (London: Cape, 1966) and *After the Armada* (Oxford: Oxford University Press, 1984). The Military Revolution, which the Dutch exploited so well in their long war with Spain is admirably summarised in a recent book with that title by Geoffrey Parker (Cambridge: Cambridge University Press, 1988). *The Army of Flanders and the Spanish Road* (Cambridge: Cambridge University Press, 1972) and *The Dutch Revolt* (London: Allen Lane, 1977) by the same author trace the detail of the war, while J. H. Elliot, *Imperial Spain* (London: Penguin Books, 1970) gives a broader view of Spain's problems. *The Count-Duke of Olivares* (Yale: Yale University Press, 1986) by the same author gives much detail about Spain's efforts to continue the war after the truce with the Dutch ended in 1621, but by far the best overview of the second phase of the war is given in J. I. Israel, *The Dutch Republic and the Hispanic World 1606–1661* (Oxford: Oxford University Press, 1982).

5 Britain and France: The Whale and the Elephant

E. H. Jenkins, *A History of the French Navy*, already referred to and Paul Kennedy, *The Rise and Fall of British Naval Mastery* (London: Allen Lane, 1976) are particularly useful, especially it A. T. Mahan, *The Influence of British Sea Power on History 1660–1783* and J. Corbett *Some Principles of Maritime Strategy* (London: Longmans Green, 1911) are available for reference. Works on the military campaigns of the period are too numerous to mention, but D. Gates, *The Spanish Ulcer* (London: Allen & Unwin) gives new material on the Peninsular War as seen from the Spanish point of view. Articles by D. A. Baugh and others in J. Black and P. Woodfine (eds), *The British Navy and the Use of Naval Power in the 18th Century* (Leicester: Leicester University Press, 1985) are most helpful. The quotations are from Correlli Barnett, *Britain and her Army* (152, 225, 231, and 268) and Richmond, *Statesmen and Seapower* (87).

6 Before the First World War

A. J. P. Taylor, *The Struggle for Mastery in Europe* (Oxford: Oxford University Press, 1954) covers late nineteenth-century European politics and the rise of a united Germany in an unforgettable way. J. Steinberg, *Yesterday's Deterrent* (London:

Macdonald, 1963) describes German naval plans and Gordon Craig, *The Politics of the Prussian Army* (Oxford: Oxford University Press, 1955) and G. Ritter, *The Schlieffen Plan* (London: Oswald Wolff, 1958) cover military preparations. These and the British reaction to them are surveyed in Michael Howard, *The Continental Commitment* (London: Temple Smith, 1972) in several chapters in Paul Kennedy (ed.), *The War Plans of the Great Powers* (London: Unwin Hyman, 1979) and in S.R. Williamson, *The Politics of Grand Strategy* (Cambridge, Mass.: Harvard University Press, 1969). Paul Kennedy, *Strategy and diplomacy 1870–1945* (London: Allen & Unwin, 1983), *The Rise and Fall of British Naval Mastery* by the same author and Martin van Creveld, *Supplying War* (Cambridge: Cambridge University Press, 1977) are helpful on prewar plans and their results in war. There is much to be gained from E. M. Earle (ed.), *Makers of Modern Strategy* (Princeton: Princeton University Press, 1944) including a chapter on Moltke and Schlieffen by Hajo Holborn. The quotations are from Taylor, *The Struggle for Mastery in Europe* (372 and 447); Kennedy, *The Rise and Fall of the Great Powers* (157) and Holborn in *Makers of Modern Strategy* (204). The War Office minute of 1905 is quoted on page 42 of Michael Howard, *The Continental Commitment*.

7 Planning for the Second World War

The strategic problems of the European powers in the interwar years have been critically examined in recent years by a number of historians. Notable contributions are Stephen Roskill, *Naval Policy between the Wars,* Volumes I and II (London: Collins, 1968 and 1976); Brian Bond, *British Military Policy between the Two World Wars* (Oxford: Oxford University Press, 1980); G. C. Peden, *British Rearmament and the Treasury* (Edinburgh: Scottish Academic Press, 1979); *The Rise and Fall of British Naval Mastery*; Paul Kennedy, John Terraine, *The Right of the Line* (London: Hodder & Stoughton, 1985); D. C. Watt, *Too Serious a Business* (London: Temple Smith, 1975) *How War Came* by the same author (London: Heinemann, 1989) in the first chapter of David Fraser, *And We Shall Shock Them* (London: Hodder & Stoughton, 1983). For strategic decisions I have also relied on chapters by D. MacIsaac, M. Matloff, M. Geyer and D. Clayton James in P. Paret (ed.), *Makers of Modern Strategy* (Oxford: Oxford University Press, 1986). John Keegan, *The Second World War* (London: Hutchinson, 1989) has useful comments on strategy, and John Terraine, *Business in Great Waters* (London: Leo Cooper, 1989) covers the Battle of the Atlantic. For the Italian campaign I have used Chester Wilmot, *The Struggle for Europe* (London: Collins, 1952); the counter to my thesis on this campaign is expressed in the final part of Sir William Jackson's *Official History of the Italian Campaign* (London: HMSO, 1988). An essay in Paul Kennedy's *Strategy and Diplomacy 1870–1945,* already referred to, deals convincingly with Japan's strategic errors before and during the Pacific War. Finally, Wesley K. Wark, *The Ultimate Enemy* (London: I. B. Tauris, 1985) comments on the performance of British Intelligence in the interwar years. I have quoted from MacIsaac (630), Geyer (575) and Matloff (683) in P. Paret (ed.), *Makers of Modern Strategy*. Other quotations are from Terraine, *Right of the Line* (76) and *Business in Great Waters* (515); Watt, *Too Serious a Business* (73); Fraser, *And We Shall Shock Them* (19); Wark, *The Ultimate Enemy* (76); and Kennedy, *Decline and Fall of Great Powers* (355 and 356). Churchill's reference to the Salonika campaign is taken from the introductory note to Alan Palmer, *The Gardeners of Salonika* (London: Andre Deutsch, 1965). The quotation from the Official History *The Strategic Air Offensive against Ger-*

many is to be found on page 91 of Terraine, *Right of the Line*. R. V. Jones, *Reflections on Intelligence* (London: Heinemann, 1989) discusses the use of scientific advice by the RAF during this period. 'John Ellis' history of the Second World War *Brute Force* (London: Andre Deutsch, 1990) appeared when most of this chapter had been written. It rightly stresses the industrial preponderance of the allies but also provides many instances of the failures by both sides to make the correct choice between land sea and air strategies.

8 The Cold War – and After?

T. H. Edzold and J. L. Gaddis, *Containment: Documents on American Policy and Strategy* (New York: Columbia University Press, 1978), Louis Halle, *The Cold War as History* (London: Chatto & Windus, 1971), J. Smith, *The Cold War* (Oxford: Basil Blackwell, 1989) and M. Dockerill, *The Cold War, 1945–1963* (London: Macmillan, 1988) cover recent history admirably. On nuclear strategy I have referred to Michael Howard, *The Causes of Wars* (London: Temple Smith, 1983) and Lawrence Freedman. *The Evolution of Nuclear Strategy* (London: Macmillan, 1981). A. Enthoven and K. Wayne Smith, *How Much is Enough?* (New York: Harper and Row, 1971) describes the interrelation of systems analysis and nuclear strategy in the McNamara era. Quotations are from Freedman, *Evolution of Nuclear Strategy* (228, 285 and 400); Enthoven, *How Much is Enough?* (172–3); and Dockeril, *The Cold War 1945–1963* (page 1). The quotations from the *Foreign Affairs* article by George Kennan published anonymously in July 1947 and from President Truman's subsequent statement to Congress about aid for Greece and Turkey can be found in Etzold and Gaddis (eds), *Documents on American Policy and Strategy 1945–50*.

Index

Aboukir Bay 110, 111
Acharnania 19
Adriatic Sea 18, 28, 40
Aegates Islands, Battle of 24
Aegospotami, Battle of 17
Africa 23, 171
Agrigentum 21
Alcaniz, Battle of 114
Alcazar, Battle of 44
Aleutian Islands 170, 171, 172
Alexander the Great, King of Macedon 20
Algiers 39, 41
Almanza, Battle of 88, 89
Alsace 69, 126, 128
Alva, Duke of 56
Amersfoort 72
Amphipolis 15
Amsterdam 64, 72
Anatolia 46
Andaman Islands 170
Anglo–German Naval Treaty 1935 149, 153
Anglo–Japanese Alliance 1902 132
Anjou, Duc de 65
Anson, Admiral Lord 97, 98, 140
Antwerp 64, 75, 78, 136, 179
Apennine Range 20, 24, 179
Apulia 25
Ardennes 147
Arginusae Islands, Battle of 17
Armada, Spanish (1588) 58–61, 81
Armed Neutrality, League of 111
Armenia 36
Arnhem 66
Arques, Battle of 65
Artemisium, Cape Battle of 11
Artois 77
Aspern-Essling, Battle of 116
Assaye, Battle of 111
Athens 2, 9–20
Atlantic, Battle of 165, 176–8
Auerstadt, Battle of 113
Augsburg, League of 87

Austerlitz, Battle of 112, 118, 139
Australia 171–3, 175, 181
Austria (later Austro-Hungarian Empire) 37–51 *passim*, Ch. 5 *passim*, 126–8, 142, 181
Azores 61, 62

Baecula, Battle of 29
Baetis, River, Battle of 29
Baghdad 38
Bahia 71, 76
Bajazet, Sultan of Turkey 36
Baldwin, Stanley 156
Balearic Islands 29
Baltic Sea 55, 67, 72, 83, 111, 113, 133
Bantry Bay, Battle of 87
Barbarossa (Khaireddin) 39–41
Barcelona 88, 89, 91, 157
Barnett, Correlli 90, 101, 106, 107, 116
Bautzen, Battle of 117
Bavaria 87, 93
Baylen, Battle of 114, 115
Beachy Head, Battle of 87, 91
Belgium 54, 56, 127, 137, 138, 146
Belgrade 35, 36, 180
Belle Isle 110
Bergen-op-Zoom 64, 70, 94
Berlin 99, 133, 188
Bismarck, Count Otto von 128
Bismarck (Battleship) 154
Bismarck Archipelago 170
Black Sea 16, 18, 135
Blenheim, Battle of 88, 91
Boeotia 11, 14, 15, 16
Borneo 170
Boston 101
Boyne, Battle of the 87
Braddock, General 101
Brandenburg (later Prussia) 87
Brasidas 15
Brazil 52, 71, 74, 76, 77, 78, 99
Breda 65, 70, 75
Breisach 69, 75

Index

Breitenfeld, Battle of 72
Brest 63, 88, 90, 94, 98, 103, 109, 110, 112
Brill 52, 55
Britain see Great Britain
Britain, Battle of 159
Brittany 62, 63
Brodie, Bernard 190
Brussels 75
Bunker Hill, Battle of 101
Burma 170, 171
Butt, D.M.B. 161, 164
Byzantium 13

Cadiz 58, 62, 70, 81, 88, 110, 112
Calais 59
Calcutta 97
Campania 26
Camperdown, Battle of 109
Canada 96, 98, 101
Candia (Heraclion) 51
Cannae, Battle of 25
Capua 26, 28
Carnot, Lazare 108, 117
Cartagena (Columbia) 93
Cartagena (Spain) 29
Carthage 20–31
Castlebar 109
Catalonia 91
Cateau Cambresis, Peace of 41
Ceylon 76, 103, 154, 171, 173
Chamberlain, Neville 8, 158
Charles, Archduke of Austria 116
Charles V, Emperor (of the Holy Roman Empire) 35, 36, 41, 45, 54
Charles Edward Stuart, Prince (Young Pretender) 94
Charleston 104
Chatham 79
Cheng-Ho 2
Cherbourg 99
Chesapeake Bay, Battle of 104
Childers, Erskine 135
Chile 52
China 1, 52, 71, 168, 170, 171, 172, 175, 185
Choiseul, Duc de 102, 106
Churchill, Winston S. 180
Claudius, M. Marcellus 28
Clemenceau 1
Cleon 15
Cleves 66
Condé, Louis Prince de 77
Colbert, Jean Baptiste 87, 88

Collingwood, Admiral 93
Committee of Imperial Defence (CID) 133–7
Constantinople 32, 34, 35, 45, 48 (see also Byzantium)
Copenhagen 113
Copenhagen, Battle of 111
Coral Sea, Battle of 166, 172
Corcyra (Corfu) 14, 19, 40
Corinth 12, 14, 19
Cornwallis, General Lord 104
Coron 36
Corsica 23
Corunna 61, 115
Crete 9, 34, 40, 154, 160, 166
Creveld, Martin van 124, 138, 179
Crimea 13, 18
Crimean War 122
Cuba 73, 93, 99
Cynossema, Battle of 16
Cyprus 13, 34, 36, 40, 43, 44
Cythera, Isle of 15
Cyzicus, Battle of 17
Czechoslovakia 146, 148, 188

Danzig 72
Dardanelles 16, 17, 113, 135
Decelea 16
Defence Requirements Committee (DRC) 150, 151, 156, 158, 165
Delium, Battle of 15
Delos, Confederacy of 13, 18
Denmark 72, 111
Dettingen, Battle of 94
Deventer 65
Dieppe 63
Dockerill, Michael 195
Dominica 99
Dönitz, Grand Admiral K. 178, 183
Dortmund 157
Douhet, Guilo 144, 148
Dowding, Air Chief Marshal Lord 159
Downs, Battle of the 76
Drake, Sir Francis 58, 62, 81
Drepana 23
Dresden 157
Dulles, John Foster 189
Dunkirk 59, 69, 70, 73, 75, 108
Dusseldorf 73
Dutch Republic see United Provinces
Duquesne, Fort 96

East India Company (Dutch) 67
East Indies, Dutch 67, 78, 170, 171

204 Index

Ebro, River 27
Ecnomus Cape, Battle of 23
Egypt 13, 15, 18, 19, 35, 36, 110, 111, 126
Eisenhower, General D. (later President) 178, 189
Elizabeth I, Queen of England 58–64 *passim*, 80–2
Elizabeth, Tsarina of Russia 100
Ellis, John 181
Emden 72
Engadine 55
England Ch. 4 *passim* (*see also* Great Britain)
Enniskillen 87
Eugene, Prince of Savoy 89

Fabius, Quintus 26
Falaise Gap 160
Falmouth 63
Famagusta 43, 51
Ferdinand, Cardinal-Infante, Don Fernando De Austria 74, 75
Ferdinand II, Emperor (of the Holy Roman Empire) 74
Ferrol 62, 81, 110, 115
First of June, Battle of the Glorious 109
Fisher, Admiral Sir John 132, 133
Fisher, Sir Warren 158, 166
Flanders 128, 160
Flanders, Army of 56–9, 69–77 *passim*
Fleurus, Battle of (1690) 88
Fleurus, Battle of (1794) 108
Flushing 60
Fontenoy, Battle of 94
France 35–41, 58–64, 74, 75, Ch. 5 *passim*, 126–38 *passim*, Ch. 7 *passim*, 185
Franche-Comté 55
Frankfurt-on-Main 99
Frederick the Great, King of Prussia 93, 96, 97, 99, 100
Frederick Henry, Prince of Nassau 70, 72, 75
Freedman, Laurence 192, 193
Friesland, Province of 72, 83
Fuller, General 29, 145

Gauls 24
Genoa 29, 93, 95, 118
Geldern 75
Germany Chs 6, 7 *passim* (*see also* Prussia)
Geyer, Michael 146

Gibraltar 67, 89, 90, 103
Goebbels, J. 150
Goering, Marshal H. 148, 183
Gorbachev, M. 187
Grasse, Admiral de 103, 104
Gravelines 60
Graves, Admiral 104
Great Britain 2, Chs 5, 6, 7 *passim*, 185–7
Greece 9–19 *passim*, 160
Gros Jagersdorf, Battle of 99
Guadalcanal 172, 175
Guderian, General H. 146, 147
Guilmartin, J.F. 31, 47
Guns 38
Gustavus Adolfus, King of Sweden 72

Hamburg 157
Hamilcar Barca 21, 24
Hankey, Sir Maurice (later Lord) 150, 158, 166
Hannibal 21, 24–31 *passim*
Hanover, Electorate of 93, 94, 96, 97
Hanseatic League 61, 62, 65, 71
Hapsburg, Dynasty of 34, 37, 40
Hasdrubal 29
Hawaii 171, 172, 175
Hawkins, Sir John 62
Helder Peninsula 110, 118
Henderson, D. 7
Henry III, King of France 63
Henry IV, King of France (Henry of Navarre) 63, 64, 80
Heyn, Piet 73, 81
Hickey Study 193
Himera, Battle of 21
Hiroshima 171, 185
Hitler, Adolf 144, 145, 146, 147, 149, 166
Hochkirchen, Battle of 97
Hohenlinden, Battle of 110
Holborn, Hajo 131
Holland *see* United Provinces
Holland, Province of 56
Hood, Admiral Sir Samuel 103, 104
Howard, Sir Michael 5, 6, 125
Howe, General 101
Hungary 36, 37, 40, 181
Hyder Ali, Prince 103, 104

Ijssel River 66
Illyria 27
India 97, 99, 100, 103, 104, 106, 110, 111, 122, 135, 136, 154, 182, 185
Indo-China, French 168

Index

Inskip, Sir Thomas 158, 166
Ireland 87, 91, 120
Iraq 185
Israel 185
Istria (Istrian Peninsula) 180
Italy 19, 20–30 *passim*, 55, 82, 89, 93, 108, 110, 113, 124, 150, 158, 179, 180
Ivry, Battle of 65
Iwo Jima 172

Japan 1, 126, 132, 143, 149, 152, 153, 154, 166–82 *passim*, 186, 187
Jena, Battle of 113
John, Don J. of Austria 43
Johnson, President Lyndon 193
Julich-Cleves 68

Kaiser *see* Wilhelm II
Kennan, George 187
Kennedy, President John F. 189, 193
Kennedy, Paul 82, 130, 132, 166, 176
Kerestes, Battle of 45
King, Fleet Admiral E.J. 177
Kinsale 62, 81
Kissinger, Henry 190
Kloster Zeven 97
Knights Hospitalier of St John 36, 42
Kronstadt 111
Kruger Telegram 129
Kunersdorf, Battle of 99

Lagos, Battle of 98
La Hogue, Battle of 87, 90, 92
Laurium 9, 18
Le Havre 102
Leicester, Earl of 58, 65
Leignitz, Battle of 100
Leipzig, Battle of (Battle of the Nations) 117
Lepanto, Battle of 34, 43, 44, 48
Lesbos 17
Leuthen, Battle of 97
Leyte Gulf, Battle of 172
Liddell Hart, Captain B.H. 145, 152
Liege 127, 138
Ligny, Battle of 117
Lilybaeum (Marsala) 23
Lisbon 61, 70, 89, 91, 115, 116
Ljubljana 181
Lombardy, Plain of 24
London 59, 156
Londonderry 87
Lorraine 126, 128, 146

Louis XIII, King of France 75
Louis XIV, King of France 79, 84, 86, 87, 90, 92, 107, 109, 120
Louisburg 94, 95, 97, 98
Louisiana 96
Lucania 26
Ludlow Hewitt, Air Chief Marshal Sir Edgar 161
Lutter, Battle of 71
Lutzen, Battle of 117

Maas, River (Meuse) 55, 136
Maastricht 73, 78
MacArthur, General Douglas 176, 181
Macedonia (Macedon) 11, 13, 20, 27, 28
Mackinder, H.J. 124
McNamara, Robert S. 193
Mago 29
Mahan, Admiral 31, 47, 81, 124
Mahomet II, Sultan of Turkey 35, 36
Maida, Battle of 113
Maitland Wilson, General Sir Henry 180
Malacca 76
Malaga, Battle of 89, 90, 92
Malaya 76, 170, 171, 182
Malplaquet, Battle of 88
Malta 41, 42, 49, 51
Manchuria 168, 170
Manstein, General Erich von 146, 147
Marathon 9
Mardonius 10
Marengo, Battle of 110
Marianas Islands 172
Marlborough, John Churchill, Duke of 88
Marne, Battle of 138
Martinique 99
Massena, General 114, 116
Maurice of Nassau 65, 66, 69, 70
Mauritius 103
Medway, River 91
Megara 14, 15
Memphis 14
Metaurus, River, Battle of 29
Metz 127
Messina 42
Midway Island, Battle of 166, 172, 175
Miletus 11
Minden, Battle of 99
Minorca 92, 97, 118
Mississippi, River 96
Mitylene 17, 44
Modon 36, 44
Mohacs, Battle of 36, 46
Mohne Dam 162

Moldavia 40
Moltke, Count Helmuth von (the Elder) 125, 126
Moltke, Count Helmuth von (the Younger) 127, 131
Moluccas (Spice Islands) 78
Monongahela, River 96
Montgomery, General Sir Bernard (later Field Marshal Lord) 178
Montreal 98, 101
Moore, General Sir John 115
Morocco 35
Morocco Crisis 137
Mortain, Battle of 160
Moscow 117
Munster, Treaty of 78
Mycale, Battle of 11
Mylae, Battle of 18, 23

Nagasaki 171, 185
Namur 88, 90
Naples (Neapolis) 27
Napoleon I, Emperor of France 108–21 *passim*
Neerwinden, Battle of 88
Negroponte 36, 38
Nelson, Admiral Lord 110, 111
Netherlands, Spanish 52–84 *passim*
Newall, Air Chief Marshal Sir Cyril 164
New Carthage (Cartegena) 29
New Hebrides 172
New York 101, 104
Nice 40
Nicobar Islands 170
Nicosia 43, 51
Nieuport 59, 66
Nijmegen 65
Nile, Battle of the 110
Nimitz, Admiral Chester R. 176
Nomonhan 168
Nordlingen, Battle of 74, 77
Nore Mutiny 109
Normandy 160
North Atlantic Treaty Organisation (NATO) 188–92, 195
Notium, Battle of 17
Numidia 30

Ohio River 96
Okinawa 172
Olivares, Count-Duke of 71, 83
Osgood, Robert 190
Ostend 66
Otranto 36

Ottoman Empire (later Turkey) Ch. 3 *passim*
Oudenarde, Battle of 88

Panama 62
Panormus (Palermo) 23
Parma, Duke of 56, 59, 60, 64, 65
Paris 65, 127, 139
Pausanias 11
Pearl Harbor 154, 169, 170, 171, 174
Peenemünde 72, 162
Peloponnesian League 14–17
Pericles 15
Pernambuco 74, 76
Persia 9–17 *passim*, 21, 36, 38, 41
Phaleron Bay 9
Philadelphia 101, 104
Philip, King of Macedon 27, 28
Philip II, King of Spain 41, 58–62, 66, 82, 83
Philip III, King of Spain 66–8
Philip IV, King of Spain 68, 71–7
Philippine Islands 68, 78, 99, 170, 171, 172, 181
Philippine Sea, Battle of 172
Pitt, William, Earl of Chatham 96–100 *passim*
Pitt, William (The Younger) 108–12 *passim*
Pittsburgh 96
Plassey, Battle of 97
Plateia, Battle of 11
Plateia (City) 15
Poland 145, 146, 152
Pomerania 99, 133
Pondicherry 99
Port Mahon (Minorca) 89, 92, 93, 97, 100, 103, 106
Portugal 58, 61, 77, 89, 91, 109, 114, 116
Potidaea 14
Prevesa, Battle of 40, 47
Provence 40
Prussia, (formerly Brandenburg) 93–117 *passim* (*see also* Germany)
Pylos 15

Quatre Bras, Battle of 117
Quebec 98, 101
Quiberon Bay, Battle of 98

Raeder, Grand Admiral E. 183
Ramillies, Battle of 88
Red Sea 40
Regulus, Marcus 23

Reval 111
Rhine River 55, 56, 66, 73, 75
Rhodes 20, 36, 38, 50
Richelieu, Cardinal de 75
Richmond, Admiral Sir Herbert 88
Ridgeway, General M. 190
Rocroi, Battle of 77
Rodney, Admiral Lord 93, 103, 104
Roermond 75
Romania 146, 152, 180
Rome 20–31 *passim*, 179
Roosevelt, President Franklin 174, 175, 181
Rotterdam 157
Rossbach, Battle of 97
Rouen 63, 65
Russia (later USSR) 1, 96, 99, 100, 101, 110, 111, 112, 116, 123, 126–8, 130, 135, 142, 143, 150, 168, 174, 185–97 *passim*
Ruyter, Admiral Michiel de 79

Saguntum (Murvedro) 24
St Malo 99, 102
St Vincent, Cape 77
St Vincent, Admiral Lord (Sir John Jervis) 110
St Vincent, Battle of 103
Saints, Battle of the 93, 104
Salamanca, Battle of 116
Salamis, Battle of 11, 12, 18
Salonika 180
Samoa 172
Samos 17
San Marcial 114
San Sebastian 61
Santander 61
Saratoga, Battle of 101, 106
Sardinia 27, 30, 118
Saumarez, Admiral 113
Savafid Dynasty (Persian) 36
Savoy 55, 66
Scheldt River 73, 179
Schenkénschans 75
Schlieffen, Count Alfred von (Schlieffen Plan) 126–31 *passim*, 138, 142
Scipio, Cornelius S. Africanus 28, 29, 30
Scullard H.H. 26
Selim I, Sultan of Turkey 36
Selim II, Sultan of Turkey 43
Serbia 180
Seringpatam 111
s'Hertogenbosch 72, 78
Siberia 168, 171

Sicily 14, 15, 16, 20–4, 27, 28
Sicily (Kingdom of Two Sicilies) 110, 113, 118
Silva Torok, Peace of 45
Singapore 152, 153, 154, 166, 169, 171
Sluis 66
Solent 60
Solomon Isles 171
South Africa, Republic of 185
Spain, Kingdom of 24–9 *passim*, Chs 3, 4, 5 *passim*
Spanish Road 55, 56, 66, 69, 74, 75
Sparta 11–20 *passim*
Spinola 65, 66, 69, 70
Spithead Mutiny 109
Stalin, Generalissimo J. 187
Steenkirk, Battle of 88
Stralsund 72
Suffren, Admiral 103, 120
Suleiman the Magnificent, Sultan of Turkey 36–43 *passim*, 46, 47
Sunium, Cape 9, 18
Suvorov, General 110
Syracuse 16, 19, 21, 28
Syria 32, 35, 36
Sweden 72, 113
Switzerland 110, 112
Szigeth 43

Tagus River 116
Taiwan 71
Tamames, Battle of 114
Taranto, Battle of 154
Tarentum 27
Taylor, A.J.P. 128, 134
Taylor, General Maxwell 190
Tchaldiran, Battle of 36
Tedder, Air Chief Marshal Lord 160
Tenerife 110
Thailand (Siam) 170
Thames, River 79, 91
Thebes 20
Themistocles 9, 13
Thermopylae, Battle of 11
Thrace 11, 13, 16
Tilly, Johan, Count 71, 72
Tirol 55
Tirpitz, Admiral Alfred von 128–32 *passim*, 138
Tirpitz (Battleship) 154
Toledo, Don Garcia de 42
Torgau, Battle of 100
Torres Vedras, lines of 114, 116
Toulon 89, 91, 92, 93, 94, 108, 109

Tourcoing, Battle of 108
Tourville, Admiral 87
Trafalgar, Battle of 112, 118
Transvaal, Republic of 129
Trasimene, Lake, Battle of 25
Trebbia, River, Battle of 25
Trenchard, Marshal of the RAF, Viscount 155, 161
Trieste 180, 181
Trincomalee 103
Tripoli 39, 47
Tromp, Marten van 76
Truman, President 4, 187
Tsu Shima, Battle of 1, 126
Tulagi 171
Tunis 39
Turkey 110, 113, 135, 186, 187 (see also Ottoman Empire)
Turnhout, Battle of 66

Ulm 112, 139
Union, Act of (1707) 86
UK see Great Britain
United Provinces (Dutch Republic) Ch. 4 passim, 86–90 passim, 102, 108
US 100–7, 123, 130, 132, Chs 7, 8 passim
USSR see Russia
Ushant, Cape, Battle of 102
Utica 30
Utrecht 72, 79
Utrecht, Peace of 92

Valmy, Battle of 107
Valtelline 55, 69, 74
Vendee 108, 117
Venice Ch. 3 passim
Venlo 75
Vienna 34, 36, 37, 38, 45, 46, 139, 180
Vietnam 187

Vittoria, Battle of 116, 118

Waal River 75
Wagenfuhr, R. 176
Wagram, Battle of 116
Walcheren Island 110, 118, 179
Wallenstein, Albrecht von 71, 72
Wandiwash, Battle of 99
Warburg, Battle of 99
Wark, Wesley 157
Warsaw Pact 189, 194
Washington, General G. (later President) 101, 104
Washington (Naval) Conference 1921–2 152
Waterloo, Battle of 117
Wellington, Duke of 111, 114, 115, 116
Wever, General (Luftwaffe) 148
Wesel 68
West Germany (Federal German Republic) 188, 191, 192
West India Company (Dutch) 67
Westphalia 78
Wight, Isle of 60
Wilhelm II, Kaiser of Germany 128, 129
William of Orange (William the Silent) 55, 56, 58, 65
William III, King of England (William of Orange) 79, 84, 86, 87, 90

Yamato (Battleship) 170, 183
Yorktown, Battle of 104, 106

Zama, Battle of 29, 30
Zeeland, Province of 56, 82
Zorndorf, Battle of 99
Zuider Zee 56, 66, 79
Zutphen 65